The New Small Garden

Plans and Plants
That Make Every Inch Count

PETER LOEWER

STACKPOLE
BOOKS

Published by
STACKPOLE BOOKS
5067 Ritter Road
Mechanicsburg, PA 17055

Printed in the United States of America

10 9 8 7 6 5 4 3 2

First edition

Cover design by Kathleen Peters

Garden designs, illustrations, and photographs by the author, unless noted otherwise

Library of Congress Cataloging-in-Publication Data

Loewer, H. Peter.
    The new small garden : plans and plants that make every inch count
/ Peter Loewer—1st ed.
        p.   cm.
    Includes bibliographical references (p.   ).
    ISBN 0-8117-2568-5
    1. Landscape gardening.   2. Gardens—Design.   3. Landscape plants.
I. Title.   II. Title: Small garden.
SB473.L645   1994
712′.6—dc20   93-43699
                                                                    CIP

CONTENTS

PREFACE

TIME WAS WHEN GARDENS COVERED VAST ACRES, RINGING ESTATES WITH EXOTIC PLANTS and serving as fitting backgrounds for various social activities and fashionable plantings, plantings that often put premiums on rarity and reflected the owner's station in life. The only folks who saw the gardens were those who owned them, the owners' friends, and those who had to work in them.

Times have changed and the days of the huge estate garden are, for the most part, over. A few large gardens remain as public parks, historic sites, or botanical gardens, and an occasional member of the *nouveau riche* will build an 8,000-square-foot house with a garden that covers an area equal to half an average-sized mall (often installed in less than a week). Since the 1960s, a few rock or movie stars have also maintained large gardens. But by now, most of the plant collections from huge estates have been auctioned off and the land divided for small housing plots or condos.

Contributing to the trend toward shrinking gardens is the life-style of a typical middle-class family, which begins a garden one year and moves out the next. Even older gardeners are on the move; rising fuel bills are forcing them into smaller homes on smaller grounds—and often to warmer climes. (Of course, as gardeners get older, managing a large plot becomes more difficult, too.) All of these trends point to the benefits of a smaller, more easily managed garden that can offer a continually changing picture over the years without ever outgrowing its frame.

Our northern garden in Cochecton Center, New York, was over thirty-three acres of land, every inch of which we attempted to cultivate (or at least give evidence of the hand of man). Each spring the tenth-of-a-mile-long driveway required pot-hole fillings and the poison ivy vines that wandered up and down the trunks of forty white pines (twenty on each side of the drive) had to be cut back. After that the desirable native plants would appear and visitors would see a country road neatly lined with ferns and flowers on either side. And so like the rest of the property, the drive eventually became a garden—but not without a yearly workout.

The surrounding fields soon gave out their siren song, and using a giant Rototiller, we tried to remove the age-old grasses in an attempt to plant various wildflowers. And so what once looked like a minor sea of grass became a gathering of only tough wildflowers, but it also became part of the garden.

After years of adding money to a pond fund, we hired a contractor to dig a one-third-acre pond in the front field on the left-hand side of the driveway. He came with bulldozers and trucks, and the yawning pit grew larger and deeper every day; Manhattan visitors soon likened it to a building excavation. The contractor was doing so well at selling fill to various construction projects within a fifty-mile radius that the pit grew to one and a half acres before we pulled the plug on his largess.

In the backyard I installed a border that wandered more than eighty feet and in some places measured six feet deep. We put in a terrace of flat fieldstones off the dining room and soon surrounded that with more plants. Then came a scree bed and various rock gardens and soon my eyes were wandering up the hill behind the house, where daffodils were naturalized; two hands with fingers held closely upright and horizontal thumbs pressed together made a frame through which to view the landscape and decide what trees should fall.

If a latter-day Capability Brown with a large inheritance had entered our domain, I would have continued my terrascaping. But as the years passed and other things became important, energy was harder to come by and time itself took a greater portion of every day.

So we moved to a smaller piece of land—only an acre on the tax maps but because of a slope it is more like two. And having learned our lesson about effort in the garden and the constraints of time, we have narrowed our sights and now have a smaller garden.

Actually, we have five small gardens. But before we try to improve Garden 2, Garden 1 is finished (as much as any garden ever can be). And it is these five gardens that have led to this book about small gardens in general.

The garden plans are based on personal experience. In the plant list, I have mentioned both our old and our new gardens, plus any tips or thoughts on the particular genus, species, or cultivar in question.

Special thanks, as always, must go to my wife, Jean, who works and works. And thanks to my good friend Peter Gentling, a font of garden knowledge; to Anne Halpin White, for answering the phone; to her brother Tom Moyer, for kindly lending me photos; to Budd Myers and John Hawkins for the marvelous container garden photos; and finally, to my charming editor, Sally Atwater, who is always a delight to work with.

INTRODUCTION

I HATE GARDENING BOOKS WITH CHARTS AND TABLES AND ENDLESS CHAPTERS ON HOW TO garden. The way I look at it is this: Any information that strays from the general should be included with the plant descriptions. So let's get right to the plants and designs for small gardens, after we take a brief look at plant names.

There is a move on in publishing—especially popular magazines—to "glitz it up and dumb it down." Many editors and publishers now believe that the public is too ignorant to deal with botanical names for plants, so they use only popular names. That's fine as long as you are dealing with common names like dahlias and delphiniums, which are actually botanical names. But as soon as you branch out into unusual annuals and perennials, you will find that common names change not only from region to region, but also from country to country.

There are, for example, seven plants known as snakeroot: common snakeroot, black snakeroot, button snakeroot, Sampson's snakeroot, Seneca snakeroot, Virginia snakeroot, and white snakeroot. Each one belongs to a different plant genus.

All the plants known to man are given botanical or scientific names—expressed in Latin—and each is unique. And they are easily understood throughout the world. In Japan, Saudi Arabia, Russia, or Chicago, *Cynara scolymus* is the artichoke and *Taraxacum officinale* is the common dandelion.

Don't worry about pronunciation. Latin is a dead language. Very few people can speak these names with impunity, and most of the time you will be using them in their written form.

Four terms are in general use: *genus, species, variety,* and *cultivar.* In print, the genus and species are set off from the accompanying text by italic type. The genus refers to a group of plants that are closely related; the species name often suggests an individual plant's unique quality or color, or perhaps honors the individual who discovered the plant. The first letter of the genus is capitalized and the species is in lowercase. (A species derived from a former generic name, a person's name, or a common name may also begin with a capital letter.)

Thus the common garden flower, the foxglove, has the botanical name *Digitalis purpurea.* The genus is Latin for "finger of a glove" and refers to the shape of the blossom. The species name refers to the usual color of the flower.

The variety is also italicized and usually preceded by the abbreviation *var.*, set in roman type. A variety is a plant with a noticeable change in characteristics that breeds true from generation to generation. A cultivar is a variation that appears on a plant in cultivation (thus a change either by chance or by design). The word *cultivar* is derived from *culti*vated *vari*ety and distinguished by roman type inside single quotation marks. And contrary to general rules of copy editing, punctuation marks fall outside the quotation marks, as in 'Foxy'.

Finally, three more terms you need to know: *biennial* means a plant lives for two growing seasons, compared with the one season of an *annual* and the many seasons of a *perennial*.

One

Designing the Small Garden

~

ALTHOUGH MANY PEOPLE SAY THAT GARDENING IS CHANGING THE FACE OF AMERICA, THE sight you usually see in the average suburb is the contemporary approach to landscaping and to gardening in general: wide expanses of manicured lawn dotted here and there with straight lines of meticulously clipped shrubs or some evergreens. Most shade trees are plunked directly in the center of the lot, and flowers are confined to the three most widely grown plants in the United States: petunias, marigolds, and impatiens.

If imagination is allowed in the suburbs, it's usually found out back in the vegetable garden. There caution is often thrown to the wind. Tepees of weathered stakes hold verdant tangles of beans and peas, and the many green shades of lettuces mix with the deep purples of eggplants and the bright reds of tomatoes.

In the cities you may see flowers planted around the base of a tree, or windowboxes overflowing with blossoming cascades, brightening brownstones and indeed the entire street. But most of the town gardens are hidden in backyards and back lots and alongside alleyways. A number of these small, out-of-the-way gardens are the most elegant of all.

There are distinct advantages to these small gardens, especially when it comes to upkeep. Unless you have a staff of gardeners at your beck and call, a large garden can easily get out of hand.

Like books, plants can multiply until the metaphorical garden shelves break under the weight. I'm a plant collector, and if I did not limit the size of my gardens, I would soon be faced with a strangling jungle of interlocking stems. But with a small garden I'm forced to consider each plant that goes into the collection—and everything looks better for it.

The meaning of small. There are many synonyms for *small,* including *little, tiny, miniature, diminutive, dwarf, pygmy, bantam,* and unfortunately, *peewee.* Except for the word *diminutive*—and in the case of the container gardens, *miniature*—the rest of these words do not in my mind have the same meaning as the word *small.*

A well-known mail-order nursery markets a miniature Zen garden that consists of a shallow wooden tray, clean sand, several rocks, and a small rake so that you can create your own tabletop Zen garden. It sells for $32. You won't find such a garden in this book, not even at $1.99.

The gardens described in this book are what I would term small. This category includes options that range from a four-by-four-foot opening in the midst of terrace tiles, to a collection of vases and urns that are home to burgeoning geraniums mixed with long tails of ivy, to an eight-foot-square rock garden, to a small garden room that measures twenty-five by thirty feet.

Starting the design. Creating a garden does not require a host of experts who descend like welcome rain from heaven but soon turn into unwanted sleet. Such people begin to badger you with their likes and dislikes, rarely listening to yours, and after many indignities, eventually leave—but not before bills are presented. Theme parks and vast estates need landscape designers, but you can take care of your own backyard by remembering just a few guidelines.

(That doesn't mean that you, as a fledgling gardener, cannot ask gardening friends for their help in approaching your particular problem. In all my years of working with gardeners, I've only met one who cared more for money than for plants.)

The first step in garden design is to take paper and pencil, then sketch a simple map of the area to be planted. As Amy Lowell wrote:

Bring pencils, fine pointed,

For our writing must be infinitesimal—

The map need not be complicated or artistically pleasing; it is only a tool to help you focus your energies and to save you time and effort. Include anything permanent in the area where your garden will be—outbuildings, fences, trees, and rocks. Also indicate the direction of the worst winter winds, obstructions to sunlight, and the path of the sun in both summer and winter.

The next step is to decide what kind of garden you want. Will it be a rock garden that bursts upon the spring with riots of color? A naturalistic garden full of American wildflowers? A small perennial border full of old-time blossoms? A combination vegetable and flower garden? A water garden? Or a garden based on a favorite theme, such as an all-white garden, a desert garden, a rose garden, or a small plot devoted to the plants of Thomas Jefferson?

At the same time, you must decide how much responsibility you want to shoulder. Gardening isn't easy, and it takes time and often a sizable investment of money, especially if you need to hire someone to help you. So if you think a certain kind of garden will sap too much of your time and energy, lower your aims and choose one of the smaller garden plans.

As you design your garden, you may find a camera to be a useful tool. My wife uses an old Polaroid camera for memory shots while creating *plein air* drawings or watercolors. Sometimes when I'm redesigning a garden or starting one from scratch, I'll borrow her camera and take black-and-white shots of the area from as many angles as possible. Back home I test new plantings and arrangements by drawing directly on the pictures with a fine felt-tip pen. That gives me a pretty good idea of how it will all eventually look.

Climbing 'Cécile Brunner' rose

Wall fountain + small pool   3 Dwarf Alberta spruce

2 baptisias   miscanthus 'Zebrinus'

Line of small rhododendrons

3 yellow potentilla

White forthysia   Oak-leaf hydrangea

A few words from the wise. Beverley Nichols was one of the great English garden writers and thanks to Robin Wilkerson of Garden Works, I have a book in my collection that Nichols published in 1939 entitled *Green Grows the City* (New York: Harcourt, Brace and Company). The last paragraph reads: ". . . So we will close these pages. And as we do so we both know, you and I, that if all men were gardeners, the world at last would be at peace." Nothing changes, does it?

Green Grows the City is about a house and yard in Heathstead, some thirty minutes from the heart of London, the garden being such a desolate strip of land that Mr. Nichols first pictured it as a cat run. The basic problem with the lot was its shape—an isosceles triangle with two sides some sixty feet long and the thirty-foot base at the rear of the house.

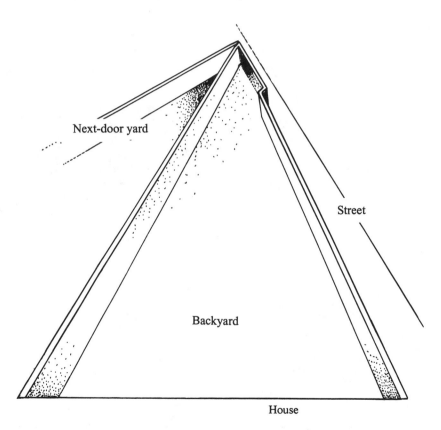

One beautiful day in July, he decided to take a sunbath in the backyard but realized that many of his neighbors could easily see him, so he brought out two screens from the house and placed them thus:

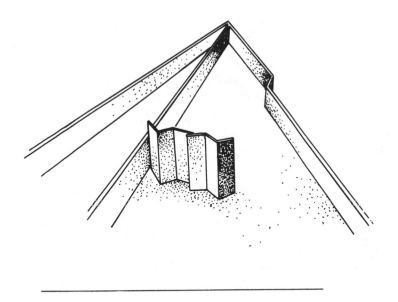

As a result of a falling screen and prying eyes from next door, Mr. Nichols went back to the house for a moment—after setting the fallen screen back in place—and looking out from a window, suddenly realized that the point of the triangle had disappeared and the garden seemed twice as large.

Eventually the design grew and two walls were constructed along with a winding pathway and circular flower beds. The backyard plan now looked like this:

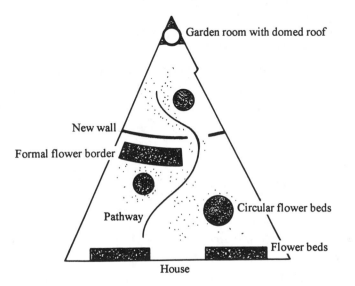

The final addition to the triangle's point was a circular garden room with a domed roof and French doors separated by wooden Doric columns—a structure probably not within the reach of most of today's gardeners. But that structure could be replaced by a small tree or a terrace with chairs and potted plants.

So when creating a small backyard garden, don't be afraid to experiment. A solution exists for most problems. Try to instill a feeling of mystery into your design so that when you are in your garden, you are removed from the problems of this modern world.

Color in the small garden. Many books written about color in the garden devote pages to the definitions of hue, value, and intensity. *Hue* is the actual color, such as red or yellow. *Value,* or luminosity, distinguishes a light color from a dark color. *Intensity,* or *chroma,* makes a color stong or weak.

I have in my hand a Nickerson Color Fan (distributed by the American Horticultural Council back in 1957), which consists of seven-by-two-inch cards, each of which is printed with forty hues. The cards are hinged at one end and open like a fan to show the results of color groupings. But I've never used it. If I got bogged down in such precise color planning, I would miss the whole fun of gardening.

There are gardeners who base plantings on whether leaves are glossy and reflect a lot of light, or dull and seem to recede into the background. I've never bothered with that approach, either. Let me sum up pages and pages of garden theory by pointing out that we quickly grow tired of flagrant colors but find subtle combinations always new.

To give you, I think, a better idea of how flower and leaf color work in both the large and the small garden, think of the two painters, Monet and van Gogh. Monet painted big, lush canvases where sweeps of different colors blend together at the edges, leaving no distinct outlines. Instead of carefully painting an individual poppy or water lily, Monet gives an *impression* of the flower (hence the name *Impressionism*), just as when you walk into a large garden, the individual flower beds meld into broad bands of color.

Not so in the small garden, as demonstrated by the art of van Gogh. Whether he depicts an individual flower, a bouquet of flowers, or a field of flowers, each blossom, each leaf is safe in its own identity. The individual seeds of a sunflower might be just a dash of brown, but they are painted in such a way that there is no question about there being seeds. The 1890 painting "Wheatfield with Crows" consists of jabs of golden-yellow paint that represent wheat stalks and heavy, dashed Vs of black for the crows—but they are all individuals.

And that's the way flowers and plants look in a small garden: each plant exists on its own, even when surrounded by dozens of others. So when you think of color on a small scale, think of working with dots of color, not broad sweeps of pigment.

When it comes to matching colors, much depends on where you live in this broad continent. Woodland gardens filled with shade call for a mix of delicate colors, while sun-splashed areas of sand and stone need bold, bright flashes of color; subtle pinks and washes of pale blue would be diminished by sun and sky.

Most colors work together if their intensities are the same. Imagine a bed of yellow, orange, red, and purple flowers, all of equal intensity. Believe it or not, this riot of color actually works. (It helps that the colors are adjacent to one another on the color wheel; such mixes usually harmonize.)

Now imagine the same mix of flowers but add some blossoms of pale blue. The blue flowers would be lost. A better match for pale blue would be pink, salmon, and pale yellow.

For me all those color problems faced by designers of large gardens are absent when dealing with the small. Just watch out for color intensity and the rest should take care of itself.

The path principle. Even a typical square backyard lot as small as twenty by twenty feet can appear much larger with the judicious use of small trees, low fences or walls, shrubbery, and wandering pathways. Consider a typical small, square lot.

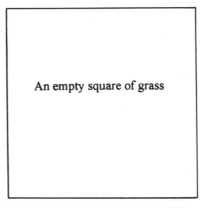

An empty square of grass

Then add some rhododendrons, a weeping pea tree (*Caragana arborescens* var. *pendula*), a small concrete bench on a flagstone terrace, and pathways.

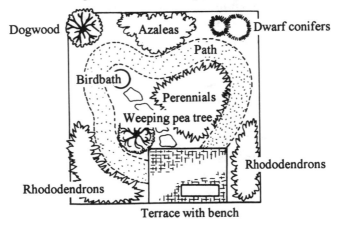

Thanks to being on a terraced hill, our one acre of land is much larger than the survey would indicate. But with the addition of winding pathways, it actually becomes a park. (I can take no credit for the pathways; they were created by Doan Ogden, a well-known southeastern landscape architect who planned our garden and the nine-acre garden next door.)

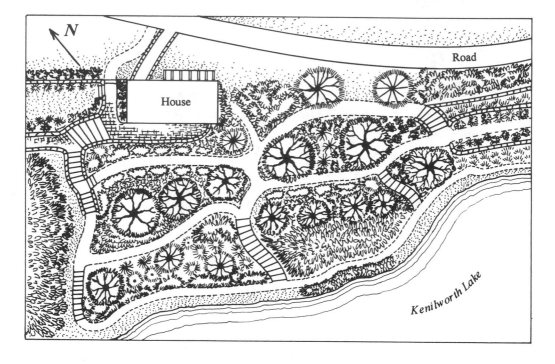

When drawing up your master plan, make sure you include pathways so that you can wander through your garden. Whether they are manicured grass, pine needles, crushed stone, railroad ties, flagstones, or a combination of these, they can be the most valuable design element in your garden.

Ornaments in the small garden. "Too much ornamentation makes a garden look busy," said garden writer and photographer Pamela Harper. "Yet we need it in small gardens even more than on large estates. Any garden can be enhanced by ornaments. Woodland gardens can get by without them, but a picture I treasure is of a white-painted wooden owl, axe-carved by a local craftsman, perched in the crotch of a tree."

Thirty years ago when most American gardeners thought of garden ornaments, a picture flashed before their mind's eye: the garden gnome, made of concrete, and dressed in primary colors of red and blue, with perhaps a yellow corncob pipe, standing alone or holding court with one or more pink flamingos. In fact *Horticulture,* one of the leading American garden periodicals of the day, carried a full-page advertisement devoted to Papa Hans and his garden dwarfs: Gustav, Otto, Hans, and Fritz (you know Fritz, he has the hat on).

And over the Atlantic, as soon as you left the stately homes of England, for every statue of Apollo or eighteenth-century stone urn decorated with floral swags out of Grinling Gibbons, there were dozens of crazy-pavings dotted with elves, rabbits, and penguins.

Today the concrete gnome is still found at the garden center. But there amidst the frogs and dwarfs are now Japanese lanterns, Renaissance putti, brass sundials, and portable fountains.

Even pink flamingos have their place. In southern Florida, in a garden of philodendrons and flowering gingers, three or five (never four) such birds in one corner can spell the difference between ho-hum and a statement.

Suppose your garden plan has been executed to perfection. Your backyard features a small brick terrace backed by a low stone retaining wall curtained with ivy, with the ground behind the wall sloping up a gentle hill. The effect is one of quiet charm—but it still needs something to set it off. Place a piece of garden sculpture on the wall and the entire mood of the garden changes.

Once the sculpture is in place, you will need a seat from which to enjoy your handiwork. "The many garden seats of the old English garden were perhaps its chief feature in distinction from American garden furnishing today," wrote Alice Morse Earle in her wonderful book, *Old Time Gardens* (New York: The Macmillan Company, 1901). The garden bench is an old concept. In a letter written in 1575 a gentleman from Kenilworth told of garden seats where he sat in the heat of summer, "feeling the pleasant whisking wynde." I have walked through many large modern gardens in the summer heat and longed for a shaded seat from which to view the surrounding beauty and feel the whisking wind, and would gladly have made use of even a wheelbarrow.

Garden ornaments should be in scale with your garden. A small Japanese stone lantern—just big enough to accommodate a candle or low-voltage light for evening viewing—is more subtle than a six-foot marble statue of the Venus de Milo, even with arms. You will find that scaled-down ornaments add depth to a small garden view; large pieces overpower it.

Five garden maxims. Here are five things to keep in mind when you design your small garden:

1. Plan for the eventual size of a plant. Visualize what it will become five or ten years from the day you plant it.
2. Match the plant to the conditions. A bush that requires perfect drainage won't be happy in heavy clay.
3. Avoid straight lines unless you are planting in an area that has a direct relationship to an adjoining building. They are never found in nature and soon become boring

to look at and impossible to maintain. A gentle and sweeping curve looks much better and is easier both to install and to keep up.

4. Break the rules. Although all the books tell you to put the large plants at the back of the border or garden area, then slot the medium plants for the middle, and place the shortest in the front, there are times and places to try the unexpected. Put a tall plant at the front, for example, so that its stems can artfully drape over the smaller plants, lending an air of mystery to the border.

5. Trust your own aesthetic judgment. After all, it is your garden and should reflect your likes and dislikes, not those of some expert you don't even know and would never invite home to dinner.

Two

Perennials

~

JUST BECAUSE YOUR GARDEN IS SMALL DOESN'T MEAN YOU CAN'T ENJOY BIG PLANTS. MOST gardeners would think the large-leafed gunnera (*Gunnera chilensis*) is too big for the small garden, that growing this plant with its six-foot-wide leaves would bring the Thought Police to the front door (not to mention using *Gunnera manicata* with its nine-foot leaves). But there it sits in a triangle of land on the west side of our home. The plot measures just five feet at the base and eight feet on the longest side, but the gunnera fits perfectly and is a show-stopper. It all boils down to design: the packed foliage of a big viburnum or the dark green of a mature arborvitae might be overbearing for the wall of the house, weighing down that corner like a black concrete ball. But the tropical, cut-edged leaves of the gunnera are just right for the spot. "It is enough, the freight should be proportioned to the groove—" wrote Emily Dickinson.

A SELECTION OF PERENNIALS

I've chosen the following perennials as favorites in my garden because their leaves, flowers, and total form are all in good proportion for the small garden. Unless otherwise specified, all these plants like full sun and a good, well-drained soil.

Anemone japonica is one of the time-honored anenomes, or windflowers, but most of the flowers sold under that name are really *A. × hybrida,* a name in use since 1894. Black and twisted roots send up stems up to three feet high with attractive large-lobed leaves and lovely flowers. There are many cultivars, but my favorite (possibly because its seedlings overrun our garden) is 'September Charm', first marketed in 1932, and 'Queen Charlotte' with three-inch pink, semidouble flowers, originally bred in Germany. Both are hardy to USDA Zone 4. After blooming, their fluffy seed heads look like pieces of dirty cotton batting and are best removed before the cold rains of late fall. In our garden, anemones have seeded themselves in the rock garden. I planted seedlings in front of our boxwood hedge, where the flowers make a beautiful picture in the fall.

Aquilegia spp., columbines, are wildflowers that can soon overrun a small garden, but there are five types worth seeking out. The first is wild columbine (*A. canadensis*), bearing fernlike foliage and graceful flowers with long red spurs and yellow faces that move about in spring breezes on wiry stems. It requires only well-drained soil and partial shade. From Maryland, 'Corbett' is a cultivar of the wild species and bears pale yellow flowers on eighteen-inch stems.

Originally from Japan, *Aquilegia flabellata* 'Nana' has lovely lilac-blue blossoms edged with white that sit on top of fifteen-inch plants; 'Nana Alba' has dainty white flowers, and the plants are even shorter.

Then there are the Music Series hybrids. The flowers of these twenty-four-inch-tall plants have longer spurs and colors of white, yellow, blue and white, and red and white. All the columbines are hardy to Zone 3.

Asparagus officinalis var. *pseudoscaber* is a dwarf asparagus that will, I'm afraid, require some searching for seed, but the plant is well worth the effort. In spring, the spears appear in front of the wall in our garden room but instead of being large and clunky, these shoots are the size of office pencils painted green instead of yellow. Even in a good year there are never enough spears to feed anything except a local contingent of the Little People, so I let them all branch out to ferns. These filmy branches stop at about thirty inches and provide an airy veil of color against the stone. In the fall, the leaves (or technically, flattened branches called cladophylls) turn yellow, and saffron crocuses (*Crocus sativus*) push their blossoms through the veil.

Aster spp. are field flowers usually too large and rangy for the small garden and best left to blend with goldenrods where they bring the glory of fall to backcountry roads—and sometimes interstates. *A. lateriflorus* grows wild along the eastern seaboard and was always special to those who knew it, but now a beautiful cultivar called 'Horizontalis' is available. This plant never tops three feet and tumbles down among other fall flowers like a moving cloud of white. The white stars are especially elegant among tiny leaves that turn a lovely coppery-purple in autumn. There are also many new dwarf varieties of the New England aster (*A. novae-angliae*) that create two-foot-high domes of one-inch flowers, so tightly packed that the leaves disappear among the petals. 'Audrey' is lavender-blue,

'Jenny' is cyclamen-red, and 'Snow Flurry' and 'Pink Bouquet' speak for themselves. Use them in clumps in the rock garden or as edging for the border. For large lavender daisies, try *A. linearifolius*. Its common name, sandpaper aster, refers to its rough texture. A well-grown plant can reach four feet, and the flowers bring great charm to any border, woodland garden, or rock garden.

Athyrium goeringianum 'Pictum', the Japanese painted fern, is listed in older garden books as *A. niponicum pictum* or *A. niponicum* 'Metallicum'. *Flora of Japan* calls it a cultivar of *A. iseanum* and lists *A. niponicum* as an entirely different plant—and so, in the world of botanical names, it goes. But whatever name you choose, this is, as Elisabeth Sheldon describes in her book *A Proper Garden,* the "handsomest of all ferns with its elegant combination of greens, grays, and dark wine red." A deciduous fern, it has broad triangular fronds that arise from a creeping reddish rootstock and reach a height of about twelve inches. It enjoys a shady, somewhat moist spot, so we grow it under a Chinese snowball tree, where it shares space with a small concrete Foo dog and tropical plants on summer holiday from the greenhouse. This fern is said to be hardy as far north as Zone 4, and I can attest to its hardiness in the Catskill Mountains.

Begonia grandis, or hardy begonia, is considered a nuisance to those gardeners in warmer climates who object to its seeding about. But the plant is welcome in mine, not only because of the pink flowers and the tan seedpods that persist into winter but also because of the marvelous bicolored leaves. The first time I saw a gardener take advantage of the reddish undersides and the bright red veining was in the Asheville garden of Peter Gentling; he planted a line of hardy begonias on a west-facing slope so that the setting sun would light up the leaves, almost as blatantly as neon signs on Times Square but with far more panache. Height is about eighteen inches and the plant thrives in partial shade. It is hardy in Zone 6 with protection. (You can also start new plants each year from the bulbils.) 'Alba' is an attractive white cultivar.

Cimicifuga species are commonly called fairy-candles or bugbanes. The first common name comes from the tall spires of small white, mostly petalless flowers, each made of countless glistening stamens. The second name refers to the plant's insect-repellent capabilities. Forget the second and concentrate on the first. There is nothing like these plants for a shady border. In the North they will take some sun, especially if the soil is moist, but in a southern garden, they need shade. Graham Stuart Thomas, one of England's greatest plantsmen, rates *C. racemosa* a good garden plant of exceptional beauty. One of the shortest of the American species is *C. americana,* which bears six-foot-high flowering stalks. Although relatively tall for a small garden, the plants are only a few feet wide and the foliage is attractive even when plants are not in bloom.

Digitalis lutea is a perennial species of foxglove. Flower spires are about two feet high and festooned with dainty pale yellow blooms in summer. *Digitalis lutea* is especially attractive when planted in bunches. Try massing yellow foxgloves in front of Himalayan honeysuckle (*Caryopteris* × *clandonensis*), a four-foot-tall shrub that bears pale blue, fringed flowers in summer to early fall. Both plants do well throughout Zone 5.

Euphorbia characias wulfenii is a subspecies that is one glorious euphorbia, considered by Gertrude Jekyll to be "one of the grandest and most pictorial of plants." Trust me, it is. But if you don't live in the eastern Mediterranean basin or in USDA Zone 9, forget it and settle for smaller, less flamboyant members of the genus, such as *E. epithymoides* or *E. griffithii*. The first, commonly called the cushion spurge, produces a foot-high mound of foliage in spring, covered with showy bright yellow bracts that surround tiny flowers. As summer advances, the yellow fades, and by the time annuals are at their best, the plant becomes a small green mound that now bears attractive, light orange seedpods.

Euphorbia griffithii 'Fireglow' bears orange-red bracts atop three-foot branches. After flowering is over, usually about the beginning of July, cut the plants back and fill the void with summer annuals.

Fuchsia magellanica comes from southern Chile and Argentina. It is reliably hardy in North Carolina's Zone 6 as long as it is protected with mulch. In my garden plants stay about three feet high and are covered with flowers—a bit smaller than the popular flowers grown in baskets—from summer until frost. For an attractive combination, mix this fuchsia with pink petunias.

Gypsophila spp., or baby's-breath, creates a cloud of blossom with its multitude of tiny flowers. Plant it in front of dwarf conifers at the edge of a wall so that the blossoms can tumble over. Baby's-breath is excellent for both cutting and drying. The single best cultivar—to date—is the white, double-flowered 'Bristol Fairy', created in 1928 and still going strong. The soil must be lean and have perfect drainage, since the roots of these plants cannot abide wet soil. To extend the bloom, deadhead before the plants set seed. Baby's-breath is reliably hardy to Zone 4.

Helenium autumnale is a native American plant known as sneezeweed because the heavy yellow pollen is so obvious as it falls from the flowers. Three cultivars are especially valuable: 'Brilliant' has chestnut-colored rays; 'Butterpat' bears brilliant yellow flowers; and 'Moerheim Beauty' has graced gardens since 1930 with brownish red flowers that fade to burnt orange. All these cultivars grow to about three feet.

Some years ago, long before autumn gardens were fashionable, I designed a garden that would begin to bloom in mid-September and—unless cut down by an early killing frost—last until the beginning of October. There were a number of asters, both tall and short, and prairie coneflowers called Mexican hats (*Ratibida columnifera* forma *pulcherrima*), but the centerpiece of the display was sneezeweed.

Helianthus salicifolius, or willow-leaved sunflower, and *H. angustifolius,* the swamp sunflower, are closely related and easily confused. Both are large plants, usually reaching six feet or higher, and both bear small, two-inch flowers that cluster at the top of each plant. In the garden, each looks like a small willow bush with a vertical emphasis—perfect for the small garden. I first saw them in a book *The Personal Garden* (Wolgensinger and Daidone, Van Nostrand Reinhold, 1975), which includes a photograph of a German garden with a striking display of eight willow-leaved sunflowers. They spread by runners so keep them in a collar and tie the stems together at the bottom; they are easily pulled out when not wanted.

Helleborus niger, the Christmas rose, and *H. orientalis,* the Lenten rose, are great plants for hybridizing, not to mention collecting. Just a few years ago they were considered specialty plants, but they are now seen in more gardens. Many catalogs proclaim Christmas roses hardy as far north as Zone 5, but unless the plants are well protected in winter with glass cloches or a heavy blanket of snow, the evergreen foliage will suffer from freezer burn. Even with protection, hellebores usually don't flower until early spring. It is only in the warmer parts of Zones 6 and 7 that Christmas roses really bloom for the holidays and Lenten roses blossom in late February. Although hellebores grow reasonably well in acid soil, they are bigger and more florific when planted near a mortared wall or stone steps that leach a little lime. At the entrance to our garden room, to the left of the steps, is a large Lenten rose that bears masses of pure white flowers. The leaves form a green fountain, making it an attractive plant ten months out of the year. The only time beauty suffers is after the previous year's leaves have shown their age and before the new year's white flowers begin to open.

Lenten roses interbreed like the gods of ancient Greece, the baby plants visible under the parent's leafy umbrella. Watch out for unusual color combinations, and if you find a winner, take care that it survives.

Heuchera spp., or coralbells, are mostly western natives that thrive in rough terrain. Although the flower stalks can reach a height of two feet, the individual blossoms are so small that five plants in full bloom look like a red haze. To see a hummingbird dashing among tiny bell-shaped blossoms is a garden treat. Deadheading results in future blossoms, so remove developing seeds. Where summers are hot, coralbells can take a little filtered shade, but they do best in sunny spots. The one thing that plants hate is wet feet so be sure there is good drainage and enough humus in the soil. Every few years break up the bigger plants or they will eventually crowd themselves out and blooming will suffer.

Among the many cultivars available are 'Chatterbox', with dozens of bright pink flowers on eighteen-inch stems; 'White Cloud', a twenty-inch plant that bears white flowers; and 'Matin Bells', bearing coral-red flowers on eighteen-inch stems.

Also, watch for *Heuchera micrantha* 'Palace Purple', bearing reddish bronze foliage and off-white flowers on eighteen-inch stems. This cultivar is hardy to -20°F and does poorly in heavy clay. Use it for border edging, in the rock garden, or mixed with wildflowers. The flowers are self-sterile, so you'll need to cross-pollinate them for seeds. For the best color on mature leaves, choose those plants with the darkest foliage.

Hibiscus moscheutos subsp. *palustris,* or rose mallow, is an American wildflower that inhabits coastal areas from Massachusetts to North Carolina. It is so tropical in appearance, it's hard to believe it can survive winter in Zone 5. The strong stems bear eight-inch leaves with shallow lobes. The hollyhock flowers bloom most of the summer, measure four to five inches across, and come in colors of pink, purple, and white with a red eye. Rose mallow reaches eight feet in the wild but is shorter in the garden. 'Lady Baltimore' is a four-foot-tall plant with large flowers. 'Southern Belle' is even shorter but smothered with ten-inch blossoms in shades of white, pink, or bright red.

Hosta sieboldiana 'Frances Williams' is a star among hundreds of hosta cultivars and species now on the market. In my opinion it's one of two hostas every garden should have. The large puckered leaves of this eighteen-inch-high plant are medium green with an uneven edge of yellow, forming a thirty-inch circle. The pale lavender flowers bloom in early summer. In our garden this

plant sits just below the large white hellebore (see above) that flanks a set of stone steps. When the threat of frost is over, I place on the steps two concrete urns, each holding a maroon-leafed flax lily (*Phormium cookeii*). The five-foot leathery, sword-shaped leaves are in stark contrast to the deeply cut, dark green leaves of the hellebore, and both set off the hosta.

Hosta plantaginea, my other favorite, arrived in England sometime in the late 1700s from China. The leaves are finely shaped, and in early autumn, the long waxy-white trumpet flowers appear, opening in the evening and sending out a delicious honeysuckle fragance. The only problem with this plant is that the blossoms tend to be burned by early frosts in northern gardens.

Oenothera is another genus of plants to consider for the small garden. Some species, such as *O. missourensis* (*M. macrocarpa*), open their blossoms in late afternoon and stay open all night. These are commonly called evening primroses. Other species, known as sundrops, bloom by day. They have simple leaves and are easily missed in the garden until high summer, when clusters of bright red buds open to four-petaled flowers, each the color of molten gold.

Sundrops are often listed in nursery catalogs as cultivars of *O. fruticosa,* a native of the eastern United States that reaches eighteen inches tall and bears two-inch flowers. *Oenothera tetragona* has foliage that turns red in the fall and has been used for a great deal of hybridizing. Cultivars include

'Sonnenwende', which bears brilliant orange-red flowers, and 'Fireworks', one of the brightest flowers in the summer garden. Care for all sundrops is minimal. Their only requirements are full sun and a well-drained soil; even in hot summers, dryness is never a problem.

Platycodon grandiflorus, the balloon flower, is native to eastern Asia. The five-petaled flowers are waxy with prominent veins; before opening, they look exactly like hot-air balloons, ready to float up to the sky above. These plants are perfect for very small gardens, since they form clumps and do not spread. Because balloon flowers are among the last plants to break spring dormancy, be sure to mark their position carefully. Cultivars include 'Album', which has white flowers; 'Blue', with two-inch, deep blue flowers; and 'Double Blue', bearing double flowers with dark veins. We have balloon flowers in our rock garden, in front of a three-foot-high dwarf Alberta spruce (*Picea glauca* var. *albertiana*) and in the border sharing space with sweet Williams (*Dianthus barbatus*) and blackberry lilies (*Belamcanda chinensis*).

Sedum kamtschaticum is valuable throughout the entire garden since the species variation is quite remarkable. It needs only full sun and well-drained soil to thrive. Called the orange stonecrop, it grows four inches high and has deep green, scalloped leaves. The orange-yellow flowers bloom from July to September. 'Variegatum' has light green foliage tinged with pink and ivory.

Sedum aizoon reaches about twelve inches high and bears flat heads of yellow to orange starlike flowers in midsummer. 'Ruby Glow', a hybrid between *S. cauticola* and *S. telephium,* is worth considering. The flowers are rose-pink in midsummer, then darken as they age. After the flowers fade, the seed heads remain, adding interest to the plant—and to the garden. The reddish stems look attractive ambling over low walls and rocks.

Sedum spectabile 'Autumn Joy' was once known as 'Indian Chief' and 'Herbstfreude'; by any name, it's a super plant for the small garden. Here is one case where familiarity has not bred horticultural contempt. The bright green succulent leaves grow on thick stalks. In spring the tightly packed heads of green buds resemble broccoli. As summer advances, the rounded flower heads expand and turn pink atop two-foot stems. When nights are colder, the spent flowers turn a lovely shade of mahogany, persisting into the coldest months and making great dried flowers for winter bouquets.

Solidago spp., commonly known as goldenrod, still gets poor reviews from most American gardeners, and even the odd extension agent still believes these plants belong only in field or forest. Many people blame this plant for hayfever, but the real culprit is the rangy and unkempt ragweed (*Ambrosia* spp.), whose ugly, small green flowers throw bushels of allergy-irritating pollen to the winds and unfortunately bloom in the same fields and waste places as goldenrod. The English know better. They have developed many cultivars of *Solidago;* more than thirty are now in cultivation, with new varieties coming every year.

Solidago canadensis is the parent for many new cultivars. 'Golden Baby' is a compact plant—about twenty-four inches high—with upright sprays of golden flowers. It blooms the first year if seed is started early in the spring. 'Golden Dwarf', sometimes called 'Goldzwerg' (*Zwerg* is German for gnome or dwarf), bears yellow flowers on foot-high stems. 'Cloth of Gold' is eighteen inches tall and bears golden blossoms. 'Golden Fleece', developed from *S. sphathulata,* reaches a height of two feet and sports wands of golden flowers.

Solidago rugosa, the rough-leafed goldenrod, grows about four feet tall in the garden, taller in nature. The golden blossoms are clustered on the tops of arching stems. A new cultivar called 'Fireworks', developed by the North Carolina Botanical Garden, offers sprays of golden-yellow flowers that light up the autumn sky.

Tricyrtis spp., from Japan, bears the unfortunate name of toad lily. This valuable member of the lily family bears no resemblance to any warty amphibian, but looks more like an artifical flower made of pipe cleaners or scraps of chenille. A late bloomer, it brightens the border in late September and October. The most common species offered by nurseries is *T. hirta,* whose one-inch mauve and purple flowers are born in the leaf axils of arching stems. Planted at the edge of the border, toad lilies are especially beautiful as they float above the lawn in what we call our garden room. 'Miazaki' bears white and lilac flowers. Toad lilies are hardy as far north as Zone 4 with protection.

Verbena bonariensis (V. patagonica) is a tall species of the mostly tropical verbenas, named for the city of Buenos Aires and now naturalized in the warmer parts of the Southeast and California. (In colder areas, you can raise new plants every season and get blooms if seeds are started early in the year.) Wiry stems grow to six feet and are topped with five-petaled flowers of rose-violet. When massed, they make a striking show.

This verbena is especially beautiful when planted in the midst of lamb's-ears (*Stachys byzantina*). I also keep plants at the base of the rock garden where the stems shoot up between the branches of ground-hugging junipers.

Woodland Gardens

~

MY OLD FRIEND BEBE MILES ONCE SAID, "THE WORD *WILDFLOWER* IS A PARADOX TO START with. Many species of tulips are wildflowers in Turkey or Greece but treasured as garden delights in the rest of the world. The bloodroot, which grows in open woods from eastern Canada to Florida to Texas, is described thusly in an English gardening book: 'Although quite hardy, it also makes a good alpine house plant.' The resident of Maine or Michigan who reads that laughs."

A SELECTION OF WOODLAND PLANTS

Considered wildflowers by at least some people, the following plants are perfect for creating a small woodland garden.

Allium stellatum goes by the common name ramp, ramsons, or wild leek. It's a lovely plant whose leaves, once bruised, smell of onion, and disappear by late summer. Small white flowers appear on twelve-inch stems. Grow *A. stellatum* under a deciduous tree so that the early spring leaves can get enough sunlight to pump nourishment back to the bulb.

Anemonella thalictroides, or rue anemone, belongs to the buttercup family. It grows to a height of eight inches and produces several small white flowers with prominent yellow stamens. This delightful plant is perfect for colonizing at the edge of a woodland garden, and it never outwears its welcome, since the leaves dry up by midsummer.

Aquilegia canadensis and *Aster lineari-folius,* listed under "Perennials," are both lovely in the woodland garden.

Chrysogonum virginianum, green-and-gold or golden-star, is another American native worthy of better press. In the North it can take full sun, but from Pennsylvania south to Florida, make sure it gets partial shade. Green-and-gold blooms from spring into summer.

Colchicum spp. are commonly called autumn crocuses, but they belong to the lily family (whereas crocuses are bulbous member of the iris family). Though beautiful in their own right, *C. autumnale* and *C. speciosum* 'Album' have produced one of the loveliest fall-blooming flowers, a hybrid called 'Waterlily'. Originally from southern Europe and North Africa, this hybrid originated in the Haarlem nursery of Zocher and Company sometime before 1905. Corms are hardy, with some protection, to Zone 4.

Coreopsis verticillata, the thread-leafed coreopsis, will grow in almost any soil. It thrives in full sun, so we put ours at the front of the border. The wiry stems can sometimes grow to three feet but are so delicate they never infringe on neighboring plants. Remove the old seed heads during the summer to encourage bloom until frost.

Dicentra eximia, called turkey corn or fringed bleeding heart, is an American native and one of the best in the genus. When given ample water and shade during hot summers, it will produce lovely pink or rose blooms from spring until the first hard frost. The foliage is attractive, too.

Eupatorium rugosum, or white snakeroot, always surprises me because it blooms profusely even in dense shade. I remember the white ageratum-type flowers glowing in the middle of autumn foliage in our woods in the Catskill Mountains. White snakeroot is especially attractive underneath a dogwood tree. It is also lovely near wintergreen (*Gaultheria procumbens*), a dainty ground cover of small evergreen leaves and nodding white bell-shaped flowers, followed by large, lustrous red berries. All white snakeroot needs is partial shade and moist—but not wet—soil. If the weather is very dry, provide some extra water.

Heuchera villosa, a southern species of coralbell, is perfect for small gardens in Zone 6. This fifteen-inch-tall plant bears sprays of tiny white bells that stand above attractively pointed leaves, many with beautiful markings. Cultivars are available in many different colors.

Hypoxis hirsuta, yellow star grass, is one of the longest-flowering plants in the woodland garden since it blooms from spring to late fall. The lovely yellow flowers last only one day but are quickly followed by dozens more. Just remove spent flowers and give the plants plenty of water when times are dry.

Iris cristata, crested iris, is also a good candidate for the small woodland garden. Across from our house is a shaded roadway, too narrow for a road and too wide for a path, leading into a woodland that has been untouched for decades. In the middle of that road—where the oaks are taller and the shade more pronounced—is a large colony of these lovely plants. When they bloom, nothing could be finer. I think they are worth a try in colder areas; mulched with leaves or pine needles, my plants survived Catskill winters.

Phlox divaricata and *P. subulata* are two species of woodland phlox. The first reaches sixteen inches in height and bears fragrant blue to lavender flowers. There are many beautiful garden cultivars, including 'Fuller's White'. The second hugs the ground and has almost become a cliché, now that it is used throughout the Northeast and Midwest as one of the first showy flowers of spring.

Polemonium reptans, Jacob's-ladder, has somewhat ferny foliage and clusters of small blue bells on one-toot stems that bloom throughout the spring. The foliage remains decorative until fall.

Sanguinaria canadensis, bloodroot, is, like most of the good things in life, fast fleeting: the pristine white flowers can bud, bloom, and fall within a week, especially if buffeted by spring rains—but what a week! There is a double-flowered cultivar originally called 'Multiplex', but that unfortunate moniker is slowly being replaced by 'Flore Pleno'. The sap is blood-red and is used in toothpaste to fight bacterial infections and plaque.

Smilacina racemosa, or Solomon's-plume, is also called false Solomon's-seal because the foliage of the two plants looks similar. The true Solomon's-seal (*Polygonatum commutatum*) is a larger plant that can make a strong statement as it arches over a garden pathway, decorated in spring with small bell-like flowers, then later with small, deep blue berries. But *Smilacina,* false Solomon's-seal, is better for all-season interest. In spring two- to three-foot-tall stems bear terminal clusters of tiny starry white flowers that turn to bunches of red berries by fall. This plant benefits from extra water during dry summers.

Tiarella cordifolia, commonly called foamflower, makes a great ground cover for a shady garden. It's a creeping plant with maplelike leaves and narrow clusters of tiny white flowers that appear on foot-high stalks in spring. The flowers lack petals and are a mass of foamy stamens—hence the common name. In the South it must have shade, and it prefers the cooler mountains to the hot and humid seashore. Never let this plant go without water.

PLAN FOR A SMALL WOODLAND GARDEN WITH ALL-SEASON COLOR

This garden is designed to sit at the corner of a seven-by-seven-foot square. To begin, you'll need a deciduous tree so that shade will be available during the summer months. Choose a dogwood (buy the Chinese *Cornus kousa* if there is any disease in your area) or one of the other smaller trees mentioned in chapter 12.

Candytuft (*Iberis sempervirens*), a mix of spring crocuses (*Crocus* spp.), and annual alyssum

(*Lobularia maritima*) provide a long season of color. Wild ferns, such as maidenhair fern (*Adiantum pedatum*), ebony spleenwort (*Asplenium platyneuron*), and Christmas fern (*Polystichum acrostichoides*), are also well suited for this site. The soil should be deep and include plenty of leaf litter and compost. This garden is hardy to Zone 4.

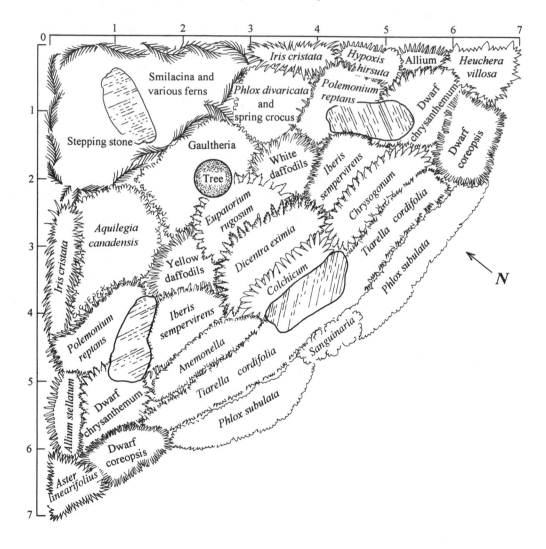

Four

Ornamental Grasses and Bamboos

I HAD A CLUMP OF GIANT EULALIA GRASS (*MISCANTHUS SACCHARIFLORUS* 'GIGANTEUS') IN our northern garden, sitting smack-dab in the middle of a thirty-foot-long English-style border. Although this fourteen-foot specimen was as tall as a small tree, the proportions worked—and this particular grass lent an air of mystery to the scene and effectively divided the border into two sections.

Regardless of the size of your garden, there's always room for at least one type of ornamental grass. The various species exhibit amazing variations on a simple blade (or leaf) of grass, and because their pollen is wind-borne and not carried about by insects, the flowers are designed to be waving plumes of grace and elegance. As an added benefit, their arching stems, called culms, make whickering sounds whenever breezes blow.

These plants are interesting almost year-round. The blades of most ornamental grasses turn various shades of brown, sepia, and tan when autumn arrives, and the floral plumes continue to wave in the wind until winter's worst finally tears them to shreds.

A SELECTION OF ORNAMENTAL GRASSES

The following plants are perfect for most small gardens and are meant to be used as focal points. I've tried making entire gardens of ornamental grasses but unless you have a large tract of land, the scale is wrong and the constant arching blades become repetitious, crying out for different leaf designs and textures.

Chasmanthium latifolium, the beautiful northern sea oats, goes to the head of the class. Doing well in full sun or light shade, this grass can reach a five-foot height but grows in such a tightly packed clump that it is never too pushy for the border. The flowering spikelets are very attractive and will stay whatever color they are when picked, whether fresh green or golden brown. On a cold and rainy day in January, my specimen stands tall, and the winds of December have yet to reduce the leaves and seed heads to tatters. Sea oats will seed about but the new plants are never invasive.

Festuca ovina var. *glauca* represents a large clan of ornamental and forage grasses with narrow pointed blades. Until just a few years ago, the most common was the original blue fescue, a short ornamental with a bluish bloom; it is useful for edging or, if set out in rows, creating a sense of pattern in a small area. Today there are many species and cultivars that range in height from four inches to four feet. From Europe comes *F. amethystina,* with three attractive cultivars, all of which grow about eight inches high: 'April Gruen', which has olive green blades; 'Bronzeglanz', with bronze blades; and 'Klose', olive and an excellent ground cover. At four inches, *F. alpestris* is well suited for the rock garden, and at four feet, the giant fescue (*F. gigantea*) is perfect at the edge of the woodland garden. Unlike the other fescues, it revels in a bit of shade.

Hakonechloa macra 'Aureola', sometimes called golden hakonechloa, originally came from the mountains of Japan, where it grows on wet, rocky cliffs overlooking the sea. Because nurserymen think that Americans

cannot deal with the word hakonechloa, most labels now read "Japanese forest bamboo." In Japan the plant is grown in pots, but the best effect is achieved when two-foot-high plants border a shaded path or walkway and the warm yellow leaves, striped green and off-white, gracefully bend to the ground. The foliage is especially striking in fall when touches of magenta appear. This grass blends especially well with hostas and ferns.

Imperata cylindrica 'Rubra', Japanese blood grass, has been around gardens for about fifteen years but is still little known. The leaves vary between one and two feet in height and can adapt to partial shade in the South. As the summer days get warmer, the blades of grass begin to turn blood-red. A mass planting (at least six plants to start) creates a startling effect and is great for the rock garden or at the front of the border.

Miscanthus sinensis 'Gracillimus', commonly called maiden grass, is one of the most graceful grasses in cultivation. Stiff culms grow about six feet high and arch out to create beautiful fountains of narrow leaves with conspicuous white midribs. Not only is maiden grass perfect for the border, it also does well in damp soil at the edge of a pond or lake. By setting plants out in two or three rows, you can produce a very effective hedge.

Miscanthus sinensis 'Zebrinus', zebra grass, belongs in every garden, large or small. It's difficult to believe that this tropical-looking grass could survive in Zone 5 winters, but it does. The leaves are not striped (as the common name suggests) but dashed with horizontal bands of a light golden brown that appear in summer when temperatures climb above 70°F. Large clumps develop over the years, usually reaching six or seven feet. A specimen planting in the middle of a lawn is very effective and not as blatant as a clump of pampas grass (*Cortaderia* spp.). The flowering panicles are large and showy with purple-silver tints, eventually fading to tan.

Molinia caerulea 'Variegata', variegated purple moor grass, also works well in small gardens. Every year a fountain of rather rigid leaves—banded with white and gently curling toward the ground—appears in early spring, often reaching a height of three feet by the end of May.

The flowering stems are striped like the leaves, but tinged with violet and light green. After the first frost of autumn, the leaves turn a light tan, and the whole plant resembles a bursting skyrocket tied to the ground rather than lighting up the sky.

Pennisetum alopecuroides is a fountain grass that forms four-foot mounds. 'Moudry', a late-blooming cultivar, grows to three and a half feet and blooms with stunning black flower heads (and it does seed about). Two new and smaller cultivars are available: 'Hamelyn' usually forms three-foot mounds, but in a lean and dry soil it may reach only eighteen inches. Then for very small gardens there is 'Little Bunny', an extremely dwarf form of fountain grass that just tops ten inches.

TWO BEAUTIFUL BAMBOOS

Arundinaria viridistriata, the Kamurozasa bamboo, is a comparatively dwarf species that grows about two and a half feet high. It's also a runner; you'll need to cut off unwanted runners with a lawn mower or clippers, or contain the wandering roots with plastic or metal collars buried at least a foot deep. This splendid plant is worth the extra effort because its narrow leaf blades have the texture of velvet—velvet striped with chartreuse green and soft yellow in spring, then fading to green by early summer. There is a clump of Kamurozasa bamboo against the wall of our garden room; I have contained its wandering roots at the front and back so that it will wander

only to the sides. Use this bamboo in pots or planters, especially on decks or patios. Unfortunately, it's hardy only in the warmer parts of Zone 6.

Sasa veitchii is called the Kuma bamboo in Japan and the silver-edged bamboo in America. This is a magnificent bamboo, one of the best for either a small or a large garden. In the fall the edges of each leaf are burned by frost and turn a pale buff or light tan, creating a variegated effect. (Because of the band of dried tissue, this bamboo retains its shape in water and is thus the only bamboo that's good for flower arrangements.) According to many nursery descriptions, the Kuma bamboo normally grows to three feet. The warmer the winter, however, the taller the plant. Under optimal conditions the culms can reach six feet. Use Kuma as a hedge or a mass planting in the corner of a low-maintenance backyard.

Kuma also makes a good potted plant, either indoors or out. This plant is said to be hardy in Zone 5 but I'm sure that is only in a well-protected spot.

GRASSES IN THE GARDEN

The following design is for a small garden that mixes ornamental grasses and bamboos with black-eyed Susans, goldenrods, and asters for an especially attractive autumn garden.

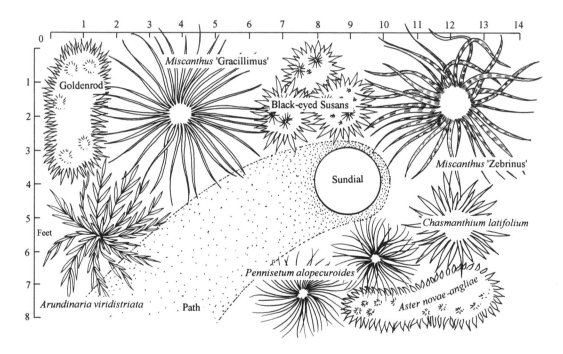

Five

Herb Gardens

~

WHAT IS THE TRUE VALUE OF A SMALL HERB GARDEN? IN *OLD TIME GARDENS,* ALICE MORSE Earle described a friend's garden in Chicago: "On a bleak day in December we both revelled in holding and breathing in the scent of tiny sprays of Rue, Rosemary, and Balm which, still green, had been gathered from beneath fallen leaves and stalks in her country garden, as a tender and grateful attention of one herb lover to another. Thus did she prove Shakespeare's words true even on the shores of Lake Michigan: 'Rosemary and rue: these keep seeming and savor all winter long.'"

Last week during Thanksgiving, my wife went to our garden room to pluck some ambrosic leaves from a small rosemary bush against the stone wall. I have added weeping love grass (*Eragrostis curvula*) for its attractive dried leaves in winter. There is also a clump of saffron crocus (*Crocus sativus*), whose late blooms are propped up by the herb's branches.

All through the seasons these fragrant, flavorful, or medicinally useful plants are tough. In high summer, for example, herb gardens are places of marvelous smells, subtle colors, the buzzing of various insects, the whirr of hummingbirds, and the flutter of butter-flies. While other plants gasp for water or wilt from the summer sun, most herbs survive and take all the punishment a vengeful climate can hand out.

For gardeners seeking instant gratification, herbs are perfect. Plants are easily grown from seed and quickly grace the garden with shades of gray, green, and purple and many touches of blue and yellow—not to mention the marvelous textures.

Herbs have few demands. Most herbal plants need only full sun, poor—not rich—soil, and near-perfect drainage. To achieve perfection, construct a raised bed of wood, stone, or brick in your small garden so that water easily percolates through the soil.

A SELECTION OF HERBS

The following herbs are a few of my favorites. Cultural requirements are the same as above, unless otherwise noted.

Achillea millefolium, yarrow, was named in honor of Achilles, who supposedly used the plant to treat his ankle. (It didn't work.) The flat floral clusters are composed of many tiny blossoms and are attractive both fresh in the garden and dried for winter bouquets. (To extend cut-flower life, make sure the flowers are open and pollen is visible before cutting.) 'Coronation Gold' grows to three feet and bears beautiful bright yellow floral heads up to four inches across. The gray-green leaves are both attractive and aromatic.

Aconitum napellus, known as monkshood or wolfsbane, has long been a personal favorite because of its use as a poison in mystery novels and additional associations with werewolves in horror films of the late 1930s and 1940s. The plant is the source of aconite, the powerful heart stimulant. The strange-looking flowers are shaped like a monk's cowl and are usually purple blue or light blue. Unlike most herbal plants, monkshood requires partial shade, moist soil, and cool temperatures. You can raise new plants from seed or by division.

Agastache foeniculum, anise hyssop, is valuable not only for the long-lasting floral spikes but also for its wonderful fragrance. Bees fly about the flowers all summer long,

and if touched on a cold January morning, even long-dead flowers will delight the nose with their sharp lemony scent. Because both fresh flowers and dried flower stalks are decorative, anise hyssop adds interest to the garden most of the year. The strong, square, three-foot-high stems never bend but stand straight and tall in the perennial border or herb garden. American Indians used hyssop leaves for medicinal teas. Plants will bloom the first year from seed. In the South, they will tolerate some shade.

Allium schoenoprasum is the botanical name for garden chives. There's nothing quite like clipping fresh chives for a breakfast omelette or to garnish cottage cheese or soup at lunch. Plants produce beautiful balls of rose to rose-violet flowers. After they finish blooming, cut them back for a second crop of flavorful leaves and lovely flowers. Grow from seed or divide clumps.

Allium tuberosum, garlic chives, are called *gow choy* by the Chinese. Bulbs produce strap-shaped leaves and twenty-inch flower stalks bearing umbels of white, starlike flowers. The blossoms impart a gentle taste of garlic and a touch of the exotic to salads; the leaves taste like onions. The flowers dry to a light brown and produce shiny black seeds that resemble marcasite. In warmer climates they will seed about.

Asclepias tuberosa, called wild milkweed, butterfly weed, or pleurisy root, is small and suitable for the wild garden or sunny border. All the species have strangely beautiful and complex flowers, but *Asclepias syrica,* the common milkweed that has naturalized in fields, is too large for a small garden. *A. tuberosa* produces flat umbels of flowers that range from bright yellow to reddish orange or orange. Once established, the woody roots are very tough and require no attention, but first-year seedlings need some protection from winter heaving. Wild milkweed is easy to raise from seed; transplant only young plants whose roots are still short. In folk medicine the roots were used to treat lung inflammations and applied to bruises. The plants provide food for caterpillars of the monarch butterfly.

Atriplex hortensis 'Rubra' is called mountain spinach, French spinach, or red orach. The leaves are a mild, colorful salad ingredient, but I grow the plants as a striking wall of color in the herb garden. Blood-red arrow-shaped leaves run up and down six-foot stems. In the fall, when the plants go to seed, they produce flaming crimson, heavy-set plumes that make excellent dried flower arrangements. Red orach is especially effective in the small herb garden when grown on a tripod of six-foot-long bamboo stakes.

Chrysanthemum parthenium, feverfew, is a short-lived perennial that usually grows to a height of two feet. It bears pungent ferny foliage and many white, three-quarter-inch daisylike flowers with pale yellow discs. Plants grow easily from seed and are drought resistant. There are a number of cultivars,

including 'Aureum', which has chartreuse yellow foliage, and 'Ultra Double White', with double flower heads. A tea made from feverfew has been used in treating arthritis, fevers, and colds but beware: some people experience allergic reactions from using the leaves.

Cymbopogon citratus, Asian lemongrass, is not only an important food item but also supplies the lemon oils found in various detergents and furniture polishes. Chopped leaves are used to flavor many Asian dishes, and the bulblike basal culm is thinly sliced, then added to soups and sauces. Most oriental food shops keep lemongrass roots in their coolers; once potted up, they will usually grow. Although lemongrass is tropical, for short periods the roots have been known to survive temperatures below 40°F. The light green grass blades reach a height of three feet and are planted out in summer, then potted up for winters in a window greenhouse or sunny window.

Dictamnus albus, the gas plant, is the only species in this genus. Other common names include dittany and fraxinella. This perennial bears unusual fringed white to rosy purple flowers with five petals atop three-foot stems, blooming in late spring to early summer. The crushed leaves smell of a mix of anise, sweet clover, and lavender, but most gardeners find it decidedly citrus in content. According to folklore, if on a warm summer's night a lighted match is held to a crushed leaf or seedpod, a volatile oil will burn with a blue flame, much like that produced by burning brandy. I have tried it but have yet to succeed. Gas plants resent being moved and should be left alone after the first planting, so choose the spot with care.

Echinacea purpurea, purple coneflower, bears cone-shaped prickly heads of bronzy-brown surrounded by petals (actually ray flowers) that are horizontal when young but soon droop (or reflex). Rose-purple flowers bloom on very stout stalks from two to four feet high, and continue until they are cut down by hard frost; deadhead to prolong bloom. The simple alternate leaves are very rough to the touch. The white cultivar is called 'Alba'.

Coneflowers are especially beautiful when at least three or four plants are grown together. They make excellent cut flowers and can easily withstand drought conditions. It takes two seasons for a large clump to develop from seed, but plants will bloom the first summer if started early. The chemicals from coneflowers are used to treat many ailments and present research points to their use in cellular defense mechanisms.

Eupatorium purpureum and *E. maculatum* are the botanical names for Joe-Pye weeds. These are very large plants; those brought in from the wild can reach a height of twelve feet or more. Yet their soft purple blossoms have a place even in the smallest herb garden. Trim the plants in midsummer to keep their height in check. I have one specimen of *E. maculatum* (so called because of purple spots and blotches, *maculae* in Latin, on the stems), at the end of our boxwood hedge, along the stone wall; it makes a nice small "tree."

Eupatorium fistulosum has given rise to a white cultivar called 'Album', endowed with the whimsical name Joe-Pye's bride by Alan Bush of Holbrook Farm. At a little over four feet tall, this new introduction is an excellent plant for very small gardens.

All three of the above-mentioned species need full sun but will tolerate some shade in the South. Unlike most herbs, Joe-Pye weeds revel in damp, moist soil. Butterflies, especially swallowtails, are attracted to the flowers. Teas made from the leaves and roots of these plants were used to treat ailments of the urinary tract and gall bladder.

Foeniculum vulgare, common fennel, is often listed as an annual, but if properly mulched, the roots often survive winters in Zone 6. Plants can reach six feet. The leaves are so finely cut, they resemble soft, waving plumes and the new growth looks like young feathers. Countless tiny greenish yellow flowers form large, flat umbels, adding to the plant's lacy effect. There is an especially attractive cultivar called 'Bronze Form', whose leaves are a deep, reddish purple that matures to bronze. Tea from fennel seeds has the taste of anise and is used to treat gastric upsets. Plant oils are known to be sterilizing agents but too much of the oil may cause contact dermatitis.

Lavandula spp. have *cachet.* Because of the felty gray leaves and the lovely flowers, lavender is probably the most popular of the fragrant herbs. Today it remains one of the primary fragrances in soaps, toilet waters, and sachets. The three species most often grown in herb gardens and formal borders are the English lavender (*L. angustifolia*), French lavender (*L. dentata*), and the Spanish lavender (*L. stoechas*). All three of these subshrubs reach a height of three feet and make perfect edgings. For an especially attractive display, try growing three or four plants together so that the foliage becomes a distinct patch of gray.

Unfortunately for gardeners in the North, these delightful plants resent the cold. English lavender can survive—but not thrive—in Zone 5 with protection; the other two are hardy only to Zone 6. All three like hot summers, full sun, and perfectly drained, sweet soil. If your soil is highly acidic, plant lavender near a stone or mortared wall, or add lime to raise the pH.

Liatris spicata, blazing-star, is an American native that produces lavender to purple flowers on dense spikes up to thirty inches high. Unlike most floral stems, these bloom from the top down, making them perfect for cut flowers. The foot-long, narrow, grasslike leaves form a dense clump and are attractive in the garden even when flowers are absent. If you give these plants moist, fertile soil, they grow much taller. I have five blazing-stars in my front border, along with three Spanish-bayonets (*Yucca aloifolia*) and three red yuccas (*Hesperaloe parviflora*). This combination looks good all season long yet requires no work except occasional weeding. The roots of *Liatris* species were once used in treating kidney and bladder ailments.

Marrubium vulgare, common horehound, is a thirty-inch-high perennial member of the mint family that is known as a bitter herb. And it's so bitter that merely touching a crushed leaf to the tip of your tongue is enough to set off the alarm in your taste receptors. The entire plant appears gray green because woolly white hairs cover both the square stems and the round, wrinkled leaves. Small white flowers arranged in whorls bloom in summer. The stems twist and turn about other plants and provide a beautiful effect. In our garden it is combined with yellow calla lilies (*Zantedeschia elliottiana*), whose large, arrow-shaped, silver-spotted leaves are in fine contrast to those of the horehound. Soil must be well drained or horehound will fail. The plant also dislikes damp weather.

Oenothera biennis is my favorite evening primrose. It was originally an American plant, but so many seeds traveled to Europe and elsewhere around the world that today, many people think it's a foreign import. These biennial plants are straggly if grown in poor, rocky soil, but given half a chance, by the second summer they become large, many-branched specimens, sometimes reaching over four feet tall. In midsummer they bear many sulfur yellow flowers that open as the sun goes down. The blossoms' lemony scent is very attractive to moths.

American Indians used the roots to treat many disorders; an oil extracted from the seed is used to improve imbalances of essential fatty acids in the production of prostaglandin.

Pelargonium is the genus of the scented geranium. These delightful plants scent perfumes and potpourris and flavor food. Scented geraniums reach a height of two feet and bear small pink or white flowers. They can be grown as annuals, but since they are true perennials, only tender, they are excellent container plants to overwinter in a sunny window. The leaves have various scents, including rose, apple, nutmeg, ginger, peppermint, lemon, pineapple, and coconut. If you like vanilla pudding, you will love it when a leaf or two is used for added flavor.

Rosmarinus officinalis, the common rosemary, is a wonderful evergreen shrub that grows to four feet. The deep green needlelike leaves have a piney scent and surround small light blue flowers in spring. This classic culinary herb imparts a marvelous taste to foods and has been used in the kitchen for centuries. Rosemary is also a good subject for topiary. Unfortunately, it is hardy only to 10°F and needs protection. If you live in the North, bring the plant indoors to a sunny window for the winter months.

Rudbeckia hirta, or black-eyed Susan, is a wildflower annual, biennial, or short-lived perennial, depending on soil and climatic conditions. Its resistance to heat and its long period of bloom make it well suited for the herb garden. These plants were used by American Indians as a root tea for treating colds and also for external applications to treat snakebites and earaches.

Cultivars of *Rudbeckia hirta* include the gloriosa daisies, which are even stronger when it comes to drought resistance; badly wilted plants will perk up before your eyes if given a dram of water. They can, in fact, be moved in full bloom. Blossoms can expand to seven inches and are lovely in varying colors that range from orange, yellow, or gold, to tan, brown, and dark red. The flowers of 'Irish Eyes' have green eyes instead of black, and 'Goldilocks' bears double golden-yellow flowers on fifteen-inch stems.

Rudbeckia laciniata, a native coneflower first described in 1753, often reaches a height of ten feet in the wild. It's not particularly attractive, but the double-flowered cultivar 'Golden Glow' is and still survives around old farmhouses and in abandoned gardens, having been around since 1913. Plants can be seven feet tall and often need staking. 'Golden Glow' has great color and charm at the rear of an herb garden, and in the small garden it is the surprise that shouldn't be there—a column of green topped with a living bouquet of golden yellow. There is also a newer cultivar (introduced in 1951) known as 'Goldquelle', which seldom tops thirty inches and is not invasive.

Santolina chamaecyparissus is called lavender cotton. This many-branched, two-foot perennial is covered with tiny silvery leaves and small heads of minuscule yellow flowers. The best use in the garden depends on the attractive color mix of gray and yellow. Lavender cotton was once used to treat worms in children and repel moths in linen cupboards.

Solidago odora, sweet or anise-scented goldenrod, is one of more than a hundred American goldenrods but is the only species I know that makes a pleasant-tasting tea when its dried leaves are steeped in hot water. Small clusters of yellow flowers appear atop slender two- to three-foot stems. Sweet goldenrod does not spread about like many of its relatives. It requires an acid soil but tolerates partial shade. In old home remedies, the leaves were used to treat colic, stomach cramps, and fever. But be warned, some people are allergic to this plant.

Stachys byzantina, lamb's-ears, is grown primarily for the silvery gray, six-inch oval leaves. Covered with dense, woolly white hairs that are very soft to the touch, they really do look like lamb's ears. The leaves were once used to dress battle wounds. Full sun is mandatory for lamb's-ears, and the soil must be really well drained and very dry—or plants start to rot. Somewhat attractive pink to lavender flowers are borne on eighteen-inch stalks, but their number is so few that blooming stems are best removed and dried for winter bouquets. Without maturing flower stalks, the plants spread faster.

Teucrium chamaedrys, or germander, is a two-foot perennial with glossy dark green toothed leaves and purple to red-violet flowers arranged in whorls near the tops of the stems. Once a popular stimulant used to treat intermittent fevers and gout, germander is best used as a low hedge. It responds to yearly trimmings and looks great in knot gardens.

Thymus includes the creeping thymes, small plants that are perfect for setting between stones or for filling small cracks in walls. They thrive in dry, well-drained soil and full sun. *Thymus praecox,* or mother-of-thyme, grows about two inches high and is evergreen in mild areas. Lemon thyme is *T.* x *citriodorus* but is often listed as *T. serpyllum.* There are many cultivars, including 'Pink Chintz', which blooms for long periods and tolerates even drier conditions than the others. Common garden thyme, *T. vulgaris,* is the most powerful spreader of the lot, so be careful when planting it in rock gardens or other places where it could overpower weaker plants. Use thyme sprigs in lentil soup.

Yucca spp. are indigenous American wildflowers that bear stout clumps of stiff, sword-shaped leaves and tall stalks of nodding, bell-shaped white flowers, usually blooming at night. In the desert (and occasionally in a suburban backyard), flowering stalks can reach twelve feet. But this spire of bloom arises from a spiky rosette that is often less than three feet in diameter and thus a fine focal point in a small garden. In the North, the evergreen yucca leaves are wonderful when dolloped with snow during a bleak winter.

Yucca filamentosa, the hardiest of the species, can endure northern winters without injury. The common name, Adam's-needle, refers to the sharp, pointed leaves and the threadlike hairs that line their edges. Once established, yucca will perform every year regardless of drought because of a very deep taproot. American Indians used this root in salves and poultices for skin afflic-

tions. A powder prepared from pounded roots, if spread on the surface of a pond, will stupefy the resident fish.

The following two cultivars of *Yucca filamentosa* are offered by nurseries: 'Bright Edge' has variegated foliage edged in yellow-gold, and 'Variegata' has leaves with creamy white stripes.

PLAN FOR A SMALL HERB GARDEN

This olitory (the original word for an herb garden) is set within a square of land measuring thirty by thirty feet. Half the area is covered with paving stones, bricks, or fieldstones.

At the center is a lozenge area of grass bordered by an annual of choice, perhaps a different one every year. The center is a perfect spot for a small garden sculpture or sundial.

Since there are many small fruit trees available today, I thought an apple tree or a quince should be included in this garden plan. Why quince? you ask. Because, I answer, the quince (*Cydonia oblonga*) is not only a good small tree with spring blossoms beyond compare, but there is nothing quite like the taste of quince jelly on homemade bread liberally dashed with butter.

The Irish juniper (*Juniperus communis* 'Hibernica') is certainly not classy enough to be included in the previous list but the cone berries are great for flavoring stews, marinades, and even gin.

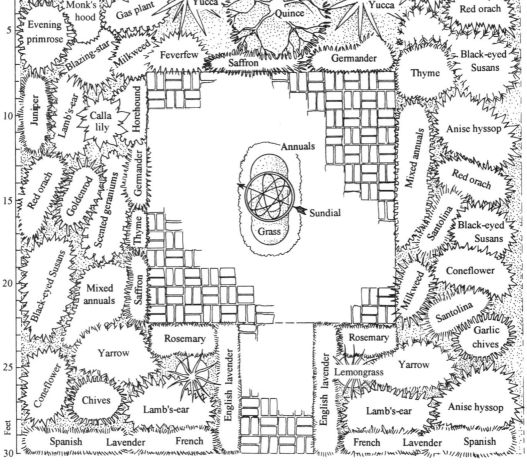

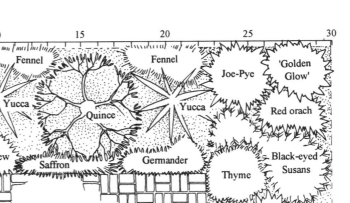

Six

Bulbs and Other Tuberous Plants

FOR YEARS I GAVE AN ILLUSTRATED LECTURE ON BULBS AND NEVER NOTICED THE AUDIENCE'S mystification when I compared a bulb to a portmanteau, both of which carry supplies: for the bulb, it's leaves, roots, and flowers; for the traveler, it's clothing, toiletries, and shoes. I've changed *portmanteau* to *suitcase* but somehow the new metaphor lacks that touch of class. Still, a bulb is basically a container for storage. It's an underground stem wrapped in a series of leaves that look like scales, forming a rounded shape that if cut open lengthwise will show embryonic leaves, a stem, and a flower, all ready to bloom when the right time comes around. Lilies, daffodils, and onions are all bulbs. Today most nurseries include corms, tubers, and rhizomes in the bulb group. Though unlike bulbs in structure, they still contain everything needed to keep the plant growing during the early weeks of development.

Corms are a series of underground stems wrapped in a round or pear-shaped package, usually flat on both top and bottom. Crocuses and gladioli are examples of corms. Tubers are modified underground stems that are swollen with stored food. Daylilies, dahlias, tuberous begonias, and potatoes are all tubers. Rhizomes are yet another underground storage system: they are horizontal perennial stems that bear roots and upright stems. Calla lilies and iris grow from rhizomes.

The marvelous thing about bulbous plants is their ability to carry an initial food supply. If you buy top-quality plants from reliable sources, usually they will all bloom the first year. (What happens the second season, however, depends on the gardener.)

There are two major requirements for growing bulbs. The first is good drainage, since most bulbs will not tolerate wet soil. The second is friable soil. Hard, dense soil can cause bulbs to pop right out of the ground, propelled by their strong root systems. If you have heavy clay soil, be sure to incorporate plenty of organic matter when planting bulbs.

Bulbs are very easy to plant. You can carry an entire garden in a paper bag while you mull over your landscape. Most bulbs go into dormancy part of the year. Their leaves turn yellow, dry up, and finally disappear. This is the time to move them if you're rearranging your garden; in fact, when dormant, bulbs are far easier to move than most garden plants. To cover any bare spots left in the garden by dormant bulbs, bring in geraniums or bedding annuals. Bulbs are easy to propagate, and many of them, like lilies, readily adapt to pot culture.

Just as a small percentage of the commercial world is greedy, there are greedy souls in the world of gardening. Instead of propagating new plants in a nursery setting, unscrupulous collectors go out into the wild, dig up native bulbs, then sell them to unsuspecting gardeners. As a consequence, many bulbs are now rare or have disappeared entirely from their natural habitat. When purchasing bulbs, look for a notice in the catalog or on the garden center's packaging that indicates nursery propagation.

FAVORITE BULBS FOR THE GARDEN

Use bulbs as you would perennial plants, sticking them in the border wherever their color, texture, or form would be welcome. Once planted, some bulbs are permanent fixtures; others must be dug up in the fall and overwinter in the potting shed or the greenhouse. Over the years I have developed some favorites, and their descriptions follow. It is an idiosyncratic selection. Unless noted, these bulbs are hardy in USDA Zone 4.

Acidanthera bicolor, the peacock orchids, have been removed from the *Acidanthera* genus and assigned a new name, *Gladiolus callianthus.* Whatever the name, they are close relatives of the glads but infinitely more attractive. The star-shaped flowers, creamy white with a dark maroon center, are pollinated at night by moths attracted to the sweet fragrance. Height is about two feet. North of Zone 7, dig them up in the fall and store in a warm, dry place. Up North, you can jump-start the season by planting each corm in a three-inch peat pot. I put a large grouping of peacock orchids in the middle of the perennial border.

Agapanthus africanus, lily-of-the-Nile, has attractive straplike leaves that arise from thick rhizomes. Leave these plants outdoors only where the ground never freezes. They are great plants for decorative pots. Flowers are blue or white and bloom for at least a month or more; the dozens of individual flowers make a globular cluster on a long straight stem. 'Peter Pan', is a dwarf cultivar that rarely tops sixteen inches with sky-blue flowers.

Allium christophii, commonly called stars-of-Persia, produces eight-inch-round balls of many small, star-shaped, metallic-pink flowers with green centers. The wide leaves look very untidy after the plants bloom, so place the bulbs behind other flowers. The dried seed heads are attractive, however. *Allium karataviense* has no common name but does have beautiful straplike leaves that enfold burgeoning balls of starry, greenish-white flowers. These bulbs do well when forced in a pot for late winter blooming.

Arum italicum, Italian arum, is a tuberous plant that produces unusual flowers, resembling ghostly Jack-in-the-pulpits, hidden behind the arrowhead-shaped leaves. By late summer, both the flowers and the leaves are gone, but in the fall foot-high stalks are topped with lipstick-red berries. Then in late fall or early spring—depending on your climate—the new leaves appear. This elegant plant looks great in front of a stone wall. Give partial shade in the South. Cultivars include 'Pictum', with dark green leaves marbled with veins of a light yellow-green. In the South, Italian arum needs partial shade.

Caladium × *hortulanum* is the botanical name for the fancy-leaved caladiums. These tropical tubers are grown for their colorful leaves, which range from white veined with green, to pink edged with red, to endless combinations of maroon, silver, fuchsia, and creamy to dead white. The flowers are interesting but resemble unattractive relatives of the Jack-in-the-pulpit. Plant heights vary from nine inches to two feet. Caladiums make great edgings and are also wonderful when massed in floral beds. Before planting, make sure the soil temperature is 70°F. The

larger the tuber, the more leaves you will have. Caladiums need partial shade up North and deeper shade in the South. I have lined our stone pathways and steps with the brighter colors as they help us to walk the garden at night.

Chionodoxa luciliae is better known as the glory-of-the-snow. This bulb blooms early in the spring and bears eight to ten one-inch star-shaped flowers on five-inch stems. The plants naturalize with ease, so remove the spent blossoms if you don't want them to seed about. 'Pink Giant' is an especially attractive cultivar that bears eight to ten rose-pink flowers on each stem.

Colchicum spp. are cormous herbs that belong to the lily family and are commonly called autumn crocuses. They are marketed in a number of lavender or mauve variations but the one I like the best is *Colchicum* 'Waterlily'. This hybrid was registered before 1927, and in my opinion nothing better has appeared on the market since. The mauve double blossoms, which appear in early October, do look like the blossoms of showy aquatic plants. The none-too-attractive leaves show up in spring. These plants naturalize well and should be planted in large groups.

Crinum spp., the crinum or spider lilies, are spectacular members of the amaryllis family. *Crinum* × *powellii* 'Album', one of the best, is hardy in Zone 6. The bulbs are very large—often over four inches wide—and produce long, medium green, straplike leaves followed in summer by three-foot-tall stalks topped with trumpet-shaped blossoms. They have a very sweet fragrance, especially at night. Plant the bulbs at least nine inches deep so that only the tops of the necks are exposed. These plants like lots of sun, even in the South. They also do well in pots; allow the roots to get crowded before you repot.

Crocosmia spp. are corms that produce arching two- to four-foot stems; the blooms appear in mid- to late summer when days are really warm. They are hardy in Zone 7 if planted in a sheltered spot; we have a large batch against the west wall of our house. The best is *Crocosmia* 'Lucifer', well-named for its brilliant red flowers. In colder areas, dig the corms after frost browns the leaves and store them in a bag of peat moss at 50°F.

Crocus includes dozens of species and cultivars, all easy to plant and dependable bloomers. My favorites for welcoming spring are *C. chrysanthus* 'Princess Beatrix', a clear lobelia blue with a golden yellow base, and *C. sieberi* 'Firefly', bearing flowers that open with rich lilac petals, each with a yellow base. Both bloom as the snows recede.

Crocus sativus, commonly called the saffron crocus, is a true autumn-blooming crocus. The blooms in late fall are followed by grasslike leaves that last well into the winter. Corms need a moist, rich soil that does not dry in summer and is laced with well-rotted manure. Plant at least five to seven inches deep; replant every three or four years. In my experience saffron crocuses are not reliably hardy north of USDA Zone 6. The bright orange stigmas of these flowers are used in a number of medical treatments and are also gathered and dried for an aromatic food color.

Cyclamen persicum is the botanical name for the desert cyclamen. Since before the time of Queen Victoria, hybridizers have worked with this particular species and changed their dainty, sweetly scented, reflexed flowers of white flushed with pink into the large, blousy blossoms traditionally given to Mom on Mother's Day. Two of the best species are *C. coum* and *C. hederifolium* (*C. neapolitanum*). The first plant blooms in late fall and early winter, when purple-magenta flowers appear on three-inch stems, held above shiny green leaves. The second plant bears pink flowers in late summer and continues blooming into autumn; the lovely green leaves are marbled with silver. Both cyclamens need well-drained soil, rich in organic matter, and a place in the shade. And both species are hardy only to Zone 6, but they also do well in pots. Unlike other tuberous plants, cyclamens grow larger every year, producing more and more flowers. They also seed about and will slowly naturalize in the garden.

Eranthis hyemalis, winter aconite, pushes its buttercup blossoms up through the snow to face the cold air of very early spring. Each one-inch-wide flower has six waxy yellow sepals (the petals have evolved into nectar-secreting areas within the flower). Bunches bloom on four-inch stems and carpet an area with gold. These bulbs need full sun but can be planted under deciduous trees, since the foliage will have faded away by the time the trees have leafed out in early summer. The tubers are usually shipped in early fall and will be especially florific if soaked in tepid water for twenty-four hours before planting. Winter aconites can be moved or divided even when they are in full bloom. If happy, they naturalize with ease.

Fritillaria meleagris, the guinea-hen flower, produces bell-shaped blossoms that droop on delicate stems. The petals bear checkerboard patterns: 'Artemis' sports a square pattern of purple and green; 'Poseidon' has gleaming white petals marked with purple checks. Their exotic appeal is outdone only by *F. michailovskyi,* a new species that has bell-shaped blossoms of burnished mahogany tipped with gold.

Galanthus spp., snowdrops, bloom a bit earlier than crocuses but last longer. Like aconites, they need a shady spot with a good, woodsy, well-drained soil. Plant new bulbs in the fall, but when time-honored plants become crowded, dig them up in the late winter or early spring and divide them. This procedure does not harm snowdrops at all, but since the roots form in August, digging them up at that time can be fatal.

There are many snowdrop cultivars, including 'Flore Pleno', which has more and larger flowers than the species, and 'S. Arnott', a new snowdrop on the scene that reaches a height of ten inches. All of the species except *G. nivens* are sometimes harvested in the wild, so be sure you know your supplier.

Galtonia candicans, the summer hyacinth, struggled in our northern garden but has done beautifully in North Carolina. If you garden in Zone 6, be sure to include this plant in your summer border. Forty-inch stems bear twenty to thirty fragrant bell-shaped flowers of white with a touch of green at the base. The flowers look like spring hyacinths but are, to my mind, far more attractive. If snow cover is scarce in your area and you don't have the time to mulch heavily, plant the bulbs in mesh bags and dig them up for storage over the winter.

Hemerocallis spp., daylilies, have long been popular war-horses of the garden, especially when you realize that more than seventy thousand cultivars have been created since the late 1800s and some thirty thousand cultivars are available today—with new varieties appearing every year. These perennial tubers bear clumps of narrow sword-shaped leaves that are often evergreen where winters are warm. The stout floral stalks bear six-petaled lilylike flowers in all colors except pure white and blue. Depending on the type, daylilies bloom anytime from late spring to autumn.

Hemerocallis fulva, the common tawny daylily, came to Europe from Asia in the Middle Ages. The plants are self-sterile and known today as the cultivar 'Europa'. All of the daylilies that line the back roads of America are descendants of *H. fulva;* they were spread not by seed but by roots (or pieces of them) pushed about by plows and bulldozers or just thrown out with the rest of the garden trash.

Daylilies are virtually carefree. They can hold dry, rocky banks together or grow with perfect ease in moist soil by a lake or stream. They have no major problems with disease, harbor few—if any—insect pests, and are reliably hardy throughout the country. Plants may be left in one place for many years, but once blooming declines and plants become overgrown, it's time to divide. You can transplant whenever you like but the best time is in early spring, before growth hits its stride.

To plant daylilies, dig a hole, then make a small mound of dirt at the bottom; spread the tuberous roots around the mound. Although tough, daylilies respond to this treatment and settle in to do a great job of blooming.

Daylilies are well suited for beds, borders, and rock gardens as well as edging walkways and carpeting slopes where few other plants succeed. There are literally hundreds of new introductions of daylily cultivars every year. Check the source lists for nurseries that specialize in these flowers.

Hemerocallis citrina blooms in summer and bears arching forty-inch leaves and fragrant yellow blossoms on four-foot stems that open in the early evening and through noon of the following day. *H. fulva,* mentioned above, is too rough for today's formal gardens. *H. lilioasphodelus,* or lemon lily, has fragrant blossoms that appear in late May and early June. A dwarf species, *H. minor,* has yellow fragrant flowers and grasslike leaves reaching a height of eighteen inches.

For small gardens no cultivar is so fine as 'Stella de Oro', with two-foot-long leaves and golden yellow flowers that bloom throughout the season. There are also many new miniature daylilies that usually stop at two feet and bloom for six weeks in the North and twelve weeks in the South. Look for 'Mayan Gold', whose golden yellow flowers sport a green throat, and 'Pardon Me', with bright red flowers.

Iris × *germanica* is the tall bearded iris most people think of when they hear the genus name. Fanlike leaves are gray-green, and flowers come in a multitude of color combinations. Plants are hardy to Zone 4. Some varieties bloom in both the spring and fall. The tall irises are over two feet high, intermediates are between sixteen and twenty-seven inches, standards are eight to sixteen inches, and miniatures are under eight inches. Perhaps the best introduction to the seemingly unlimited colors available is to order a mix from a nursery special offer.

Iris cristata, the dwarf crested iris, is a wildflower hardy to Zone 5 that blooms in early spring. It thrives in early-season sun, then in the open shade provided by deciduous trees. The species is six inches tall and bears lavender-blue flowers with a two-inch yellow crest. A white form is 'Alba'. In areas with little snow cover, mulch these irises.

Leucojum autumnale is the botanical name for the autumn snowdrop. I have a soft spot in my heart for flowers that appear in the fall, so this is a favorite. Louise Beebe Wilder called it a "rare, little autumn-flowering bulbous plant [from] Portugal, Morocco, and the Ionian Isles." Be sure to plant them—in groups of at least a dozen—in front of a low rock wall or a sunny border. Otherwise, the nodding white flowers so characteristic of the snowdrops will be lost to view.

Muscari botryoides, or grape hyacinth, looks like a bunch of grapes hanging upside down. It blooms in midspring and comes in bright blue, pale blue, or white. *M. comosum* 'Plumosum', feather hyacinth, was introduced from the Mediterranean region in 1612. The name derives from the petals, which are fringed as though cut with a tiny scissors.

Narcissus is a genus that includes daffodils, narcissuses, and jonquils. Daffodils have flowers with wide trumpets (or cups), narcissus flowers have short trumpets, and the flowers of jonquils have the shortest trumpets and the sweetest scent. Listed at the end of this chapter are thirteen *Narcissus* species and cultivars, ranging from dainty (like the captivating *N. triandrus* 'Hawera') to very large (*N.* 'King Alfred').

The time of bloom is a very important consideration for the design of a small bulb garden: Some *Narcissus* bloom in early April and at month's end; others are still pushing up flowers well into the middle of May.

Tulipa includes far more beautiful and ususual flowers than most gardeners would believe. There are always the familiar tulips with the brightly colored, waxy petals, found in parks and formal gardens. But those bulbs must be replanted every year or so and are a great deal of effort for so small a return. Wild or species tulips, however, multiply and naturalize on their own. These diminutive relatives are at home in the rock garden, as edging for a formal garden, or even planted between paving stones. They require full sun (partial sun in the South),

good soil that is laced with organic matter, and perfect drainage.

Among the species to try are *T. eichleri,* with showy lipstick-red petals and bright yellow centers, and *T. vvendenskyi* 'Tangerine Beauty', whose petals are an even more brilliant scarlet—and whose leaves not only are rippled at the edges but bear maroon adornments. For a less-than-four-inch beauty, try *T. pulchella* 'Persian Pearl'. Its delicate petals are magenta rose with a greenish tint; inside they are cyclamen purple, dashed with buttercup yellow at the base.

Zephyranthes candida is commonly called the swamp lily of La Plata or the zephyr lily. The first name is derived from a South American region; the second refers to the west wind (the bulbs were discovered in the New World).

This perennial bulbous plant has teninch rushlike leaves that surround lovely, pure white starlike flowers that open in late August and continue to bloom until October. Zephyr lilies require a fairly rich soil, with lots of organic matter mixed in. During the summer months, give them plenty of water.

Zephyranthes drummondii and *Z. pedunculata* are perfect for the evening garden, since they both bloom in the cool night air. The first bears white lilylike blossoms on foot-high stems. The second has three-inch-long pink flowers on five-inch scapes.

Both species' flowers have a sweet fragrance.

PLAN FOR A SPRING BULB BED

A few years ago, my wife and I designed a new bulb bed that included daffodils, narcissuses, a few of the lesser-known spring bulbs, and one species of tulip.

First we built a retaining wall with stones lugged by hand from an old wall in our nearby woods. Using a total of seventy-two stones of all different sizes, I made a sixteen-by-eight-foot rectangular terrace that was even with the rising backyard at the rear and twenty inches above the original soil at the front.

After the stones were in place (the larger stones at the bottom and tilted slightly toward the rear for stability) I dug up the original soil, turned the hunks of turf over, roots up. Next I added ten bags of topsoil and four bags of composted cow manure, mixed it thoroughly, and left it all to settle before planting the bulbs.

When choosing bulbs, we considered the length and time of bloom. We wanted flowers from the beginning of April to at least the end of May. We also wanted a permanent arrangement of flowers that would last for a number of years without needing a great deal of care. True, the leaves of the past-blooming plants would have to remain as bulbs ripened but by that time annuals could be scattered about for camouflage. And the perennial border and the other flower beds would also distract from the browning leaves.

I transplanted a small arctic willow (*Salix purpurea* 'Nana') to the right of the bed, knowing that it would add interest all through the year. This willow grows about three feet high and three feet wide, and can be pruned if it gets out of hand. Then we watered the bed well and looked forward to the coming spring flowers.

The following spring was ushered in by a major sleet storm, followed by another massive attack on March 30. But on April 8 the crocuses began to bloom. The next day the temperature dropped to 16°F. But on April 11, the crocuses opened again to a bright spring sun. On the day that income taxes are due, the *Chionodoxa* 'Pink Giant' opened its petals and on April 24 the fritillaries and the tulips started their display. Meanwhile seven patches of daffodils were acting out the Wordsworth poem by "fluttering and dancing in the breeze."

By May 14 a few late frits were still nodding their blossoms; four patches of late-blooming daffodils were wide open and the tulips were finished. By the end of May a bunch of *Narcissus jonquilla* 'Lintie' were still hanging on. And as they dried, the tulip leaves had turned a beautiful shade of burnt sienna, adding another touch of color. As seedpods formed on the various plants I carefully cut them off, thus guaranteeing extra strength for next year's show.

A final spring frost hit on the night of June 3. On the next day I seeded some tender annuals in among the bulbs, brought out other plants from the greenhouse, and when the last of the bulb leaves died back, I moved in a host of geraniums.

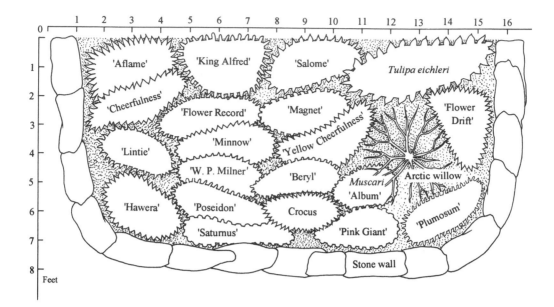

The following is a list of bulbs used in the spring bulb bed:

Chionodoxa chrysanthus 'Pink Giant'. 5″ to 8″, early, rose-pink flowers.

Crocus chrysanthus 'Princess Beatrix'. 3″, very early, lobelia blue flowers with a golden yellow base.

C. sieberi 'Firefly'. 2½″, early, lilac with a yellow base.

Fritillaria meleagris 'Poseidon'. 10″, middle, white flowers checkered with purple.

F. meleagris 'Saturnus'. 10″, middle, red-violet flowers.

Muscari botryoides 'Album'. 8″, middle, white form of the grape hyacinth.

M. comosum 'Plumosum'. 8″, late, featherlike grape hyacinth.

The following are arranged by height:

Narcissus 'Salome'. 18″, middle to late, white petals with a coral-pink cup.

N. 'Aflame'. 17″, early, white petals with a small red cup that has an orange eye.

N. 'Flower Record'. 16″, early to middle, white with an orange, red-rimmed cup.

N. 'King Alfred'. 16″, middle, large yellow trumpet.

N. 'Cheerfulness'. 15″, late, white with a creamy yellow center.

N. 'Magnet'. 14″, early, white petals around a yellow trumpet.

N. 'Flower Drift'. 14″, middle, double white flower; tufts of orange between petals.

N. 'Yellow Cheerfulness'. 14″, late, primrose yellow flowers.

N. 'Beryl'. 10″, early, primrose yellow with a globular orange cup.

N. 'Hawera'. 8″, middle to late, three to five lemon yellow flowers on each stem.

N. 'Minnow'. 7″, middle, miniature with white petals and a yellow cup.

N. 'W. P. Milner'. 7″, early, a miniature warm white trumpet.

N. 'Lintie'. 7″, late, yellow with a flat orange crown.

Tulipa eichleri. 8″, early, scarlet petals with a yellow-margined center.

Seven

Ground Covers

~

IN AMERICA, GROUND COVERS HAVE BECOME BIG BUSINESS. STATE HIGHWAY AUTHORITIES have backed away from spraying defoliants and weed killers along roadsides and turned to plants that require little maintenance. Some states have successfully used mass plantings of wildflowers, planting both annuals and perennials in great drifts of color. Others have planted ornamental grasses. But some efforts have been deplorable: the Commonwealth of Pennsylvania, for example, let loose the invasive crown vetch (*Coronilla varia*), which promises to cover everything in sight.

The ground covers I have chosen to describe (with one exception) are better behaved than crown vetch and suitable for a plot smaller than a highway right-of-way. In fact, you can create a charming garden using nothing except various ground covers.

Fall is a great time to plant perennials, but in most areas of the country, spring is the best time for planting out ground covers: the plants are then geared up to grow after spending the last six months in dormancy.

Before planting, make sure the soil is properly prepared. Remove existing weeds and till the soil or at least spade it up by hand. If you have heavy clay, make sure you add compost. Dig the soil to a depth of six inches. While you're working, keep the plants well watered and in the shade.

Today almost everyone wants instant gratification but when it comes to ground covers, that could be expensive—to fill a hundred square feet with large pachysandra plants would require about eighty plants. Most rooted cuttings are packed four or six to a unit and if planted on six- to ten-inch centers will fill in an area in two years. If you are purchasing plants in four-inch pots, increase the distance to twelve to fourteen inches. Instead of planting out in a haphazard manner, plant in staggered rows. Next mulch the bed with shredded bark, shredded leaves, or a commercial product, such as Nature's Helper. Do not use peat moss, which tends to dry out and repel moisture.

A GROUND COVER SELECTION

Aegopodium podagraria, known in England as ground elder, is an aggressive spreader. Christopher Lloyd, the great English gardener, said that if describing this plant as a gift horse, remember it belongs to the Trojan breed. Luckily, the cultivar called 'Variegatum' spreads at a fast crawl rather than running rampant.

A good garden friend once gave us a clump of the variegated ground elder (also known as bishop's weed or goutweed). We used it on an inhospitable slope in full sun, so it never took, but nevertheless I take great exception with nurseries that describe this plant as being "carefree and vigorous"; it's more like "raping and pillaging."

One day—in a fit of pique—I threw a clump into the nearby white pine woods, where the soil was poor and light was filtered all year by needles. The leaves seemed to glow in the shade, and over the next few years, the plant slowed its spread. So my advice is to eschew the sunny use of bishop's weed and plant it in the shade.

Alchemilla vulgaris, lady's-mantle, sometimes masquerades under the species name of *A. mollis* because many gardeners (and nurserymen) think *vulgaris* means "vulgar"; rather, it means "common to many places." Use lady's-mantle along the front of the border and as a ground cover. The cupped leaves are covered with tiny silken hairs that catch and hold drops of dew that reflect sunlight and roll about like drops of mercury. The chartreuse flower sprays are also attractive. Though it is hardy to Zone 4, provide shade and moist soil south of Zone 7.

Asarum Shuttleworthii is, for most American gardens, the best of the wild gingers. It's a native plant from Virginia, south to Georgia. Unlike the hardier species, *A. canadense,* this plant is evergreen and hardy to the warmer regions of Zone 5, especially when protected by snow. The shiny green heart-shaped leaves make an excellent ground cover, especially in good, acid soil with plenty of shade. The odd flowers look like little brown jugs and lie directly on the ground, where they are seldom noticed. They are pollinated by beetles as they scurry across the earth and seedling plants often naturalize. The rootstocks have a ginger odor and a hot spicy taste. In winter the leaves turn a lovely shade of purple.

Athyrium filix-femina, the hay-scented fern, is said to be an aggressive and invasive plant. I would never introduce it into a perennial border or a rock garden full of precious alpine plants, but it's perfect for carpeting a small bank where little else will grow, or at the edge of a woodland glade where other plants are out of character. Its true beauty comes in the fall, when the sensitive fronds react to frost and turn a wonderful shade of light brown with a golden glow. Add to this the wonderful scent of fresh-mown hay, and it will always be welcome in our garden.

Bergenia cordifolia hails from Siberia and Mongolia, where it tolerates temperatures of -30°F. When exposed to chilly winds below 0°, however, the leaves turn brown and burn at the edges; in winters above 0°F, they turn a reddish bronze. Bergenias prefer partial shade in the summer and a moist, well-drained soil with humus or leaf mold. Their large overlapped leaves are a perfect foil for ferns. As a bonus, bergenias bear rose-pink, waxy blossoms in early spring.

Calluna vulgaris is the only species of heather. Called lings in England, this evergreen grows about eighteen inches high, forming a small mound of foliage. The scalelike leaves overlap each other, lying closely along the stem. Heathers bloom between late June and November. There are a surprising number of cultivars. 'Foxii Nana' blooms between August and September bearing mauve flowers on four-inch-high plants; 'H. E. Beale' reaches a height of twenty-four inches and is covered with large, double pink flowers from August to November; and the pink flowers of 'Mullion' start to bloom in late July and persist through September. Some varieties of *C. vulgaris* are known for the unusual

foliage colors, including 'Aurea', with chartreuse leaves; 'Blazeway', with beautiful copper-colored foliage; 'Gold Haze', with leaves of gold; and the silver of 'Silver Queen'.

Cornus canadensis, bunchberry or creeping dogwood, is for northern gardeners who get tired of hearing about plants that will thrive only in the South. This beauty loves colder weather and actually languishes where summers are hot. In the spring creamy white bracts hover above a whorl of oval leaves a few inches high. The blossoms closely resemble typical dogwood flowers and are followed by clusters of red berries in autumn. The plants need a moist, humus-rich, acid soil. Bunchberries spread slowly by underground runners.

Epimedium spp., the barrenworts or bishop's-hats, are marvelous plants to grow along walls or the edges of pathways. Both the leaves and the flowers (which resemble a bishop's miter), sit on strong, wiry stems. The leaves, though not truly evergreen, have a papery texture and last well into winter, especially where temperatures usually stay above 20°F. The plants are hardy to Zone 5 and thrive in partial shade. *E. grandiflorum* is about one foot tall, with heart-shaped leaves that are bronzy when young, then turn green. The flowers are yellow. 'Alba' is a white form, and 'Rose Queen' bears rose-colored flowers on ten-inch stems.

Erica spp. are the heaths. Like heathers, they are small evergreen shrubs bearing hundreds of pink, red, lavender, or white flowers. Unlike heathers, however, heaths have slightly urn-shaped flowers and tiny leaves that stick out from the stems like pine needles. Plants need an acid soil and excellent drainage. They do poorly where summers are too hot and dry.

Erica carnea, the spring heath, is usually hardy to Zone 6 but will survive in Zone 5 with adequate protection. Like heather, it is acid-loving and thrives under cool, moist conditions. The flowers appear from late fall to early spring, depending on winter temperatures. In my southern garden the cultivar 'Springwood White' has been in bloom since the beginning of December and will continue at least to mid-April. Two other cultivars of *E. carnea* are 'King George', blooming with crimson flowers from January to May, and 'Springwood Pink', with pink flowers blooming from February to April. Probably the hardiest heath is *E. tetralix,* which has gray foliage and rosy flowers that bloom from late June to October; it is able to survive a Zone 4 winter.

Hedera spp., the ivies, are great ground covers if kept under strict supervision. In Zone 7 and the warmer parts of Zone 6, ivy—when left to its own devices—spreads like an oil spill on calm water and must be cut back periodically.

In Zone 5 the winter cold tempers ivy's aggression, especially if there is no snow cover and plants are exposed to chill winter winds. Except for Persian ivy (*Hedera colchica*), *H. pastuchovii* from Russia, and common English ivy (*H. helix*)—and two of its cultivars, '288th Street' and 'Thorne-

dale', originally from an area north of Chicago—most ivies are not reliably hardy under those conditions.

For warmer climes (Zone 6) there is 'Buttercup', whose leaves are yellow in the sunshine but turn dull green in the shade. This fast grower makes a superb ground cover and is especially attractive allowed to grow on a wall. 'Deltoidea', often called sweetheart ivy, bears heart-shaped leaves of dark green that turn purple-bronze in the winter. A slow-growing ground cover, it is especially suited for rock gardens. For a variegated form, look for 'Stardust'. The leaves have a slim edge of white and are blotched with two tones of green.

Iberis sempervirens, the perennial candytuft, needs well-drained soil in full sun. The one-foot-high woody stems bear thin glossy leaves that are evergreen even in the colder parts of Zone 5. In spring clusters of four-petaled fragrant white flowers appear. Crawling over the ground, candytuft will tumble over the edge of a wall and slowly root in clefts and crevices. To keep plants blooming, deadhead old flowers; if they are cut back, they will bloom twice.

Juniperus spp., the carpet junipers, are conifers that make great ground covers. *Juniperus communis* var. *depressa,* the ground juniper, is a low evergreen shrub about three feet high with sharp blue-green needles. Plants artfully spread about and look especially grand when tumbling over walls. 'Aurea' has vivid golden yellow foliage that slowly turns to bronze as the summer passes. *J. horizontalis* 'Bar Harbor' follows the contours of the land and weaves its way among rocks, and also is attractive when hanging over the edge of a wall. Its blue-green foliage turns a lovely purple-blue in the winter.

Juniperus procumbens 'Nana', an ornamental conifer discovered in the mountains of Japan about a hundred years ago, is my favorite ground hugger. The foliage is a fresh green in spring, turning a blue-green in summer, and bronzed in winter. The needles are sharp, but unfortunately not sharp enough to keep deer from devouring the plant. This conifer will eventually cover an area approximately ten to twelve feet in diameter. If you put an obstacle in its path, the branches will work themselves up and over it. In our northern garden, one plant circled part of our scree bed. Today in our southern garden, one specimen hangs over the edge of a stone wall and another sits in a pot.

Lamiastrum galeobdolon 'Variegatum', commonly called the yellow archangel, is still called *Lamium* by most nurseries and books. The evergreen leaves are attractive during the summer but turn to something special in winter, when they are liberally splashed with silver then edged with maroon. Some nurseries call this plant a "vigorous grower." That means it will spread if left uncut. But under trees this is a great plant for covering ground. Spikes of small yellow snapdragon-like flowers appear in spring.

Pachysandra terminalis and *P. procumbens* are the two garden species of pachysandra. Unfortunately, most garden centers stock the first, a Japanese native, and ignore the second, a beautiful American species. It's true that in shady places, nothing beats Japanese pachysandra for covering ground. ('Green Carpet' is hardier than the species and has glossy deep green, slightly larger foliage; 'Silveredge' is variegated.) But compared with its American relatives, *P. terminalis* seems coarse and pushy. *Pachysandra procumbens,* commonly called the Alleghany spurge, has a far subtler leaf color, and the individual plants seem to meld, like pieces of a puzzle that are perfectly matched. The foot-high plants bear oval leaves that are gently toothed, and areas of lighter green touched with silver mark the dark green surface of each leaf. The flowers have a purplish cast and consist mostly of stamens making a mass of sparkling bloom. Alleghany spurge is evergreen in areas south of Zone 6.

Parthenocissus quinquefolia, Virginia creeper, is usually considered a vine. But one year I cut down a white pine that was home to a creeper and, not wanting to lose the vine, carefully pulled the tendrils away from the bark and laid it on the ground. Later I returned to find the vine wandering over the ground and taking root. Either full sun or partial shade will do and the leaves turn a glorious shade of red in autumn.

Rubus calycinoides is known as the crinkle-leafed creeper. The attractive leaves are round and puckered, green in the summer and a bronzed maroon during the winter. Unlike most members of the rose family, it has inconspicuous flowers and no thorns. It is another rampant ground cover, sending out arching branches that soon root at the nodes and spread out again from there. For covering a bank or an enclosed area where escape is impossible, nothing is better. Give this creeper full sun or partial shade. 'Emerald Carpet' is a cultivar with deep green summer color. Unfortunately, it is reliably hardy only from Zone 7 southward.

Tussilago farfara, coltsfoot, is one of the toughest ground covers known. It should never be mentioned in the same breath as plants that are termed delicate, demure, or dainty. The small golden, daisylike flowers of early spring are always welcome, but the leaves are large and extremely insistent. Use it to carpet poor soil and areas of shaded ground but keep it within bounds by planting it between concrete walkways and house foundations.

Vinca minor is myrtle or common periwinkle, a trailing evergreen with shiny leaves and lovely five-petaled flowers of periwinkle blue that appear in both spring and fall. Throughout the Northeast, especially in old cemeteries, myrtle has been growing for centuries. It grows in all but the worst soils, rooting wherever a node touches the ground. Though it tolerates some sun, this plant is happier in partial shade or growing at the edge of a woods. In our northern garden, myrtle grew under a tall white pine. In early spring, the first flowers would appear, opening on and off for weeks. There are a number of cultivars, including 'Alba', with white flowers, and 'Atropurpurea', bearing blossoms of dusty rose. 'Bowles Variety' has deep lavender-blue flowers, and 'Multiplex' has double flowers of purple-blue.

TWO NOTABLE VINES FOR THE GARDEN

There are many vines available for the home garden but most are greedy in their growth habits and reach for far more than the gardener with a limited space can give. But there are two that can be kept within reasonable bounds.

Hydrangea anomala subsp. *petiolaris,* the perennial climbing hydrangea, grows with great dignity, clambering up and over a small wall, up a high wall, or up a tree trunk. The climbing hydrangea not only climbs, it also rambles and thus makes a very effective ground cover. A deciduous climber, it bears yellow-orange bark that peels much like a birch tree's, and the stems

aerial roots cling to any vertical surface. The dark green leaves are two to four inches wide on long slender petioles. The flowers are typical hydrangea blooms, flat-topped clusters six to ten inches wide. This vine looks best when set against a stone wall. It wants ordinary, moist garden soil and full sun in the North but it readily adapts to partial shade, especially in the South. It will not bloom in dense shade. Pruning will keep it under control.

Lathyrus latifolius, the wild sweet pea or perennial sweet pea, has compound leaves and climbs with tendrils. The gray-green, winged stems have narrow paired leaves and are hosts to many upright stalks, each holding twelve or more sweet-pea-like flowers. Blossoms appear in clusters and bloom in the summer. There are a number of cultivars, including 'Snow Queen' and 'White Pearl', both dazzling white; 'Red Pearl', with red flowers; 'Roseus', bearing rich pink flowers; 'Pink Pearl', with light pink flowers; and 'Splendens', having flowers of dark purple and red. Vines can grow ten feet or so but can be curled around to keep them contained. A number of older books on growing vines suggest planting sweet peas along the bottom of clematis and rose vines and allowing the climbing stems to cover over the sparse bottom branches of the others. Try plants along the base of an old wall or to cover the ugliness of cyclone fencing. Provide ordinary, well-drained garden soil in full sun.

PLAN FOR A SMALL GARDEN OF GROUND COVERS

The following garden consists of various ground covers that wind along fieldstone (or brick) pathways and is meant to suggest solutions to shady sites other than the usual pachysandra monoculture.

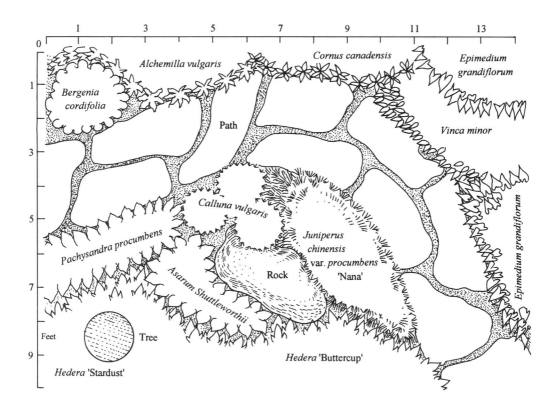

Eight

Alpine Gardens

~

MY HORTICULTURAL ROMANCE STILL PAYS COURT TO THE ROCK GARDEN PLANTS AND alpines, those charmers that peek up at me from rock crevices or beguile me from stone walls.

Alpine gardens can be glorious, but mountain springs are so short and mountain summers are dry, so most alpines bloom early in the year, many while snows are still melting. To attract a fair share of bees, their flowers are large and colorful. And because of the short growing season and poor mountain soil, most of these alpine plants are small.

Years ago, when labor was cheap, many estate gardeners thought nothing of moving tons of granite in an effort to duplicate the look that's found by climbing the average mountain. Taking a cue from the photographs of plant explorers, these gardeners created three-foot mountains in perfect scale and miniature imitations of the Reichenbach Falls—before Sherlock Holmes and Professor Moriarty had plunged over the edge—as background for plants like the edelweiss (*Leontopodium alpinum*), in pursuit of which young men plunged to their deaths.

Budd Myers has been a gardening friend for years. He grows hundreds of species of truly rare alpines (starting most of the plants from seed) in an area measuring about fifty feet square. By using the natural terrain of his sloping backyard, and a bulldozer hired to remove the surface earth, he created a most fitting environment without resorting to imported rocks.

Another rock garden friend, with few rocks on his property, bought a truckload of various shapes and sizes. Referring to photographs of a rocky rill some distance from his home, he laid out his new garden rocks so that they would look natural. If you don't believe this is important, take a look at the studio rocks manufactured for the background of almost all science fiction movies of the 1950s and notice how artificial the setup looks.

I learned much from these gardens: how to get the correct soil mix (by adding plenty of gritty material); the best way to move rocks with the least amount of effort (using leverage and crowbars instead of brute strength); and which societies had seed exchanges (see the Appendix). I also learned that it was not necessary to toss about tons of rock because these plants demand not rocks but good drainage. Whether they come from the Himalayas, the Andes, the Rocky Mountains, or the Alps, alpine plants will not survive in soggy soil; they need water but it must pass quickly over the roots.

Alpine plants have long root systems that work their way down toward the bottom of the bed to find both air and moisture. When temperatures fall in the evening, the stone and gravel chips cool, moisture condenses, and the roots get water. Plants that would die in regular soil will survive with proper drainage.

If you have a flat backyard with a base of clay (or worse), surround a space with a low wall of rocks, fieldstones, or even brick or concrete blocks. Poke holes in the bottom every few inches and fill the enclosed space with the proper soil mix. And if space is at a premium, you can always grow alpines in a trough or container garden (see chapter 10).

There are a bewildering number of plants suitable for rock gardens. The many rock garden societies sponsor seed exchanges, offering average listings of well over 1,000 species a year (in 1992, the American Rock Garden Society listed 6,316 entries.)

In Budd's garden alone, I saw edelweiss from the Alps (*Leontopodium alpinum*), blooming cyclamen from the Middle East (*Cyclamen hederifolium*), dwarf tulips from Central Asia (*Tulipa urumiensis*), blue Himalayan poppies (*Meconopsis betonicifolia*), alpine poppies (*Papaver burseri*), *Aster alpinus* from the Balkan Peninsula, and a prickly pear cactus from the Great Smoky Mountains (*Opuntia humifusa*).

PLANTS FOR AN ALPINE GARDEN

The following plants are available from the nurseries listed in the Appendix. All of the plants are fairly common except for *Meconopsis* spp., which I include just for the adventure. All have proved to be hardy in Zone 5.

Acer palmatum 'Red Pygmy' is a beautiful dwarf Japanese maple originally from Holland. The leaves consist of narrow straplike lobes of a bright reddish maroon;

in summer they turn more purple. After twenty to twenty-five years, a tree will reach about six feet high and six feet wide, but can easily be pruned.

Androsace villosa, the rock jasmine, will come tumbling over the edge of a garden wall with a jumble of rose-pink, or sometimes white, four-petaled flowers. The leaves are gray and densely covered with fine hairs. As befits a plant that revels in walls, rock jasmine loves lime. This plant is easily propagated by seed.

Artemisia schmidtiana var. *nana* forms a six-inch-high by twelve-inch-wide mound of beautiful silver-gray foliage. It also bears small yellow flowers in summer, but the leaf texture and color are what make it so valuable in the rock garden. 'Silver King' is a Japanese cultivar that forms a ball of silvery-white, cut leaves.

Aquilegia spp. are at home in the wild garden and the formal border but there are a number of European species that excel in the rock garden. Look for the lovely yellow *A. aurea,* a native of Bulgaria that grows about fifteen inches high. Or try *A. alpina* 'Alba Nana', a dwarf form from the Alps that reaches about six inches high and bears pristine white flowers. 'Nana', the diminutive cultivar of our own native columbine, *A. canadensis,* is perfect for the rock garden.

Bletilla striata is a reasonably hardy orchid that surprises gardeners with its tough beauty. This terrestrial species (most orchids are epiphytes and grow high up in trees) will bloom every summer with shocking-pink flowers that resemble a miniature cattleya (the corsage orchid of senior proms). Here the flowers cluster on top of eighteen-inch stems. In Zone 5 the plants need a heavy winter mulch. 'Alba' is the white form.

Calceolaria 'John Innes', the slipper flower, is only six inches tall by nine inches wide. A miniature version of the popular Easter plant, this species bears yellow flowers whose lips are lightly dotted with red. Slipper flowers are so tropical in appearance, it's surprising to see them in the garden. Without adequate drainage these plants soon perish, so the rock garden is their perfect home. Provide plenty of mulch in Zone 5.

Calluna vulgaris, described in chapter 7, is commonly called heather. Although it's a small shrub, I've included it with alpine plants because it is well suited for rock gardens. There are many cultivars. I've had success with 'Blazeaway', a golden yellow, foot-high mound of evergreen needlelike foliage that turns orange in winter, and 'Golden Carpet', which turns reddish orange when the cold arrives. Both have tiny bell-like flowers that appear in late summer; the first has mauve flowers, and the second has reddish purple blooms. They are marginally hardy in Zone 5 when given a spot protected from harsh winter winds and, of course, well-drained soil.

Chamaecyparis lawsoniana 'Minima' is one of the best dwarf conifers for the small rock garden. It reaches twenty inches high and twenty-four inches in diameter after ten years. The green, fan-shaped foliage grows at an astonishingly slow rate of one and a quarter inches a year. Protect it from heavy snow, which may break its branches.

Coreopsis auriculata 'Nana' is the small version of the bluegrass daisy, an eight-by-six-inch plant that bears one-and-a-half-inch bright orange daisies. Though not truly a rock garden plant, it fits the scale of its diminutive neighbors. I was introduced to this plant by Eleanor Saur of Hillsboro, Ohio; it was found in the wild by Dr. Lucy Braun near Maysville, Kentucky.

Cytisus spp., the brooms, are best described as evergreen whips covered in early summer with pealike blossoms of pink, yellow, or white. They are spectacular in bloom. *Cytisus* × *kewensis,* eight inches high by four inches wide, is one of the hardiest. Grow it close to a wall so that the stems can drape over the edge.

Dianthus spp., or the pinks, are popular spring-blooming, mat-forming perennials. The spicy-scented, five-petaled flowers are especially attractive to swallowtail butter-flies. *Dianthus petraeus* subsp. *noeanus* bears fringed white flowers; *D. alpinus* has larger blossoms of pale pink to light purple, de-pending on the plant. Seeds germinate with ease and often self-sow.

Doronicum cordatum, leopard's-bane, is a small plant measuring about six by ten inches, blooming with bright yellow daisy-like flowers in late spring. Plants will bloom a second time if spent flowers are removed.

Draba spp., the Russian mustards, are tiny plants from the Arctic Circle and the steppes of Central Asia and are usually found only on rugged mountain peaks. The four petals of the bright white or yellow blossoms open after their expanding buds have actually melted the surrounding snow with self-generated heat. Even on chilly days in late March, the flowers have a sweet smell; only a few flies will be attracted by the scent because most self-respecting bees are still asleep in the hive.

Erica carnea, the snow heath, requires the same care as *Calluna.* Their leaves are more needlelike than those of heathers. In addi-tion, they usually cannot withstand winters north of Zone 6. 'King George' grows about twelve inches high and bears crimson flowers from January to May. 'Winter Beauty' is one of the best, producing pink flowers from mid-February to April.

Festuca ovina var. **glauca** blue fescue, is one of the best ornamental grasses for the alpine garden. Its stiff blades are silvery blue, and the plants resemble eight-inch-tall balled-up hedgehogs lying in wait for the gardener.

Every year there are more species and cul-tivars, including the four-inch-tall *F. alpes-tris* and *F. amethystina* 'Bronzeglanz', or bronze sheep's fescue.

Heuchera spp., the coralbells, demand a well-drained soil with lots of sun. Some of the smaller cultivars are perfect for the alpine garden. One of the best is the compact *H. cylindrica* 'Alpina', a native of the Northwest with greenish white flowers on ten-inch stems. The miniature hybrids, resulting from a cross between *H. pulchella* and *H. hallii,* bear light pink flowers on eight-inch stems.

For something new, try a bigeneric cross between *Heuchera* and *Tiarella* (foamflower). This unique plant bears leaves streaked with maroon and gray, plus eighteen-inch spikes of starlike flowers. First discovered in Nancy, France, in 1917, the proper name is × *Heucherella tiarelloides.*

Hemerocallis spp., the daylily, is usually too large for rock gardens but *H.* 'Good Fairy of Oz' measures twelve inches high and six inches wide, and its rose-colored flowers are in perfect scale with the alpine garden.

Hypericum olympicum, St.-John's-wort, measures nine inches high by twelve inches wide and bears many one-and-a-half-inch golden blossoms with dozens of sparkling stamens that float above satiny petals.

Hypoxis hirsuta, star grass, grows ten inches high by six inches wide. This American wildflower revels in dry soil and bears bright yellow flowers one-half inch wide. Star grass is a member of the iris family and has corms rather than the grasslike roots that you would expect from the leaves.

Meconopsis spp. are familiar to diehard rock garden enthusiasts who are well schooled in growing difficult and demanding plants. The only species type I ever had luck with was *M. horridula,* so called because the stems are covered with spines. Of easier cultivation is *M. cambrica,* the common but still beautiful Welsh poppy. This four-petaled charmer comes in many shades of yellow and orange. It will seed about but is easily controlled.

Ophiopogon planiscapus 'Arabicus', six inches high and six inches wide, is a member of the lily family. The plants are grown not for the small blue flowers but for the striking dark purple, almost black leaves. Unfortunately it's not always hardy north of Zone 6, so be sure you mulch in colder areas.

Papaver burseri, often sold as *P. alpina,* is a lovely little poppy with a sweet scent that will seed around the garden. Once established, it is always there. Like most poppies it resents disturbance, so start seeds in peat pots or sow directly in the garden.

Phlox subulata, moss pink, carpets a wall or bed with bright pink, purple, and white flowers of early spring. If such floral intensity showed forth in July, most gardeners would overlook these little flowers, but because their colors insult a brown and barren world, they will always be welcome. For the purists there is a special white cultivar called 'Sneewichen' that measures three inches high and nine inches wide and is covered with tiny white flowers.

Picea glauca 'Echiniformis', seven inches high by nine inches wide, is another dwarf conifer that makes a great focal point—albeit a small one—in a corner of the alpine bed. It originated from a witches'-broom, an aberration that sometimes appears on conifers in which one branch becomes a miniature of the parent (or a monstrosity), and was thought to resemble an occult mode of travel.

Platycodon spp., the balloon flower of Japan, has produced one small cultivar, *Platycodon grandiflorus* 'Mariesii', which grows to twelve inches high by six inches wide. Plants bear pastel blue five-pointed flowers. Before they open, the buds resemble tiny hot-air balloons.

Solidago spp., the goldenrods, have never been criticized for being too short. But in the Rocky Mountains, nature cross-bred a few of these flowers and created one that is especially suited for alpine gardens. *Solidago spathulata* var. *nana* is six inches high by eight inches wide and looks like one of its larger relatives but seen through the wrong end of a telescope.

Teucrium chamaedrys, germander, is an

aromatic, eighteen-inch-high subshrub that produces two-lipped, pink flowers starting in May and frequently lasting until August. An ancient herb, it makes an excellent small hedge; space plants about six inches apart and clip frequently during active growth. North of Zone 6 they need a winter mulch.

Tsuga is the genus of the hemlocks. Although these conifers are large in the forest, nature has produced a number of very small cultivars. At the rear of our garden, snuggled against the rising bank, I planted a group of the dwarfs: *T. canadensis* 'Cole', a creeper that will follow the out-

lines of every rock and depression in its path; 'Jervis', a hemlock with dense foliage of deep green that grows about an inch a year; and 'Gentsch White', whose fresh growth in spring is tipped with an icy white.

Tulipa tarda is a four-inch-high wild tulip from central Asia. It bears white-petaled flowers with hints of bronzed green above a yellow base. Bulbs need a hot, dry place during the summer months in order to bloom well the following spring. This is one species tulip that should be in every alpine garden.

STARTING AND PLANTING AN ALPINE GARDEN

The following plan is for a small alpine garden measuring five by ten feet. Site it on a gentle rise that gets full sun for at least half the day. If you are lucky enough to have a steep hillside, all the better.

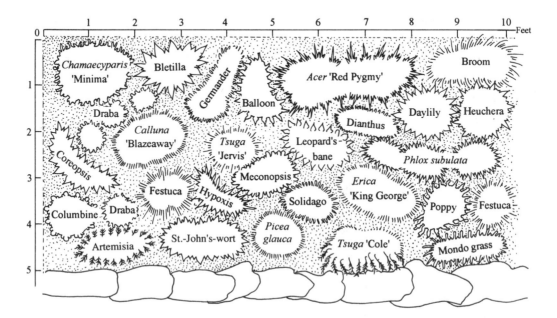

It's best to begin work in the fall. After choosing the spot, remove the turf and soil to a depth of about ten inches. Place the excavated dirt on a piece of plastic sheeting. If you are digging up part of the lawn, you can use the turf elsewhere, or consign it to the compost heap. Break up the subsoil with a heavy-duty pitchfork or long steel shaft. Make sure there are no roots left from weeds; these wiry fibers can travel many feet in their search for water and food.

Next, make a low wall using pieces of fieldstone salvaged from old stone walls and foundations, or purchased stones (find a dealer who carries a large selection of rock). Even concrete blocks will do; I've built low walls of these blocks and capped them with flat fieldstones picked up from walks through the stony fields of the Northeast. But to my mind, flat fieldstones are the best for building such walls. If the rocks are carefully placed, their weight helps to hold them in place. Have delivered a small load of crushed stone or pea gravel to mix with the soil for improved drainage. Now you're ready to build.

Some gardeners can start at one end of a plot and walk out a perfect curve. If you aren't one of them, use a garden hose to mark a gentle semicircle. Then make a single pile, about eight stones high, to mark the height of the wall. Stretch a string across the site—parallel to the bank—to the other side, and mark it. One of the tricky things about building a wall is keeping it level with the terrain, so this step is very important.

Choose the largest stones—between fourteen and eighteen inches wide, eighteen to twenty-four inches long, and three to four inches thick. Lay each stone along the inside curve of the hose and remove soil so that the back edge is about an inch lower than the front. That way, the rainwater will flow into the bed along the sloping rocks and reach the enclosed soil. More important, the slight tilt will strengthen the wall.

If your soil is reasonably soft, excavate at least eighteen inches for the first course of stones to give the wall an extra-firm footing. If the base is packed solid, you can lay stones directly on the ground.

Place the bottom stones as close together as you can, and fill all the gaps with a mixture of dirt and gravel. Once you have laid the initial ring of stones, alternate the next layer of stones so that each gap between stones in the first layer is covered by a stone in the second layer, and so on: two over one, and one over two. Fill all the gaps with a soil and gravel mix.

Pile stones layer upon layer until the wall reaches a height of about thirty inches. Use the flattest stones to finish off the top. The wall should be so strong that you can easily step on the top without a wiggle; you want a comfortable place to sit and look at the plants.

Now fill the cavity. Throw in the little stones you have gathered from your other gardens but were too lazy to haul off. Add broken pots, bits of broken glass, and other pieces of solid trash that have accumulated over the years.

Then add the fill. Mix your excavated soil in a wheelbarrow with some builder's sand (usually available in bags from the local lumberyard). Add leaf mold (if unavailable, use composted cow or sheep manure) and gravel chips measuring half an inch across or less. For every full load of soil, use a half load of sand, a half load of mold or manure, and a full load of chips.

After you have filled half the hole with the mix, wet it thoroughly with the hose to help settle the soil into the rubble on the bottom. Let it sit overnight before adding the other half of the soil mix.

Curb your impatience: plant nothing until the following spring so that the mix has time to settle. Once the plants are added, make sure they get plenty of water and some shade the first few days. I make little shady shelters out of the plastic mesh containers used to sell strawberries and blueberries.

Nine

Japanese Gardens and Moss Gardens

TO KNOW THE POPULARITY OF JAPANESE GARDENS IS TO KNOW THAT A 1993 TELEVISION science fiction series called "Babylon 5" includes in its gigantic eight-mile-long, outer space platform a Japanese stone garden where Earthlings and Aliens can seek spiritual enlightenment and relax from the chores of navigating deep space.

There are dozens of Japanese gardens in arboreta across the United States. Not bad for a style that must compete with more familiar British and continental designs, including cottage gardens, herb knots, and grottoes.

Japanese gardens are beautiful any time of the year. At winter's end, the flush of new growth brings a watercolor intensity to shrubs, small trees, and spring flowers. By early summer, when evergreens are a vibrant green and flowers are blooming, such a garden looks like an oil sketch. But when fall arrives, the sketch becomes a full-blooded oil painting, with the colors of autumn almost flung at the canvas. Finally, in winter a Japanese garden becomes a stark etching, with all colors reduced to beiges and browns, blacks and whites.

I remember visiting the Brooklyn Botanic Garden's Japanese Garden one day in mid-December. The air was cold (about 22°F) and most of the pond was frozen. Yet one small section close to the Torii (a gateway to heaven usually built near a shrine) remained clear of ice. A number of ducks had crammed themselves into the open water like commuters on a rush-hour train. Underneath the cover of ice, the hazy forms of bright orange and spotted goldfish made slow serpentine curves.

There were other colors, too: the light browns of the ducks, the diluted greens of the pine needles glowing through the snow, and the lacquered red of the Torii. Everything else was white on the canvas. The garden was beautiful, yet not one flower was in bloom.

The Japanese islands have been crowded for centuries, and population stresses are reflected in three religious philosophies: Shinto, Buddhism, and Zen.

Shinto appeared before the seventh century and taught that man was a part of nature along with the animals of the woods and the foundations of nature itself: rocks, water, and plants. Later, Japan adopted much of Chinese culture, including Buddhism, a philosophy that not only embraces nature but even teaches that the spirits of the departed can join with nature.

Finally, Zen, a form of Buddhism that arose in India and came to Japan in the fourteenth century, taught that only by self-knowledge and introspection could mankind find truth. It was the Zen monk and artist Sesshu (1420-1506) who brought Buddhism to the garden. He withdrew to a rural temple, where he studied the placement of stones, especially those with flat tops, in a garden.

Stones are endowed with the spirit of nature and represent timelessness, quietness, and stability. There are correct ways to arrange them: A large stone at the garden's center with a smaller stone in the two-o'clock position is good, but if the smaller stone is at the three-o'clock position, the arrangement is bad. If there are more than two stones, they should be arranged in odd-numbered groups of three, five, or seven. One stone in the center of a bed of raked gravel can represent a ship at sea.

Even stepping-stones have a history. They were developed by sixteenth-century tea-ceremony masters to pave the way to the teahouse without causing damage to a silken slipper, a grass stain to a kimono, or injury to the surrounding moss gardens.

Artificial light is very important in Japanese gardens, which are meant to be enjoyed at night. Tea-masters introduced stone lanterns to light the way to ceremonies. The most popular lanterns were those designed to view the snow as it fell upon the garden. In our northern garden, we had an inexpensive snow lantern made of concrete. I wired it with a low-voltage lamp so that its glow would be reflected in the falling snow.

Bamboo fences are another important feature of Japanese gardens. Every fence pattern has a name all its own. *Koetsu sode-gaki* is a long, low, sloped fence used to divide various parts of a garden. *Shiorido* uses shaved bamboo in long strips to make diagonal latticework.

Water is sublime in the Japanese garden. The reflections of water and the sounds it makes are as important as the plants. If water was not available at a garden site, lakes were built to contain it. If space was limited, ponds were used instead. If the garden was small, then stone basins were used. And if water was unavailable, dry streambeds could be constructed using a serpentine pathway of stones. Even the outline of the lake had meaning; an irregular design gives visitors the impression that the view is constantly changing.

PLANTS FOR A JAPANESE GARDEN

"Less is more," said architect Ludwig Mies van der Rohe, who took the phrase from Robert Browning. Never has the phrase been more apt than in the act of choosing plants for the Japanese garden. Most of the following plants are small and consist of shrubs, small trees, and a few special perennials.

Rhododendrons, azaleas, and small conifers are very popular in this country, and there is usually a good selection of small trees at nursery centers. Surprisingly, American gardeners often have an easier time finding plants for Japanese-style gardens than for English gardens. In addition to the plants listed below, there are others in the chapters on ground covers (like the small grasses) and dwarf conifers that will fit into a Japanese garden scheme. Unless noted in the descriptions, all of these plants are hardy in Zone 5.

Abelia chinensis is an attractive shrub from China. Plants grow to about five feet high and have small toothed, oval leaves. Terminal clusters of small white, fragrant flowers appear in early summer. *Abelia* × *grandiflora,* the most vigorous of the species, bears pink and white flowers. 'Francis Mason' is a small rounded cultivar measuring about four feet high and four feet wide. It bears light pink flowers and green foliage that turns to yellow as summer advances. All abelias need full sun and a well-drained soil that is rich in organic matter. They are not hardy north of Zone 6 or 7.

Acer japonicum, the full moon maple,

will reach a height of twenty-five feet when planted in open ground. It's a deciduous tree or shrub with a rounded, bushy, broad form. The many-lobed leaves are green in summer and red in autumn; clusters of small purple-red flowers appear in midspring. There are many cultivars, each with a distinctive leaf pattern or unusual colors in both summer and fall. Japanese maples grow in full sun or open shade. Soil should be moist, of reasonable fertility, and well drained. Trees can be pruned regularly for the small garden.

Aucuba japonica, the Japanese laurel, is evergreen and attractive throughout the winter. Mature specimens can reach ten feet; the shrub in our garden is some twenty years old and only four feet high—but what a splendid four feet! Clusters of small purple flowers appear in early spring and are followed by red berries if a male plant is present. (The flowers are dioecious; that is, male and female flowers are on separate shrubs.) 'Variegata' is a lovely cultivar with gold-spattered evergreen leaves. 'Crotonifolia' has leaves splashed with various shades of yellow. Japanese laurel requires partial shade, especially in the South, and the soil must be well drained and rich in organic matter. These shrubs need protection from the wind in Zone 6 and are not hardy in the North.

Berberis thunbergii, the Japanese barberry, can reach a height of seven feet. This deciduous, arching, densely packed shrub has thorns and small shiny leaves that turn red in autumn. In warmer climates the shrubs are evergreen. Clusters of small pale yellow flowers are followed by bright red berries. Cultivars are available that have gold, rosy, or red leaves all season. 'Crimson Pygmy' has leaves of deep purplish red. These bushes thrive in full sun but adapt easily to partial shade, especially in the South. They tolerate poor, dry soil. Japanese barberry makes an excellent hedge. In our garden it is a companion to the Japanese laurel.

Cephalotaxus harringtonia, the Japanese plum yew, can grow to fifteen feet if it isn't pruned. This evergreen, spreading conifer is similar to a yew but with slightly larger needles that are dark green above and gray beneath. Oval red fruits follow the flowers; male and female blossoms are on separate plants. Plum yews are adaptable to hot, dry climates and are hardy to Zone 6 in protected sites. The cultivar *C. fortunei* 'Prostrata' is a somewhat hard-to-find prostrate spreader. This plant grows to three feet high and has a six-foot spread. The one-inch fruits are an olive green. Plants are not hardy north of Zone 7.

Chaenomeles × superba, the Japanese flowering quince, is a cross between *C. japonica* and *C. speciosa.* This deciduous, four-foot-high spreading shrub has very sharp thorns and is a suitable alternative to a formal fence. Flowers are red, pink, apricot, or white. They are followed by yellow fruits, which are excellent for making jelly. Provide shrubs with full sun to partial shade, in moist but well-drained soil. Prune out any dead wood; flowers are produced on the previous year's growth, on new and old wood. Our Japanese quince survived a bitter cold spell that hit our garden in mid-February. The frost burned many of the blossoms, but luckily some of the buds survived.

Corylus avellana 'Contorta', or Harry Lauder's walking stick, has survived for over thirty-five years in our side garden. It's one of the plants that originally attracted me to this house. In the summer the large, floppy leaves are often attacked by Japanese beetles, and as a shrub or small tree, it fades easily into the background. But come autumn, when the tattered leaves fall and the corkscrew stems are visible, there's nothing else like it in the garden. Then, in late winter, when the two-inch catkins hang like dangling earrings, every garden visitor wants that tree. It is a slow grower and often expensive, but well worth the wait and the cost. In a small area it makes an attractive focal point. The only requirements for this plant are full sun (or partial shade in the South) and water during dry spells.

Ilex crenata, the Japanese holly, is a fifteen-foot-tall evergreen shrub or small tree with a densely branched habit. It bears small, glossy, evergreen leaves and dull white flowers that are followed by small black berries. Many cultivars are available. 'Convexa' is conical in shape and reaches a height of six feet; 'Stokes' remains dwarf, and a twelve-year-old tree is only three feet tall and four feet wide. Provide full sun to partial shade.

Ilex serrata, the Japanese winterberry or finetooth holly, is a deciduous shrub that reaches eight feet high. Leaves are glossy, green, and toothed. Many bright red berries appear in autumn; male and female flowers are borne on separate plants. Hollies do not transplant well, so use containerized plants. 'Xanthocarpa' has yellow fruits; the fruit of 'Leucocarpa' is white. Provide full sun to partial shade and any good garden soil.

Juniperus chinensis, the Chinese juniper, can reach a height of fifty feet, but there are many cultivars available in a wide range of sizes. Shapes range from pyramidal or columnar to mounded or low and spreading. The young leaves are like needles; mature leaves are scalelike and medium green, blue-green, gray-green, or golden. Trees have peeling bark. 'Ames', a broad-based pyramidal tree reaching six feet, needs no trimming. 'Kaizuka', the Hollywood juniper, has a twisted form and makes an unusual hedge. These conifers need full sun but tolerate a wide range of soils. They can survive hot, dry conditions, even in cities.

Juniperus horizontalis, or the creeping juniper, is not only a good ground cover and an excellent plant for a conifer garden but also a suitable candidate for the Japanese garden. These prostrate evergreen conifers have a low, spreading, or creeping habit. Leaves are scalelike and typically bluish green. Prune shrubs to promote bushy growth. 'Bar Harbor' is a popular cultivar that hugs the ground and weaves between rocks; its leaves are steel blue. 'Glauca' covers an area with a dense carpet of blue-green

foliage. Both are beautiful hanging over the edge of a wall.

Kalmia latifolia, mountain laurel, reaches a height of ten feet but is a slow grower. This evergreen shrub or small tree has many branches with deep green, glossy oval leaves that measure up to five inches long. Clusters of complex white or pink flowers (colors on individual plants are variable) bloom from late spring to early summer. Provide partial shade and moist but well-drained acid soil that is rich in organic matter. Mountain laurel is beautiful planted at the edge of a wood and can live a century or more. Even when the trees are old, they can be pruned; cutting back the bottom branches encourages new growth. The very contemplation of lichen-stained bark on an old laurel can convince the gardener that he or she is in Japan.

Pieris japonica, the lily-of-the-valley bush or Japanese pieris, is an eight-foot-high evergreen shrub with glossy deep green oblong leaves. Hanging clusters of small creamy white flowers appear in spring. It does best in full sun with midafternoon shade or in partial shade. For best results, provide a somewhat acid soil that is rich in organic matter. Remove spent flowers to prevent seeds.

Pinus mugo var. *mugo,* the mugho pine, never tops ten feet and is an excellent landscape conifer with an attractive silhouette. This shrublike evergreen bears many spreading branches. The needles are long and bright green, the cones are small. Give mughos full sun. They can tolerate dry, sandy soil. *P. mugo* var. *pumilo* forms a fifteen-inch bun in four years.

Pinus strobus, the eastern white pine, can reach a height of 120 feet or more. But if properly pruned in its fast-growing youth, this evergreen conifer forms a pyramid that can become a serviceable hedge. Long, soft, blue-green needles grow in groups of five. Even on low-growing cultivars, six-inch cones can appear, their tips often white-tipped with rosin. There are many suitable cultivars for the Japanese garden. 'Horsford' is a dwarf form with smaller needles that grows into a bun; 'Prostrata' bears normal foliage but has a completely prostrate habit, always seeking the horizontal and never sending up a vertical leader. Provide full sun and well-drained soil of average fertility, but this conifer adapts to very thin, moist, and even poor soil. Transplant carefully and never let the roots dry out.

Pyracantha atalantioides, fire thorn, is an evergreen shrub with spiny branches that reaches a height of fifteen feet unless it is pruned. Glossy, three-inch-long oblong leaves surround flat clusters of white hawthornlike flowers in late spring. Red berries follow in autumn and persist into winter. Plants produce more berries in full sun. Fire thorns prefer a moist but well-drained soil, though they can withstand somewhat dry conditions. They are hardy to Zone 6.

Rhododendron catawbiense, the mountain rhododendron, begins life as an evergreen shrub but often becomes a small tree reaching a height of twenty feet. The six-inch-long oval leaves are very glossy above. Clusters of lilac-purple, bell-shaped flowers appear in late spring. Use this tree as a specimen plant or in a line of background shrubs. Provide partial shade and a moist acid soil that is rich in organic matter. These plants are very shallow rooted, so be careful when cultivating and be sure they get additional water during droughts. This American native is valued for its hardiness, surviving in Zone 5. *Rhododendron catawbiense* is the parent of many Catawba hybrids. Flowers are now available in white, fuchsia-purple, magenta, violet, rosy lilac, Persian rose, and red.

Rhododendron fortunei, the cloud brocade rhododendron, reaches a height of twelve feet. This evergreen shrub has broad leaves that are a glossy deep green above and smoky blue beneath. Clusters of fragrant pink, funnel-shaped flowers appear in the spring. Partial shade is the key, plus moist, acid soil rich in organic matter. It is not hardy north of Zone 6.

Rhododendron williamsianum comes from southwestern China. It's a rounded evergreen shrub bearing round leaves about an inch long that are apple green on top and silvery beneath. A fully mature plant is only four and a half feet tall. They bloom in early spring with bell-shaped, pink blossoms. The new shoots are often damaged by late frosts, so plants do best in a protected place. If frost threatens, we cover our shrub.

Rhododendron obtusum, the Hiryu azalea, is a four-foot-tall shrub that is semievergreen with a few leaves persisting to the following spring. This dimorphic plant has two sets of leaves: one-inch, elliptical dark green leaves in spring that are followed by more oval leaves in summer. Flowers come in various shades of rose, magenta, red, or red-violet, depending on the cultivar, and bloom in spring. 'Amoenum' has bright wine-red, double flowers; with leaves that turn red in winter, it has a deserving place in our garden. These shrubs need partial shade, and moist soil rich in organic matter and moderately acid. Most hybrids are not hardy north of Zone 6.

Sophora japonica 'Pendula', the Japanese pagoda tree, is usually twelve to fifteen feet tall with a spreading habit. Ferny compound leaves surround drooping clusters of pale yellow pealike flowers in spring. (Trees may not bloom until they are quite a few years old.) Provide full sun and well-drained average soil. These deciduous trees can withstand city conditions.

Taxus cuspidata, the Japanese yew, can reach a height of forty feet but is usually an evergreen shrub or small tree. Spreading and upright branches have soft, flat, narrow and lustrous leaves that are dark green above and light green below. Inconspicuous spring flowers release clouds of pollen and are followed by scarlet berries (really arils) in autumn; male and female flowers are borne on separate plants. Give Japanese yews full sun to partial shade and moist but well-drained soil on the alkaline side. The cultivar 'Nana' is a low spreading bush that grows three feet tall and six to ten feet wide. It is often used for foundation planting and, if it gets out of hand, responds well to trimming.

Taxus × *media* 'Densiformis' grows about eight feet tall and is an evergreen hybrid between *T. baccata* (the English yew) and *T. cuspidata*. The rounded form is made up of dense, lateral branches that bear flat leaves and red berries. This plant is hardier than the English yew. Provide full sun to partial shade and moist, well-drained soil.

PLAN FOR A SMALL JAPANESE GARDEN

In addition to trees and shrubs, the plan for a Japanese garden includes balloon flowers (see chapter 2), hostas (see chapter 2), and horsetails (see chapter 11). Balloon flowers (*Platycodon* spp.) are Japanese to begin with and the flowers are delightful. Hostas (*Hosta* spp.) are favorites for this type of garden because of their marvelous leaf textures, in this case a feature more important than flowers. Horsetails (*Equisetum* spp.) have an architectural strangeness that is especially appealing in an oriental garden.

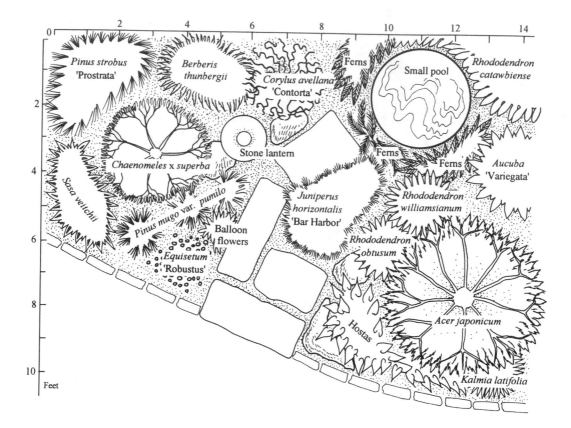

PLAN FOR A DRY STREAM GARDEN

This garden only suggests the presence of water. A small creek or stream runs with gravel or small stones instead of water. With the addition of a bamboo fence or a screen, it takes on a very oriental character. Many suburban lots have drainage ditches in the rear of the property. By filling the ditch with river stones and planting small conifers and ornamental grasses along the edge, it becomes an attractive addition to the garden instead of a liability. The illusion is heightened by placing flat stepping-stones through the gravel "water." The accompanying plan also includes a small pool. (See chapter 11 for more information on pool liners.)

Among the plants to be considered for such a garden are the bamboos, including the beautiful Kamurozasa bamboo (*Arundinaria viridistriata*), with its beautiful mix of chartreuse, yellow, and pale green. The striking green-and-tan Kuma bamboo (*Sasa veitchii*) and the larger ornamental grasses are perfect for this garden scheme. They include the various cultivars of *Miscanthus;* variegated prairie cordgrass (*Spartina pectinata* 'Aureomarginata') with five- to seven-foot sweeping blades edged with a pale brownish yellow; and the common but still desirable Ohwi Japanese sedge grass (*Carex morrowii* var. *expallida*), which bears variegated leaves edged with white. The newer cultivars of Ohwi sedge—including 'Aureo-marginata', with golden yellow striping, and 'Old Gold', with green and gold stripes—are also excellent additions.

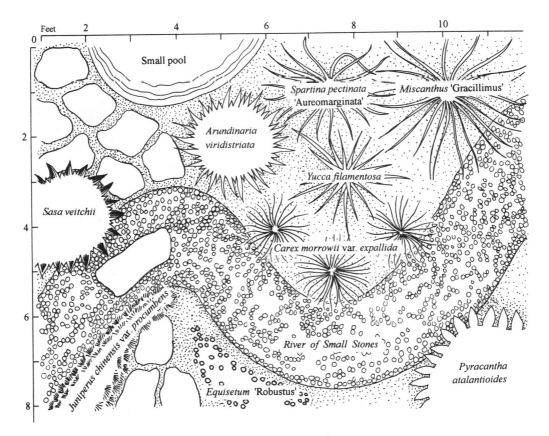

THE JAPANESE MOSS GARDEN

Back in 1907, Nina L. Marshall wrote the following tribute to mosses in her delightful book entitled *Mosses and Lichens:* "The blackened embers of the picnic fire are hidden with golden cord-mosses and the roadsides in the woods and the slopes to the lake are carpeted with sturdy hairy-caps. The crumbling roofs of deserted cottages and the unused well-sweep and old oaken bucket are decorated with soft tufts of green."

I hesitate to mention this particular Japanese approach to gardening because so many Americans, when confronted with moss growing either in their garden or, heaven forbid, in the lawn, immediately call the county extension agent and attempt to kill it. They should not. Instead, sit down and take it as an excuse not to mow the lawn.

There is a beautiful moss garden next door. It was created over many years by the late Doan Ogden, a brilliant landscape architect who, with his wife Rosemary, brought moss plugs from the nearby woods and slowly turned a thirty- by fifty-foot area that consisted of sparse grass and some large white oaks into a garden of contemplation that inspires the visitor at all times of the year. The only maintenance needed is removing fallen leaves so that the moss does not go into dormancy from lack of light.

But not all moss gardens must be big; they can also be a world in miniature. Small rocks become mountains, and the mosses change from tiny plants to thickets of impenetrable green. The yellow blossom of a tiny star grass (*Hypoxis hirsuta*) assumes the proportions of the Liberty Bell.

Friends in the mountains of North Carolina created such a garden by collecting all the rocks from nearby walking tours and the mosses from an area eventually to be cleared for a pond and small botanical garden. There are a number of small hostas and wildflowers, including pinks (*Dianthus* spp.) and bluets (*Hedyotis purpurea*), but by far the largest number of plants in the garden is the mosses.

Most mosses need shade because they have poorly developed water distribution systems, and the hot sun can dry them out before water reaches thirsty cells. Haircap moss (*Polytrichum commune*) will grow in open fields, but in that environment the grass provides some protection and helps to collect and channel the morning dew to the mosses below.

When mosses become dry, they fold up their leaves, which markedly changes their appearance. But once the plants have water again, the cells quickly swell and the mosses revert to their normal size.

Mosses reproduce by releasing spores from little containers called peristomes. Looking at different peristomes—each genus has a design all its own—is like looking at a Paul Klee etching of Turkish minarets. These fanciful capsules are edged with teeth that vary from four to sixty-four, always being in multiples of four. When the weather is damp, the teeth are closed tightly together; when it is dry, they open up and the spores are shaken to the winds like salt cast from a saltcellar.

Mosses can easily exist on bare rock. By threading their rhizoids, or tiny roots, into microscopic pores in the rock's surface, they can remove elements for nutrition and eventually create soil. Even airborne dust is trapped by the leaves of the mosses and eventually combines with pieces of old and dehydrated plants to form dirt.

WOODLAND MOSSES FOR THE GARDEN

The following mosses are common to most temperate woods and not in any danger of extinction.

Andreaea petrophila, the stone-loving andreaea, was named in honor of the German botanist G. R. Andreae. The species is from *petra,* or rock. This plant grows best on granite or slate in shady, damp places. They are among the first colonizers to settle on these inhospitable surfaces.

Bartramia pomiformis, or apple moss, gets its species name, *pomum* (apple) and *forma* (form), from the plant's tiny spore cases, which look like little apples. The genus was named in honor of John Bartram, the great botanist from Pennsylvania. There are thirteen known species of apple moss in North America, most of which are found growing in rock clefts.

Dicranum longifolium, the fork moss, gets its generic name from the Greek word for flesh-hook or fork, referring to the unusual formation of the teeth on its spore case. The species name refers to the very long leaves. This moss is among sixty-five species of *Dicranum* in North America; at the turn of the century, six were found within the limits of New York City. The plants grow only in high-altitude rocky regions and are sometimes found at the base of trees.

Hylocomnium triquetrum, the triangular wood-reveller, makes an excellent plant for a moss garden. The common name is the English translation of the Greek generic name, and *triquetrum* refers to the shape of the stems. This moss grows with a luxuriant delight only on wood. I placed it in a rock crevice that holds its wooden base.

Hypnum crista-castrensis, the ostrich-plume feather moss, is so called because the plants are plumelike. The Greek term *hypnum* suggests that these mosses were once helpful in promoting sleep; the species name refers to the shape of the branches. The spore capsules are large, curved, and held horizontally.

This bright yellow-green moss is common in mountainous regions and grows on soil and rotten wood.

Hypnum splendens, the arched feather moss, is a beautiful combination of gold and green leaves on reddish stems. This splendid plant is common on rocks in the deep woods and on nearby fallen stumps or rotten logs. Miss Marshall wrote of them:

> Glittering with yellow, red and
>   green,
> As o'er the moss, with playful
>   glide,
> The sunbeams dance from side
>   to side.

Leucobryum longifolium, the pincushion moss, looks so much like a pincushion that little imagination was needed for the name. The generic name is Greek for "white moss," which refers to the unusual pallid green. Plants look pale because the cells containing chlorophyll are surrounded by larger transparent cells that carry water and protect them from heat.

Polytrichum commune, the haircap moss, gets its generic name from *poly,* "many," and *trichum,* "hair." Pliny called this plant golden maiden-hair because of the golden gloss the leaves exhibit when dry. The fringed edge on the sporecaps are said to resemble a lady's tresses—hence the common name.

Haircap moss has been used in lieu of expensive feathers to stuff pillows. It was the first plant to be recognized by early botanists as not having true flowers.

Thuidium delicatulum, the tiny cedar moss, was named for its close resemblance to a miniature cedar tree (*Thuidium* is an ancient name for a resinous-bearing evergreen. This moss was well known to Linnaeus, the great Swedish botanist who devised the binomial system for naming plants. He called it *delicatulum* because of its dainty appearance. Tiny cedar moss enjoys damp shady places and runs over stones, earth, and rotten logs.

Moss gardens are not for everyone. They require a delight in the small, in fact a complete shunning of the bravado—not to mention a shady spot beneath some tall trees. But for those gardeners who have the inclination for creating a world in miniature, the moss garden is the answer.

Ten

Container Gardens

~

BACK IN 1969 I BOUGHT A SMALL BOOK WITH BLACK AND WHITE PHOTOGRAPHS ENTITLED *Pots and Pot Gardens* by Mary Grant White. It's still a mainstay in my garden library after twenty-four years.

According to Miss White, tomb paintings from ancient Egypt portray men using earthenware pots for growing plants. In one fresco a wall decorated with flowerpots forms the backdrop for grape pickers from El-Bersheh. And fragments of flowerpots from Classical Greece have been dug up around the temple of Hephaistos in the Athenian Agora.

"Greeks do not seem to have made gardens as we understand them, being hampered, no doubt, by the rocky nature of their soil," wrote Miss White. "Such ornamental gardening as did exist had great religious significance, often taking the form of sacred groves dedicated to some god or goddess."

It was the cult of Adonis that led to midsummer festivals during which earthenware pots were sown with quick-growing seeds like fennel, barley, or lettuce, then placed around a figure of the god. When seeds sprouted, everyone rejoiced that Adonis had come back.

Pots. When our descendants dig through the rubbish piles of today, in among the beer cans, pop bottles, and air freshener buttons they will also find millions of plastic flowerpots, many with imitation gold rims. Such pots work well for the commercial grower but there is no excuse to use them in the home.

Every year the front and back terraces are filled with pots from our collection, and many empty niches are, too. Sometimes I use plastic pots as liners but most of the pots in our garden are earthenware.

Each pot is washed and scrubbed after every use. Sanitation, including periodic washings, is very important because fertilizer salts tend to build up around the edges of clay pots. I use kitchen pot scrubbers and strong soap, then rinse well before air drying.

Clay breathes. It allows air and water to pass through the walls just as air and water pass through garden soil. It's difficult to overwater plants when using clay pots. (I'm convinced that more damage is done to plants by lethal overwatering than any other mistreatment.) Clay lasts longer than most plastic, which becomes brittle with age. By noticing the algae or fertilizer-salt deposits that form on the outside of clay pots, you can predict problems long before the plant itself shows signs of trouble.

Finally, clay pots are heavier and less likely to topple in a mild breeze or fall over because you (or the cat) brushed them in passing. (A large clay pot is very heavy, of course. As a practical matter you may need to switch to plastic for your big potted plants. Look for a new lightweight terracotta-style pot called Eura Cotta. Made of polyurethane foam, these pots and windowbox planters are decorated with a traditional Greek frieze and look a lot like clay but they weigh about eighty percent less than a typical terracotta pot.)

Check antiques shops and garage sales for old clay pots, bowls, and jardinieres. If you find a fancy pot without a drainage hole, put two or three inches of coarse gravel in the bottom, then place a piece of plastic tubing cut to the pot's height against the side. Add soil mix, pot the plant, and water well. Using a wooden dowel as a dipstick, measure the water supply periodically; when the stick comes out completely dry, water again.

Troughs. To grow a lot of plants in a limited space, use a trough, like an old soap-stone laundry tub set on some flat rocks or partially buried. The larger tubs are very heavy, however. A friend of mine gave me such a tub and it sat in the back garden for years, waiting for enough manpower to move it.

The Styrofoam trough. For a lightweight trough, nothing beats a Styrofoam carton, an invention many of my rock-gardening friends attribute to Charles Becker, Jr., of Philadelphia. Such a container may not sound appealing for the backyard, but once it's completed, you will never know that it's made of plastic.

First, buy a Styrofoam container of the kind that the bright young things use to carry beer to the beach. Any sturdy Styrofoam box will do. You'll also need asphalt roof paint, epoxy resin (buy the epoxy in cans because tubes are too small—and expensive), a sack of builder's sand, and something for texture, such as aquarium gravel, pea gravel, bits of oyster shell, or marble chips.

Using a sharp wood saw, cut the sides of the box down to a height of about six or eight inches. Paint the bottom inside and out with asphalt roof paint. Then, using a brace and bit, drill at least twelve half-inch drainage holes in the bottom, each about four inches apart.

Next, mix equal parts of the epoxy resin and hardener. (I suggest you wear gloves for this step.) Make just enough glue to paint one side of the trough at a time. Apply a thin coat: if you use too much glue, it will dissolve the Styrofoam. Use an aluminum pie tin for a mixing bowl, and if you have any epoxy left over, set it on ice to inhibit the chemical reactions.

While the glue is still tacky, dribble a mix of sand and gravel over the epoxy. Use additional glue for the edges so that none of the Styrofoam shows through. Allow at least thirty minutes for the epoxy to set. Clean up excess glue with water, but be sure you do it before it hardens.

Now follow the same procedure for the other sides of the box. The next day, shake off the excess mix and touch up any bare spots with more epoxy and more mix.

To finish the top edge, make a thick paste of epoxy and sand and apply a quarter-inch layer with a putty knife. Use a knife to add texture to the partially hardened material.

Wait another day, then set the finished trough in place. Use two bricks underneath to hold it above the surface and to promote good drainage. Put broken crockery or plastic screening over the holes, then fill the trough with planting mix.

The hypertuffa trough. For a heavier trough, try hypertuffa (named by F. H. Fisher, former president of England's Alpine Garden Society), a mix of one part Portland cement, two parts builder's sand, and one part milled peat moss. You will also need scrap lumber and wire mesh from the hardware store.

First decide on the size of the trough and make a wooden form. Then blend the ingredients thoroughly. Gradually add water; the mix should be viscous, not runny. Let it sit for five minutes. Put a one-inch layer in the frame and set in the wire mesh an equal distance from the sides. Add more of the mix to make a one-and-a-half-inch layer all over the bottom, then set the inner frame in place. Use wooden plugs for drains. Push damp sand into the corners of the wooden frame so that when the frame is removed, the sand will flake away, leaving worn, rounded corners rather than sharp edges.

Fill the rest of the cavity and lay plastic over the top. In twelve to eighteen hours, remove the inner frame, carefully pulling out the side pieces, and remove the drainage plugs. Replace the cover. Twenty-four hours later, remove the outer form. Brush the sides and top to remove any large bumps; take extra care, as the cement is still green. Carefully cover the trough with wet burlap or plastic and leave it for three more days. Then remove the outer framework and clean out the drainage holes. Leave the trough alone for at least another week to let it harden completely.

Cure the trough by filling it with water and adding one-half teaspoon of potassium permanganate crystals (available from drugstores). Using a paintbrush, coat the outside with the solution. Let the trough sit for a few hours, then rinse it well and let it sit outside for two more weeks before planting.

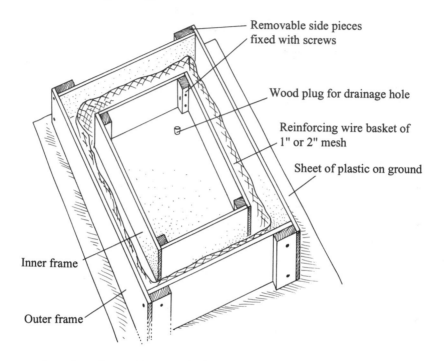

Removable side pieces fixed with screws
Wood plug for drainage hole
Reinforcing wire basket of 1" or 2" mesh
Sheet of plastic on ground
Inner frame
Outer frame

You can make other shapes for troughs by using a wooden form set on a large piece of butcher's wrap. Use less water in the mix to make it thicker, then spread the mix over the form.

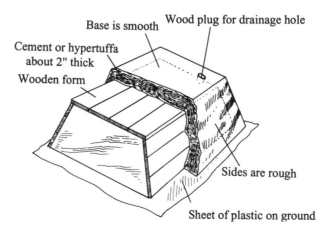

Base is smooth
Wood plug for drainage hole
Cement or hypertuffa about 2" thick
Wooden form
Sides are rough
Sheet of plastic on ground

In addition to troughs, you can easily make artificial stone planters for growing tiny alpines. Dig a hole in the ground and line it with stones, some of which you push two inches into the sides and bottom of the hole. Then mix one part cement, one part builder's sand, and two parts moistened peat. Fill the hole with the mix and let it cure for a week before you dig out the planter. Tap away the stone fragments, leaving holes for setting in plants. Cover the planter with damp burlap for another five days. Finally, soak it in a pail of water for a few days, and you are ready to plant.

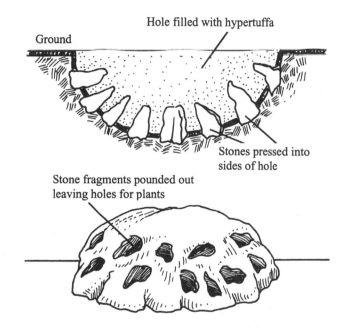

Many creative gardeners make unusual pots by cementing pieces of stone together and experimenting with various formulas. For example, some add premixed cements to sphagnum moss; others use perlite instead of sand in a hypertuffa formula. For more information on these and other methods, contact the local chapter of the American Rock Garden Society.

Planting and watering containers. Just to make things simpler, I've used variations on the same soil mix for years. I buy large bags of sterilized potting soil and builder's sand, and composted sheep or cow manure. Then I mix the three together in equal amounts. Except for alpines, which require more grit for drainage, this mix seems to work well for almost any potted plant.

Once plants are potted, watering begins. The soil in pots and troughs will dry out faster than garden soil so it's a good idea to check your pots every day, especially during hot summers. Be prepared to water every day.

Always use tepid water for watering plants, especially when they are growing in the hot summer sun. Cold water is a shock to their root systems in the same way cold water can shock you.

There are other ways to get water to the plant besides the watering can. For example, you can set a small custard cup slightly in the soil, then place a wick (of fiberglass or the kind used for kerosene lamps) with one end in the water and the other end in the soil so that the roots can absorb what they need. Or in very hot weather, you can leave ice cubes on the soil surface; the ice will slowly melt and quench the plant's thirst.

Gradually all the water running through the potted soil tends to leach out important nutrients and soluble salts, and if these aren't replaced, the plant will eventually suffer. There-fore, feeding potted plants with a good soluble fertilizer is very important. It really doesn't matter what brand you use, as long as the ratio is about 10–10–10 or 20–30–20. The three numbers represent the amount of usable nitrogen, phosphorus, and potash in the fertilizer mix. For example, 5–5–5 contains five percent nitrogen, five percent phosphorus, and five percent potash; the rest of the solution consists of inert ingredients.

Plants need nitrogen for strong stems and healthy foliage, but too much leads to rampant growth at the expense of flower, fruit, or seed production. Phosphorus helps plant tissue to ripen and mature; a phosphorus deficiency can cause stunted growth. Potash helps plants in the early stages of growth by strengthening tissue and making it more resistant to cold; too little potash results in poorly developed root systems and stunted plants.

Don't start fertilizing until the plants are really growing. Even then I dilute the formula by half, and I never use it more than once every two or three weeks. Remember, less is more.

Lilies in pots. One of the most elegant additions to a small garden is a large pot over-flowing with blooming lilies. Few perennials take to pot culture with the ease of these magnificent flowers. Once in containers, they can be moved around the terrace or garden with ease, bringing glorious color to hitherto dark corners. Then, when the flowers fade, you can move the containers back to a less conspicuous spot.

In every garden we've always included *Abeliophyllum distichum*. A member of the olive family, it is called the white forsythia because its four-petaled honey-sweet white flowers resemble those of the forsythia. After its early spring bloom is through, the layered foliage of this bush provides a dark green background for a series of jewel-tone lilies.

In amongst the thicket I always plant a number of Japanese gold-banded lilies (*Lilium auratum*). In late summer, their tall arching stems bear dozens of pure white fragrant flowers, each banded with gold that radiates from the flower's center. Every petal is set off by stamens that are drenched with rich chocolate-red pollen. 'Platyphyllum' has ten-inch flowers with waxy white petals dotted with crimson specs as though a toothbrush loaded with pigment has been splashed across each golden band. 'Opala' bears pure white flowers.

But before the heat of late summer arrives, I also place pots of lilies at the base of the bush. For bloom in June and July, I include Asiatic lilies, offered in a wide range of bright colors, including maroon, yellow, orange, pink, and white plus such pastels as cream, pale peach, coral, and pink. Some nurseries feature naturalizing mixes; try planting some directly in the garden and the rest into pots. Especially attractive is *Lilium* 'Admiration', its creamy white blossoms with maroon spots on twenty-inch stems—and great on a moonlit night.

Lilium canadense, an American native, is lovely in containers. Commonly called Canada lily, it bears orange-yellow to red flowers in late June.

In July and August both the early orientals and the Aurelian hybrids bloom. Jan de Graaff, one of the great lily hybridizers of all time, created the Aurelian strain, including the spectacular 'Moonlight Strain' and 'Golden Splendor'.

'Casa Blanca', an oriental lily, blooms in early August and features fragrant ten-inch flowers with pure white petals and burnt red anthers. They blossom atop five-foot stems. Another oriental lily, 'Strawberry Shortcake', bears six-inch, sweetly fragrant flowers the shade of ripe strawberries and edged with creamy white. Only twenty-four inches high, this dwarf hybrid is perfect for pots. 'Little Pink' is another short variety, perfect for the edge of the border or for pots.

Lilies that bloom in August and September include the various hybrids of *Lilium auratum* and the magnificent *L. formosanum.* This second species bears six-inch-long, sweetly fragrant white blossoms atop four- to six-foot stems. It hails from Taiwan, yet is hardy in this country as far north as Zone 5 if protected with mulch. Because it blooms so late, it requires special protection in the North from early frost. In addition, this species is susceptible to a virus infection called lily mosaic, so do not plant it with other lilies. 'Little Snow White' is a cultivar with large solitary, paired, or multiple flowers on nine-inch stems. If grown from seed sown in September, this lily will bloom the following summer. It is especially well suited for pots.

Buy or order your lily bulbs as early in the spring as possible. If they arrive and you are not prepared for them, store them in the refrigerator or another cool place. In spring our refrigerator often has seed packets in the butter compartment, seed flats in the freezer, and bulbs in the crisper.

I use straight-edged black plastic pots for lily bulbs. When the buds have developed to the point of showing color, remove the pots from the bed and place them in decorative pots.

Use large pots that are at least fifteen inches deep and hold about a cubic foot of soil. The bulbs must be planted deeply, since many lily stems bear roots above the level of the bulb. Also, lilies are heavy feeders and need a good deal of soil.

Although many garden writers claim that soil drains perfectly when there is nothing in the pot bottom except a small hole, I've found healthier root growth if, when potting up, I put at least an inch of pebbles or broken pottery in the bottom of the container. Use a planting mix of good potting soil, sand, and composted manure or shredded leaves, and add a dash of lime.

Put about two inches of soil mix in the bottom of the pot, then set the bulb in place. With small bulbs you can plant three in an eight-inch pot. Then fill the pots to within a half inch of the top. Gently firm the soil.

Water the pots well and place them directly in the soil in a protected nursery bed. They will need at least six but preferably eight hours of sunlight a day. Water well and feed with a liquid fertilizer once a month.

After the bulbs have stopped blooming, move the pots back to the nursery bed to allow the foliage to ripen. Then either plant the bulbs out in the garden or place them in a deep cold frame or another cold but protected place for the winter.

For a special touch, plant some crocus bulbs around the edges of the lily pots. The early-season blossoms will provide welcome color before the lilies appear.

Roses in pots. The selection of roses you can grow in containers is enormous. Hybrid teas, miniature roses, tree roses (of *Alice in Wonderland* fame)—in fact, almost all roses are suitable for container gardens.

Rose roots need air, so the best pots are terracotta, wood, or unglazed ceramic, with at least one hole at the bottom for drainage. Suitable sizes vary from ten inches wide and a foot deep for miniatures to sixteen inches wide and eighteen inches deep for a tree rose. The planting mix should be two parts soil, one part builder's sand, and one part composted manure, compost, or other organic matter (except peat moss). Mix in about one-half cup of bonemeal at planting time.

Make a small mound of soil at the bottom of the pot. Spread the roots out over the mound and cover them with dirt, so that the crown of the rose and the soil level are about two inches below the edge of the pot. This extra space makes watering much easier and allows room for a layer of mulch, which helps keep the roots cool. Roses need four to six hours of sunlight a day but the roots should not bake in the hot sun; give the pots shade by putting them inside slightly larger containers or grouping them behind more tolerant plants.

Japanese maples in pots. Many Japanese maples (*Acer* spp.) can be grown in containers with only an occasional pruning to keep their size within bounds. Some of the most beautiful Japanese maples are under seven feet high, and at least six that I'm familiar with stop at three feet. In a neighbor's garden, a beautiful specimen of the red lace leaf maple (*A. palmatum dissectum atropurpureum*) is planted in a redwood tub that measures about sixteen inches across and twelve inches deep; around the edge is an assortment of houseleeks (*Sempervivum* spp.), mostly *S. tectorum*.

One of the most graceful of the smaller Japanese maples is *Acer palmatum* 'Kamagata', which bears two-inch five-lobed leaves that are lightly toothed at the margins. In the spring the leaves are a rusty red, becoming bright green in the summer; when autumn arrives, they are flushed light orange with sparks of red. *A. palmatum* 'Hoshi kuzu' has unusual light green leaves that look more like those of a fig than a maple. About two inches long and two inches wide, they turn a golden-yellow in the fall. *A. palmatum* 'Goshiki kotohime' has a variegated leaf that resembles a Jackson Pollock painting: The green is splashed with red, pink, white, cream, and a touch of yellow.

The only problem with potted Japanese maples occurs when winter temperatures fall below 14°F; at this temperature the roots are severely damaged. If you live where winter temperatures rarely fall below zero, the container can be enclosed in layers of bubble wrap or set within a larger box that is then filled with a nonabsorbent insulation like polystyrene peanuts. If there are many days of below-freezing temperatures, bury the pot in a below-ground container or a box within a box. Mulch the pot heavily on top, or store it in a shed or a porch where it stays cold (about 40°F) but above freezing.

OTHER PLANTS FOR POTS

In addition to lilies, roses, and Japanese maples, most of the plants mentioned in this book will grow in pots—if given the proper pot, watering, soil, and placement.

Specialty geraniums, calla lilies, cannas, asparagus ferns, petunias, and all kinds of summer bulbs are well suited for containers. You can even grow hostas in pots; just return them to the garden in the fall so that the roots overwinter in the ground. The following plants also do beautifully in pots.

Amaranthus 'Tricolor Perfecta' makes a colorful display in any container garden. Last summer my next-door neighbor put a ten-inch clay pot with three of these plants in front of a trellis made of stout, dried grapevines. Then he set out a pot of *Cobaea scandens,* cup-and-saucer vine, so that the vine's satiny purple-blue flowers were suspended in front of the yellow, green, and crimson leaves. The effect was bright and beautiful.

Canna × *generalis,* the common garden canna, is attractive in pots, especially when combined with *Tagetes patula,* the French marigold. For an effective summer display, plant a ring of marigolds around two cannas in a twelve-inch terracotta pot. French marigolds range in height from eight to fourteen inches and come in orange, yellow, gold, and mahogany-red. For smaller pots there are also dwarf cannas. They reach a height of thirty inches but bear regular-sized pink blossoms that bloom ninety days from seed.

Cordyline australis, the cabbage palm, starts out as an elegant seedling tree with long arching leaves. It's often planted in the midst of pots of geraniums. If kept in a frost-free area over the winter, in some twenty years it will occupy a fourteen-inch-wide container. When it reaches an unmanageable height, it can be air-layered; even the shortened version is a show-stopper, especially in the middle of the perennial border.

This tree is hardy in London and the south of England, so having a specimen in your garden will add a British touch.

Cucurbita pepo 'Zucchini', the hybrid zucchini, grows beautifully in a fourteen-inch pot. After forty-five days the cultivar 'Gold Rush' will produce hordes of bright yellow fruits (they are especially delicious sliced raw for salads). Plant three seeds in a three-inch peat pot.

Remove two seedlings and set the strongest plant into a large pot. Don't stint on water, especially when summer temperatures climb. Apply a liquid fertilizer every ten days or so when the plant is bearing fruit.

Helleborus orientalis, the Lenten rose, is a wonderful plant for pots. Use a twelve-inch clay pot and set a well-grown hellebore in the center. Around the edge plant three specimens of *Bergenia cordifolia* 'Purpurea' (Gertrude Jekyll admired this cultivar for its marvelous winter color). The deeply cut, glossy, dark green leaves of the hellebores are in sharp contrast to the rounded leaves of the bergenias.

Be sure to water often, since hellebores like damp soil.

Nerium oleander, better known as olean-der, starts blooming in early spring and continues until well into December. In areas with freezing temperatures, it must spend the winter indoors, but as soon as days warm up again, it will bloom anew.

A three-foot-tall oleander planted in a twelve-inch terracotta pot makes a beautiful display.

Phormium colensoi, mountain flax, is easily started from seed. Within three or four years a plant will fill a ten-inch pot.

Phormium tenax 'Variegatum', the varie-gated form of New Zealand flax, will reach a height of four feet. Its sword-shaped white- and yellow-striped leaves add a sense of rhythm to the garden scene. These plants thrive in warm areas, especially when grown in plastic pots sitting inside other pots filled with water.

Picea glauca 'Conica', the dwarf Alberta spruce, is a fine small conifer.

Lend drama to almost any house by plant-ing one in a substantial pot on either side of a front stoop. Or plant *Juniperus procumbens* 'Nana', the dwarf Japanese juniper, in smaller pots. Its fresh green, sharp foliage turns blue-green in the summer and bronzed in winter.

Pittosporum undulatum, the Victorian box, reaches a height of forty feet in the wild, but when kept in a pot probably grows to just eight feet; if it gets too tall, it can easily be trimmed. You can start plants from seed. The pale yellow flowers, which give off a night fragrance, usually appear within four years.

Sequoia sempervirens 'Adpressa', a dwarf sequoia, grows in a fancy terracotta pot that sits outdoors all summer and fall, then spends December in the living room dressed like a Christmas tree.

While we lived in the North, this tree spent most of the winter in our green-house, but here in the South, it goes out to the garden room.

ALPINE GARDENS FOR TROUGHS

Budd Myers introduced me to growing alpine plants in troughs. He has a wonderful collection of troughs that contain both common and rare plants, with as many as twenty-three plants in one eighteen-by-twenty-four-inch container.

Plants range from dwarf conifers to tiny bushes to alpine perennials that provide a burst of color in the spring, followed by sporadic outbursts throughout the summer and still more color in autumn. A selection of his trough plants appears in "Alpine Gardens," chapter 8.

Ruth Samotis, a rock-gardening neighbor from Hendersonville, made me a square trough that measures twelve by twelve inches. It contains one of the smallest of the dwarf conifers (*Abies balsamea* 'Nana'); a dwarf, shrubby elm tree (*Ulmus* × *elegantissima* 'Jacqueline Hillier'), originally from Birmingham, England, and named in honor of Harold Hillier's mother (of Hillier's Arboretum fame); and two small but elegant alpine snowbells (*Soldanella alpina*), which I grew from seed. The elm could grow as high as four feet but can be pruned to remain in scale.

Eleven

Water Gardens

~

ANYONE WITH A SMALL GARDEN HAS ROOM TO INSTALL A PLASTIC WASHTUB TO HOLD A tropical water lily, or half a wine keg in which to grow a collection of small aquatic plants. One of the most imaginative water gardens I ever saw consisted of five wooden tubs sunk into a slight slope, their edges hidden by pieces of flagstone. The first tub received a slight trickle of water from a garden hose, which overflowed into the next tub down the line via a short length of plastic tubing that was hidden by other stones. The last tub dripped water onto a lovely mixed planting of cardinal flowers (*Lobelia cardinalis*), sensitive ferns (*Onoclea sensibilis*), and various species of primrose.

If you shy away from such a large project, a single buried tub, ringed with flat stones and fed a mere trickle of water from a garden hose hidden under stones or plants, is enough to lend a small degree of comfort to an otherwise hot afternoon or evening.

In her book *Wall and Water Gardens* (New York: Charles Scribner's Sons, 1928), Gertrude Jekyll wrote: "On a still summer day nothing is more delightful, apart from the admiration of lovely plant and flower form, than to sit quite still and listen to the sounds of the water of the little rills."

Miss Jekyll goes on to describe the houses of Imperial Rome that included tanks of water combined with beds of flowers, the walled and fountained courts of Spain, and the reflecting ponds that mirrored garden temples in elegant English estates.

But Americans had their say, too. "Water in a landscape is as a mirror to a room, the feature that doubles and enhances all its charms," wrote Neltje Blanchan in *The American Flower Garden* (New York: Doubleday, Page, and Company, 1909). "Whoever may possess a lake, a pond, or a pool to catch the sunbeams, duplicate the trees and flowers on its bank, reflect the moon, and multiply the stars, surely will."

Building a water garden. The evils of plastic in the environment have been many but there have been a few benefits, too. One of these is the development of PVC (polyvinyl chloride) and rubber pond liners. Gardeners can now build a decent-sized pond for a very reasonable price. And if installing such a pool seems like too much trouble, there are free-form fiberglass pools or tubs that will fit easily in a shallow depression dug in the ground.

When siting the pool for your garden, choose a level spot that gets at least half a day of full sun; shady pools cannot support blooming water lilies or most of the other flowering aquatic plants. If possible, locate your pond close to an electric outlet to allow for the installation of a pump, not only to filter the water but to perhaps support a small fountain, or a set of lights to illuminate the pool at night.

Consult one of the many water garden catalogs or your local nursery and choose a liner. There are at least three types. PVC liners are black, twenty mil (one-thousandth of an inch) thick, and usually guaranteed for five years. Rubber liners are black, forty-five mil thick, resistant to ultraviolet rays, and guaranteed for twenty years. GeoPond liners are black, sixty mil thick, resistant to ultraviolet rays, punctures, and tears, and guaranteed for thirty years. Stick to the black liners; turquoise or blue will make your pond look completely artificial.

The cost of a ten-by-fifteen-foot PVC liner for a pool measuring about six by eleven feet and eighteen inches deep retails for less than $100. A rubber liner of the same size costs just under $150, and a GeoPond liner costs just under $300. That's not bad when you consider that just a few years ago, only wealthy landowners could afford the luxury of concrete pools.

Here's a simple rule of thumb for figuring how much liner to buy: Add twice the depth plus two feet (to allow a one-foot overlap on each side) to your maximum width. Do the same for the length.

To make your pool, first dig a hole eighteen inches deep and remove all the rocks, pebbles, or other debris. If the pool is large, use a garden hose to lay out the shape. Use a string and a line-level to make sure your excavation is level; nothing is more disconcerting than a pond that is full at one end and one or two inches low at the other. To help in future cleanings, slope the sides to the center and slope the bottom to one end. If you plan to grow some bog plants, dig out a shelf about eight inches wide and ten inches from the top edge; you can extend it either partway or all around the entire pool.

Next, using a sharp-edged shovel, cut a shallow twelve- to fifteen-inch trench around the edge to hold the excess liner. Put a half-inch layer of sand on the bottom and use more sand on the sides to fill any holes left by stones. If you have especially rocky soil, lay a layer of fairly thick commercial polyethylene over the sand before you put in the liner.

Drape the liner into the depression, placing bricks or stones on the sides to hold it down. Start filling it with water. As the pool fills, gradually remove the stones to allow the liner to fit tightly into the hole. Once the pool is full, trim the exposed liner; leave an eight-inch overhang and cover that with a layer of fieldstone slabs or other stone. If you want a formal look, you can lay stone paving on a bed of mortar. Before you put fish in the pool, let the water settle for a week. You can use a siphon to empty the pool if it needs cleaning, but most such pools can be left all season long.

Problems with algae. Some years ago I asked the head water gardener at the Brooklyn Botanic Garden about preventing algae.

"Algae," said Mr. Michael Ramirez, "is something you have to expect in any new aquarium or pool. Initially you're going to get algae. Usually when you begin such a garden, you may not have many higher plants that are established and growing and acting as competitors, so algae becomes the dominant vegetation. But later, once everything is planted and fish are added (I try to avoid snails because, being vegetarians, they can be disfiguring to plants), the water reaches a condition of desired clarity.

"Have patience, and over time it will be difficult, or almost impossible, to get that pea-soup type of algae to repeat itself. You can use filters that will strain all that minute algae out of the water, but it's going to come back again once the pump is turned off until it's all in balance.

"And it's important to realize that chlorinated water is bad for plants and fish, but the chlorine will dissipate if the water is left to sit for forty-eight hours or so, depending on the size of the container and the temperature of the water."

If the algae in your small pond is getting out of hand, try adding green food coloring; the dye will reduce the amount of light below water and thus keep the algae in check.

Planting in pools. Plant the plants in water gardens in individual black plastic pots, never directly into a submerged soil. Use an ordinary garden topsoil that is on the heavy side. Do not use commercial potting soils or mixes in the containers, since these often contain vermiculite, perlite, and other fillers that will float. The water lilies in the big outdoor pools are always planted in large square and rectangular boxes made of cypress, and those boxes last for years.

Plant tropical water lilies when the water is above 70°F, and hardy lilies when the water is above 60°F. Water lilies will go into a rest period if they are subjected to a sudden drop in water temperature, so when adding or changing water in your pool, make sure you add lukewarm water.

Individual fertilizer bags can be made of cheesecloth or even newspaper, then filled with a handful of 5–10–5 or 10–10–10, and stuck in the wet soil. If the water is chlorinated, let it sit forty-eight hours before adding fish or plants.

The chief problem of an outdoor pool results from dead and dying vegetation that falls into the water. Always remove organic material before it begins to rot.

LOTUSES AND LILIES FOR THE WATER GARDEN

Nelumbo is that majestic flower, the lotus, the blossom in which Buddha sits. It's a blossom steeped in the fragrance of far-off lands. The lotus produces a seed-pod whose seeds are still used as food in Asia. Two species are grown in water gardens: *Nelumbo lutea,* the American lotus, and *N. nucifera,* the East Indian lotus.

Nelumbo lutea produces large pale yellow flowers and plate-sized leaves up to two feet across. *Nelumbo nucifera* bears even larger leaves than its American cousin; the fragrant flowers are pink, rose, or white. Cultivars include 'Rosea Plena', which bears large, double rose-pink flowers; 'Shiroman', which opens with large, double cream-colored flowers that are pale green in the center but become pure white as they age; and 'Alba Grandiflora', a very large flower with pure white rounded petals.

Smaller cultivars, such as the tulip lotus (*Nelumbo nucifera* 'Shirokunshi') and the popular 'Momo Botan', do well in a twelve-quart plastic bucket; others need at least a thirty-quart pot.

Both the blossoms and the leaves of lotuses stand well out of the water. Flowering begins in early June in the deep South and July in the North with the fragrant blossoms opening in the morning and closing by midafternoon. Lotuses require five to six hours of sunlight a day. They rarely produce much bloom the first year and must have temperatures in the 80°F range to begin the sequence of bloom, which lasts six to eight weeks. Lotuses are practical to grow from Zone 3 southward (north of Zone 3, the summers are too short) and are hardy as long as the rhizomes are below the level of ice. When planted in buckets and tubs or in shallow pools and ponds, they must be brought into the basement for the winter, since the water around them is likely to freeze.

Start lotus roots, or rhizomes, in shallow water. Fill a plastic tub halfway with soil. Add fertilizer or prepared fertilizer tabs, then fill with soil, stopping about four inches from the top. Plant the banana-shaped root at an angle with the bud pointed up. Make a slight depression in the soil surface and carefully position the tuber. Cover the tuber with two inches of soil at the bottom or heavy end and leave the growing end one-half inch above the soil. Do not damage the bud; if it breaks, another may not sprout. Lower the container into the water until the tuber is two inches underwater. As the plant grows, gradually increase the depth to six to twelve inches.

Nymphaea includes both the hardy and the tropical water lilies. Hardy water lilies are perennials and can be left outdoors year-round as long as the water in your pond does not freeze to the bottom. If it does, you'll have to lift the pots from the pond and store them for the winter in your basement. Tropicals are tender plants and in climate zones colder than Zone 10 are usually treated as disposable annual flowers. They can be stored underwater in a warm greenhouse, and with the increasing daylight of spring new leaves will appear. But not many home gardeners have the facilities or space for this sort of storage. They actually go into a decline when water temperatures fall below 70°F.

Most of the water lilies need five or six hours of full sun a day. The blossoms, many of which are fragrant, float upon the water's surface, opening in the morning and closing in the afternoon for three or four days. A healthy plant produces flowers all summer long. Many water lilies, especially the tropicals, make excellent cut flowers.

To plant water lilies, fill a container half full of topsoil. Carefully set the rootstock on the soil, then add more soil, pushing it around the roots, keeping the crown free of soil. Cover the soil with a half inch of pea gravel or very small stones, still keeping the crown uncovered. Then saturate with water. Gently lower the tub into the water.

Among the hardy white water lilies available to gardeners is *Nymphaea* 'Marliacea Albida', which bears superb fragrant white flowers. It has a six- to eight-foot spread and is excellent for the small pond. *Nymphaea* × 'Virginia' produces nonfragrant white double flowers and spreads up to twelve feet. Use a ten-quart container for the first and a fifteen-quart container for the second.

Nymphaea 'Fabiola' offers a classic pink flower with a slight fragrance. It spreads to six feet. 'Pink Sensation' spreads up to twelve feet and bears large light pink flowers that remain open late in the afternoon. Use a ten-quart container for the first and a fifteen-quart container for the second.

Nymphaea 'Charlene Strawn' spreads to twelve feet and needs a bit less sun than most varieties to flower. Its beautiful, yellow-gold fragrant flowers bloom above the water's surface. 'Sunrise' bears very large yellow flowers that stay open late in the afternoon and also spread to twelve feet. Use a ten-quart container.

Nymphaea 'Ellisiana' bears many-petaled, deep red flowers on plants especially suited for small ponds, spreading up to six feet. They are best for northern ponds, since temperatures above 95°F cause the flowers to burn. 'James Brydon' has a glorious and fragrant cup-shaped red flower on a plant that spreads up to twelve feet. Even so it can adapt to a smaller pond. Use a ten-quart container for the first and a fifteen-quart container for the second.

Nymphaea 'Graziella' is called a changeable lily because it's nearly yellow when it first opens, then changes to a copper bronze. Spread is about six feet. A bit less than full sun is needed for flowering. Use a five-quart container.

A view of our autumn garden shows (from top) a mix of asters, including New England asters (Aster novae–angliae) moved from the fields and the warm-pink cultivar 'Alma Potschke'; all-yellow sneezeweeds (Helenium autumnale 'Butterpat'); prairie coneflowers (Ratibida columnifera), a biennial or short-lived perennial with flowers that resemble Mexican hats; and at the bottom, some short asters (Aster novi-belgii 'Professor Kippenburg').

Purple moor grass (Molinia caerulea 'Variegata') is a long-season ornamental grass that provides garden interest throughout the year. The variegated leaves are attractive in late spring, the blossoms appear in early summer, and leaves persist well into winter. The flowers at right (above) are Stokes' aster (Stokesia laevis), an American wildflower. The conifer is a very young Juniperus 'Skyrocket', which reaches a height of six to eight feet in ten years with a width of only one foot, making a column that's perfect for the small garden. In the fall (below) the arching tan leaves of purple moor grass become a bursting rocket, especially when planted in front of hay-scented fern (Dennstaedtia punctilobula).

A small woodland garden consists of (from left) the leaves of a Japanese Jack-in-the-pulpit (Arisaema tripetallum), *with a lady fern* (Athyrium Filix-femina) *standing behind; an Alleghany spurge* (Pachysandra procumbens); *the tiny Scott's spleenwort fern* (Asplenosorus ebenoides); *Braun's holly fern* (Polystichum braunii); *smooth-bladed Hart's-tongue fern* (Phyllitis scolopendrium) *overshadowed by Christmas fern* (Polystichum acrostichoides); *and some Southern worm-wood* (Artemisia abrotanum) *at far right. There are seedling hostas with variegated foliage in the rear, various violet leaves, and a species of* Ligularia *at bottom left. Over fifteen plants happily coexist in a space less than five feet wide and three feet deep.*

Here railroad tie steps are lined with caladiums
(Caladium 'John Peed' and 'White Queen').
The armillary sphere is surrounded by red salvias
(Salvia 'Bonfire') and mixed-color petunias.
This garden lasts all summer long and needs only
the deadheading of the petunias.

Marge Martin's Asheville garden is highlighted
by a marvelous bird sculpture by Bill Heise,
a bird bath, and an ancient snake plant (Sanse-
vieria trifasciata) that is brought out every
summer.

My front garden during August consists of (from left) a short but unknown cultivar of Miscanthus, *gayfeather (*Liatris pycnostachya *'Alba'), Spanish-daggers (*Yucca gloriosa), *the orange blossoms of butterfly weed (*Asclepias tuberosa), *and the leaves of the Nippon daisy (*Chrysanthemum nipponicum) *that begin to bloom in mid-September. The phlox in the background are seedlings from the wild.*

Another view of my front border, this time showing (from the left) the yellow Hemerocallis *'Ida Miles', the night-blooming daylily (*H. citrina), *the seven-foot orange daylily (*H. altissima), *white shasta daisies,* Miscanthus *'Morning Light', achillea spotted with butterfly weed (*Asclepias tuberosa), *fennel 'Bronze Form', and more miscanthus, all fronted with the black-blooming grass* Pennesetum *'Moudry'. The garden measures less than ten feet wide by six feet deep.*

My herb garden sits in front of an old wall and features plants that include Achillea *'Hope'*, *lamb's ears* (Stachys byzantina), *the silver leaves of* Artemisia *'Silver Mound', and to the right,* Russian sage (Perovskia atriplicifolia), *a long-blooming perennial that in combination with some ornamental grasses can be an entire garden. At the edge of the wall is Japanese blood grass* (Imperata cylindrica rubra) *and a white rose bush,* Rosa *'White Meidiland', that is easily clipped when it gets too large.*

Because of limited space, my herb garden is continually changing. But for color I use tender and perennial bulbs, corms, and tubers because if cared for, they will always bloom and can be moved with ease. Here a golden calla lily (Zantedeschia elliottiana) *blooms above some common horehound* (Marrubium vulgare).

The Japanese garden of Ross and Betty Parks in Asheville is ablaze with azaleas and wildflowers in May. Although it looks large, the L-shaped piece of land is less than fifty feet long and as narrow as twelve feet.

Dwarf conifers provide year-round color, beautiful shapes, and small stature. In my rock garden a dwarf Alberta spruce (Picea glauca var. albertiana 'Sander's Blue') serves as the background for some autumn crocus (Colchicum spp.). The spruce will be four feet high with a two-foot width in ten years. ▼

▲ I planted an entire garden in a space eight feet wide and about four feet deep. The back window of the garage was trellised for blue morning glories (Ipomoea spp.). The tree is a cabbage palm (Cordyline australis) grown from seed; it will come inside for the winter. The white phlox is 'Mt. Fuji', and the arching leaves are various daylily hybrids. The small tree in the background is a weeping birch (Betula pendula 'Tristis').

A spring view of my northern scree bed features dwarf alpine plants mixed with dwarf conifers and, along the bottom edge of the stone wall, early-blooming pinks (Dianthus spp.), globeflowers (Trollius europaeus), and Euphorbia epithymoides. At far right is dwarf iris (Iris pumula 'Alba') backed by dwarf asparagus (Asparagus officinalis var. pseudoscaber).

A midsummer view of the scree bed shows ferns among the conifers, with hosta 'Piedmont Gold', dwarf asparagus, and various perennials at the bottom of the curved rock sides. The area measures twenty feet along the back of the semicircle and holds hundreds of plants.

In the fall the scree bed's small Japanese maple (a cultivar of Acer palmatum) is watched over by "Fat Persian Cat," a sculpture by Richard H. Reccia (1888–1983) from the Boston Museum. Behind the cat is a dwarf Scotch pine (Pinus sylvestris 'Viridis Compacta') that will reach six feet in fifteen years of growth. The weeping grass is cord grass (Spartina pectinata 'Aureo-marginata').

The scree bed under its mantle of snow still has color and texture. The ornamental grasses, dwarf conifers, and small shrubs add winter interest.

A statue of St. Fiacre (the patron saint of gardening) by Becky Grey stands beneath a Japanese maple cultivar in a circle of stone with a six-foot diameter. Creeping junipers (Juniperus spp.) and a collection of sedums and sempervivums grow at his feet. It's a focal point in John Cram's Asheville garden of annuals and perennials.

A great combination for the small garden that lasts an entire garden season consists of Sedum *'Autumn Joy' at left and frost-tinged cord grass (Spartina pectinata 'Aureo-marginata'). Even in winter the burned flower heads of the sedum contrast with the light tan of the grass blades.*

A terracotta rabbit peeks out from a line of fancy-leafed caladiums, houseplants in pots, with ferns and hostas in the background.

Our first spring bulb bed was a mass of color from early April to late May yet it measured only seventeen by eight feet. Here many varieties of narcissus, fritillaries (Fritillaria meleagris 'Artemis'), and the vibrant reds of Tulipa eichleri chased away fears of returning winter. After the bulbs were finished, the space was filled with various annuals, including pots of geraniums.

An old half wine cask in Dr. Charles Brett's Greensboro, North Carolina, garden is home to various ivies and a rose, 'Bonica '82'. This procumbent shrub rose will reach a height of about three feet with a six-foot spread. That and a line of clipped boxwood shrubs and some elegant lawn furniture are all that's needed to make an empty terrace into a lovely small garden.

Moss-covered bricks invite the stroller past white astilbes, begonias, hostas, roses, and various evergreen shrubs in Dr. Charles Brett's backyard garden.

Even the smallest garden has room for one of the most beautiful of the old European roses, 'Rosa Mundi' (Rosa gallica versicolor). *It grows only about three by four feet but adds a big dimension to your garden: it's the oldest striped rose in rose history.*

A concrete Foo dog oversees Plantago major *'Purpurea' and the ground cover* Ajuga *'Bronze Beauty', turning a neglected corner of a garden into a small but beautifully colored autumn spot.*

Every summer the New Zealand flax (Phormium tenax 'Variegatum') leaves my greenhouse to take up residence in a section of the perennial garden. Here the stiff-leaved flax sits between two dwarf false cypresses (Chamaecyparis pisifera 'Filifera Aurea'). These conifers will be just three feet high by four to five feet wide after ten years. They are fronted by Italian geraniums (Pelargonium 'Skies of Italy') and the rambling vines of the white form of the wild sweet pea (Lathyrus latifolius 'Alba'). The leaves of Aster tartaricus *are upper left.*

A small and decorative vegetable garden in the French manner includes young beet plants (Beta vulgaris) and an edging of the wonderful loose-leaf lettuce 'Lollo-rosso', a variety that will grow many weeks without bolting to seed. If the beets bolt to seed, replace them in summer with borage (Borago officinalis) for use in the autumn.

One of the most valuable evergreen flowering ground covers for the small garden is the Lenten rose (Helleborus orientalis), here an unknown hybrid in Peter Gentling's Asheville garden. Used in a mass, as an edging, or in a pot, this is a spectacular and long-flowering plant.

The rock garden of Dr. David Lincoln takes advantage of what was once a grassy slope and now features many rock plants grown from seed, all packed in a space less than twenty feet long and fifteen feet wide.

The perennial part of the rock garden combines astilbes, blanket flowers, gayfeathers, salvias, hostas, and shasta daisies, balanced by carefully chosen stones and railroad tie steps.

A concrete stone box that measures four by four feet contains the far-reaching roots of Equisetum 'Robustus'. *For summer and fall color, use the hardy begonia* (Begonia grandis).

Both formal and wild gardens of small size can feature black-eyed Susans (Rudbeckia *spp.*). *I temper my collection with the addition of gold-banded lilies* (Lilium auratum).

For the focal point of a small garden nothing is more beautiful than a tree peony (Paeonia suffruticosa), here an unknown pink cultivar. Even when not in bloom, this elegant shrub sports beautiful leaves and interesting branches tipped with red buds in winter.

Spring daffodils bloom next to a dwarf hemlock (Tsuga canadensis *'Cappy's Choice'*)*, which will reach an eighteen-inch height in ten years. The conifer behind is* Chamaecyparis obtusa *'Pygmaea Aurescens'*, *a plant that turns a rich copper-bronze in late fall and will reach twenty-four to thirty inches in ten years. As the garden year marches on, the night-blooming daylilies* (Hemerocallis citrina) *in the rear reach a height of three feet. Directly behind the terracotta garden watcher, one ornamental grass* (Deschampsia caespitosa *'Fairy's Joke'*) *offers him shade—and the daffodils are never missed.*

My collection of various tender succulents summer on a concrete table on the downstairs terrace. When temperatures are kind, move your collection of potted houseplants outdoors to create a garden in almost any corner.

One of the most tropical-looking trees for North American gardens is the staghorn sumac (Rhus typhina). Kept clipped, it becomes a background shrub, or left alone, it's a small tree that can reach a height of twenty feet. The autumn color is spectacular.

A rock cleft stuffed with wild mosses, tiny seedling ferns, and some wandering hens-and-chickens (Sempervivum soboliferum) becomes an entire garden.

A very small moss garden created by Majella Larochelle in the mountains of North Carolina. Native mosses, tiny shrubs, and very small dwarf conifers: a world in miniature comes to life.

One of the author's small water gardens consists of a kidney-shaped plastic pool measuring six by four feet and filled with water-loving plants, including a number of wild sedges (Carex spp.) gathered from roadside ditches. Among the flowers are iris, columbines (Aquilegia spp.), and polka-dot plants (Hypoestes phyllostachya). The yellow flower is an interloping hawkweed (Hieracium spp.)

A small water garden at the North Carolina State University Arboretum is designed with a townhouse in mind. The pond is outlined with slate and contains water lilies, cannas (Canna spp.), four-leaf water clover (Marsilea malica), and even a clutch of water hyacinths (Eichhornia crassipes), beautiful when contained but dangerous in the wild. Outside the pond are ornamental grasses (Chasmanthium latifolium), cut-leaf sumac (Rhus typhina 'Laciniata'), plus evergreen shrubs. Photo by L. A. Jackson.

A corner garden whose outline was made with a garden hose. Eventually the Japanese maple and the shrubs will fill in and meet, while the edging can continue to be annuals that provide bloom all summer long. Photo by Tom Moyer.

A small backyard garden in Raleigh, with mixed perennials, herbs, and annuals. The low walls are flat stones, and the pathways have terracotta tiles in the shape of cats. Photo by L. A. Jackson.

Flowerpots and a silver urn filled with ornamental grasses fit perfectly on the edge of a terrace. The flowers below are Achillea millefolium in pots, this plant's invasive tendencies thereby kept under control. Photo by Elvin McDonald.

A trough garden designed by Budd Myers becomes a miniature delight. This is an experimental trough that contains many standard plants that are kept trimmed. It includes a Pinus rigida, Potentilla fruticosa 'Abbotswood', and a yellow-variegated yew. Photo by John H. Hawkins.

Another of Budd Myers's trough gardens, this time a home to sixteen plants including two tiny conifers (Chamaecyparis obtusa filicoides *and* Juniperus communis echiniformis), Spiraea japonica *'Gold Mound', and a dwarf cranberry,* Vaccinium macrocarpon *'Hamilton'. Photo by John H. Hawkins.*

Budd Myers displays all his troughs on what he calls the Trough Terrace. Six are made of hypertuffa and the seventh is a soapstone sink. Photo by John H. Hawkins.

Plastic dishes filled with a mix of cheerful annuals change three steps into three charming gardens. Photo by Peter Gentling.

A small backyard garden features mostly white flowers, here white nicotiana, cleome, vinca, phlox, feathery ornamental grasses, and a touch of color with blue salvias. Photo by Tom Moyer.

Even under winter snow, the backyard town garden of Linda Yang shows the copper trellis (designed by her husband), the knot garden, bird feeders, the black hole of the pond, and seeds on perennials, all enclosed by stone and concrete block walls. Photo by Linda Yang.

The perennial garden of Dr. Bill Holloway in Greenwood, South Carolina, features lilies, liatris, coreopsis, and many annuals, all set out in white wooden boxes. The boxes are the right height and properly spaced to make his garden wheelchair accessible. Photo by Francis Worthington.

Tropical water lilies are either day-blooming or night-blooming. The very fragrant blossoms stand above the water's surface and bloom all summer. Tropicals all make excellent cut flowers.

Among the night-bloomers are *Nymphaea* 'Juno', a beautiful large white, needing a bit less than five hours of sun to bloom and spreading to twelve feet, and 'Red Flare', with red-tinged foliage and flowers with dark red petals and stamens of deep maroon, needing full sun. Use a fifteen-quart container.

The following day-blooming tropicals are listed in water lily catalogs:

Nymphaea 'Mrs. George H. Pring' bears large white flowers that rise above lightly speckled leaves, taking slightly less than full sun and spreading to twelve feet. *N.* 'Evelyn Randig' has classic deep magenta flowers and variegated foliage; it needs full sun and spreads to twelve feet. *N.* 'Daubeniana' is blue, taking slightly less than full sun and spreading a little over six feet; it is also highly viviparous, a fancy word that means small plantlets form where the leaf blade meets the leaf stalk. The first two lilies need fifteen-quart containers and the third needs a five-quart container.

OTHER WATER-LOVING PLANTS FOR POOL OR BOG

Bog plants thrive in shallow water or at the edge of a pond, lake, or stream. For direct planting in your water garden, use good garden soil with some humus added. If plants are in containers, fill the container within a few inches of the top with soil, then push in the roots of the plant, and tamp the soil. To keep the soil from dirtying the water, cover the surface with a one-inch layer of pea gravel or small stones. Saturate the pot with water, then lower it gently into the pool or pond, to the correct depth. If necessary, place bricks or fieldstones under the plant to raise it to the desired level.

Acorus calamus 'Variegatus', variegated sweet flag, has a thick rhizome that produces slender, fragrant sword-shaped leaves striped with yellow about two and a half feet high. The tiny flowers twirl about a green spadix

(it looks like the "Jack" in a Jack-in-the-pulpit flower) that appears on the edge of the leaf. The rhizomes are very aromatic and were once used in hair oils. Plants do best in full sun, but even in the North they will adapt to dappled shade. Sweet flags also do well in boggy soil or shallow water to six inches deep. *Acorus gramineus* 'Variegatus', a miniature version of variegated sweet flag, never tops eighteen inches. The swordlike leaves are arranged like a fan, with stripes of white and green arising from a nonaromatic rhizome. Small but beautiful.

Caltha palustris, the marsh marigold, reaches a height of two feet and bears succulent heart-shaped leaves. In very early spring, loose clusters of bright yellow flowers appear. Each flower is about an inch across and has five waxy petals. Give these plants full sun until the leaves appear, then partial shade. They will luxuriate in moist soil or a few inches of water. Be careful with placement since these plants go dormant in summer.

Canna × *generalis* includes the water cannas, hybrid members of the genus. They have rhizomes similar to the well-known bedding plant favorites but are suited to wet conditions. The six-foot stems are clothed in large upright leaves and, in the heat of summer, produce spikes of showy large-petaled flowers in warm colors. Give water cannas full sun and plant them in either boggy soil or water up to six inches deep. Good cultivar choices include 'Endeavour', whose flowers are a clear red; 'Erebus', with pink flowers; 'Ra', which bears yellow blossoms; and 'Taney', with bright orange flowers. A group of newly introduced hybrids developed at Longwood Gardens—called the Longwood hybrids—are especially lovely, with slender leaves and salmon, yellow, or red flowers. Water cannas are tropical plants, so unless you live in Zone 10, you'll need to winter the roots indoors.

Chelone glabra, the turtlehead, grows about four feet tall and bears narrow, oval leaves up to six inches long. Toward summer's end, clusters of white (or sometimes pink) flowers resembling turtlelike snapdragons appear. Provide full sun to light shade. Plants will grow in any moist, humusy soil but do best along the water's edge.

Eleocharis montevidensis, the spike rush, is a perennial that reaches a height of about one foot and produces tall, quill-like leaves that grow in a clump. The flowers are non-descript brown buttons. Provide full sun and plant in boggy soil or up to two inches of water. Spike rushes are hardy to Zone 6.

Eleocharis tuberosa (E. dulcis), Chinese water chestnut, grows three feet tall and bears clumps of tubular stems and straw-colored catkins in summer. The corms are the water chestnuts used in Chinese cooking. Give plants full sun to partial shade; grow them in boggy soil or in water up to one foot deep. They are not hardy north of Zone 9.

Equisetum hyemale, the horsetail or scouring rush, is a tough perennial that usually grows about four feet tall. You'll find it in the wild along streams, lakes, ditches, and the edges of old railroad beds. The evergreen shoots grow from a rhizome and have such a high silica content that in pioneer days they were used to clean and polish pots and pans. The conelike caps produce spores instead of seeds. Horsetails thrive in full sun to partial shade and boggy soil. They will also grow in a few inches of water, either in containers or, if you section off the area, at water's edge. These ancient rushes are very, very invasive, so plant them within an eight-inch plastic collar or perhaps set them in a plastic pail or dishpan. In addition to the larger horsetails, there are some that stay very small. *E. scirpoides,* the dwarf scouring rush, has three-inch-high threadlike stems. It is perfect for miniature water gardens and bonsai but, like the rest of the genus, is very invasive.

Eupatorium purpureum, Joe-Pye weed, was mentioned with affection in the chapter on herb gardens, but it deserves a note here because it's another plant that is especially beautiful at the water's edge. This ten-foot perennial with large terminal clusters of tiny purplish flowers does well in damp or wet soil and is twice as beautiful when reflected in a shimmering pond.

Iris pseudacorus, the yellow water iris or yellow flag, grows about five feet tall with sword-shaped, light green leaves. Many yellow flowers bloom on tall, stout scapes. Provide full sun and moist or boggy soil. These irises excel at the pond's edge and in water up to ten inches deep.

Iris sibirica, the Siberian iris, reaches three feet in height and has clumps of sword-shaped leaves. Flowers come in many shades of blue, and a few cultivars bear lovely white flowers. Plants do best in full sun to partial shade. They adapt easily to boggy conditions and can grow in water up to four inches deep.

Lobelia cardinalis, the cardinal flower, bears spikes of striking bright red flowers in summer that can reach a height of six feet. In nature they grow along the banks of a stream and in the garden do best in boggy soil. Provide partial shade to full sun. In the cold North, wet but mulched soil is necessary for the winter.

Matteuccia struthiopteris, the ostrich fern, grows three feet tall and bears large fronds that grow from a central crown and resemble green ostrich feathers. These plants are partial to woodland shade and a moist soil, rich with organic matter. A group of ostrich ferns will soften the edge of any pond or pool.

Miscanthus sinensis 'Gracillimus', or maiden grass, is a perennial ornamental grass that can reach a height of seven feet. Its thin arching blades have narrow white midribs. The flowers form short plumes with that shimmer in the sunlight just before opening. Give them full sun and a moist, fertile soil. In a few years they become very large specimen plants. Many ornamental grasses do well when planted directly in the water.

Nymphoides peltata, the floating-heart, has three-inch leaves that float on the water's surface and are variegated with maroon. Five-petaled yellow flowers sit above the water on short stems. These plants need full sun to partial shade and grow in water a foot deep.

Osmunda regalis, the royal fern, is doubly effective when reflected at the water's edge. This perennial grows to five feet tall. The long fern fronds arise from a central crown. Give these ferns light shade and a moist soil that is especially rich with organic matter. Mature specimens are difficult to move, so start with young plants.

Scirpus tabernaemontani 'Zebrinus', or the variegated bulrush, has two-foot-high round stems with sharp points that resemble porcupine needles. On this cultivar the stems are banded with white. The leaves are brown sheaths at the base of the stem. Plants need full sun to partial shade and grow in boggy soil or shallow water. If green stems appear, remove them at the rhizome. Bulrushes are striking plants but are not hardy north of Zone 6.

Thalia dealbata is an unusual native American plant with flowering scapes (or stems) that reach a height of eight to ten feet with light blue-violet flowers in summer. Its graceful, broad, oblong leaves resemble those of cannas but are on taller stems. Provide full sun to partial shade and plant in boggy soil or up to one foot of water. This beautiful plant also does well in a pot set inside a larger pot full of water. The red-stemmed thalia (*T. geniculata*) has leaves supported on red stems, again with flowering spikes up to ten feet tall. These tropical plants are not hardy north of Zone 10.

Typha includes the cattails, which reach a height of about seven feet, depending on the species. The leaves are upright, slender, and look slightly grassy from a distance. The familiar large brown catkins appear in the heat of summer. Plants like full sun but adapt to partial shade. They must have boggy soil or up to ten inches of water. The wild species of ponds and backwaters is *T. latifolia* and must be treated with respect because they are very, very invasive. Being rampant is not a problem in a small pond but when allowed to conquer a large area of water, these plants know no bounds—and once estalished are almost impossible to get rid of. The cultivar 'Variegata' has vertical green and white stripes on the leaf, and is less invasive and even more attractive. *Typha angustifolia,* the narrow-leaved cattail, has more graceful leaves than the wild species. *T. minima,* the miniature cattail, grows to only two feet and has very narrow leaves and small catkins.

Zantedeschia aethiopica, the calla lily, is often called a tender perennial but if given plenty of mulch will survive in Zone 7. The beautiful, arrow-shaped leaves of glossy green top three feet. The elegant flowers have always been symbols of sophistication: the milky white spathes surround golden yellow spadixes and look like large white Jack-in-the-pulpits. Callas like full sun to light shade and grow in boggy soil.

PLAN FOR A WATER GARDEN

This plan features a six-by-four-foot oval pond made of a six-by-ten-foot butyl rubber liner, the edges lined with flat fieldstones. A bubble-type fountain is at the center and assumes the gardener can install an electric outlet nearby.

Another choice for a water garden is the use of a watering trough that's made of black plastic instead of galvanized steel. Again the edge is camouflaged by flat fieldstones.

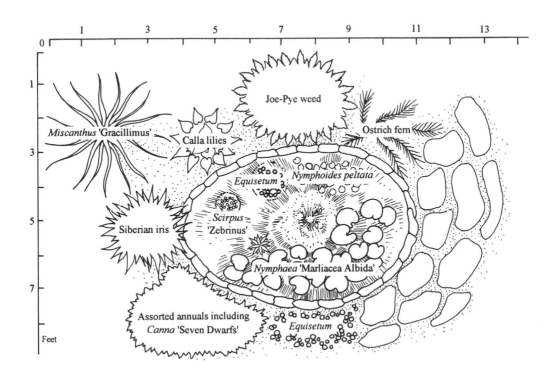

PLAN FOR A BOG GARDEN

Even if you don't care to have an open pool, the same liners can be used to transform a dry plot of land into one that will remain wet. This opens up the garden door to a host of plants that resent deep water but are especially happy at the water's edge or in boggy soil.

Just as with making a small pool, a hole is excavated, this time to a depth of twelve to fourteen inches. Next line the cavity with a PVC liner. (In this case it's not necessary to spend the extra money for a butyl rubber liner.) Roll back the liner edge a few inches. Then, instead of filling the hole with water, fill it with the excavated soil with some added compost or other organic material. Keep the bog area slightly below ground level so that when it rains, the surrounding runoff will continually saturate the bog soil. If additional water is needed, the hose does the job.

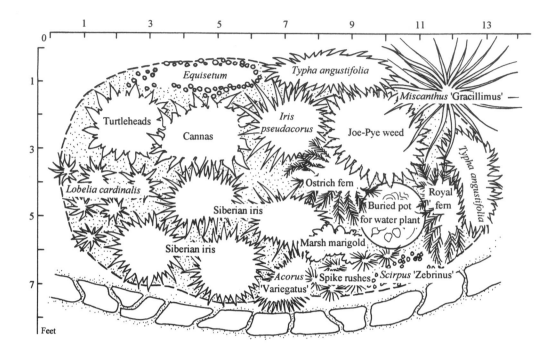

Twelve

Small Trees

~

YEARS AGO, WHEN FAMILIES STAYED IN ONE PLACE FOR A GENERATION OR MORE, TREES were planted for the future. Today families move from city to city and town to town, never staying in one place long enough to enjoy the aesthetic return on planting a tree. Others feel it's simply too much trouble to be involved with such a project.

Indeed, waiting for an oak to mature can take a generation or two, but the growth rate of a tree depends entirely on the species: some are slow, some intermediate, and some remarkably fast. And gardeners often forget that even a shrub can be fairly large, large enough, in fact, to dwarf a small tree. A weeping birch cultivar, for example, can often grow beneath the towering branches of an old lilac shrub. (At the other end of the scale the diminutive heaths and heathers, often thought to be herbaceous plants, are actually shrubs, even though a pair of typical gardener's feet could easily crush them to the ground.)

Even one tree can lend a feeling of age to a garden, acting as a focal point in the design. I had a lovely five-foot-high weeping birch (*Betula pendula* 'Youngii') that I set out in our garden in 1981. Within two years it dominated the scene, and by the end of six years, it stood eight feet high and its weeping branches covered a twelve-foot circle. On hot summer days the tree was a cool, green haven, and in the fall it became a shower of golden leaves. But in winter, when the branches sparkled with hoarfrost or were coated with ice, it was the most beautiful sight of all.

Today, most perennials are sold in containers, but small trees and shrubs are often balled and burlapped or arrive bare-root.

Containerized plants can be transplanted almost any time during the growing season (although I wouldn't suggest planting in the middle of a heat wave or a drought). Just be sure to water the root ball thoroughly before removing the plastic container. When you remove the container, check the root system: if the roots are compacted and growing in a ball from sitting within the container, pull them apart.

If plants are balled and burlapped, make sure the root ball is well watered. If it's not completely saturated, most of the water will roll down and off the wrapping and the root ball will dry out. As long as the roots are watered carefully, balled and burlapped plants can wait for weeks—or even months—until planting day.

Trees and shrubs that aren't more than two or three years old may be shipped bare-root. This means the supplier has washed the soil off the roots, then lightly wrapped them in a ball of sphagnum moss, shredded wood, or even paper strips, and soaked them thoroughly before shipping.

When you receive such a plant, open the wrapping immediately to see if the packing has dried out and add water if necessary. Then place the plant in a cool, shady spot. Soak the roots thoroughly in a pail of water for at least twenty-four hours before planting. Never leave the plants in water for days on end, however, or the roots will rot. How long the roots will last with just occasional soakings depends on the plant. But if you can't get around to planting in a few days' time, dig a trench about six inches deep, then place the plants on their sides two or three inches apart at a 45-degree angle. Water well, then cover the roots with dirt and tamp it down with the heel of your shoe. This time-honored practice is known as heeling in.

Planting out. Use the following steps for planting a containerized or b&b tree or shrub.

1. Pick a planting day that is cloudy, preferably after a soaking rain. Dig a hole large enough to allow six inches of space all around the root ball. (Always plan on a larger hole than you think you'll need; the old adage "never put a ten-dollar tree in a five-dollar hole" is still the rule.) Put the excavated soil on a tarpaulin or piece of plastic to make cleanup easier.
2. Dump a pailful of well-rotted or composted manure into the bottom of the hole and work it in; never use raw commercial fertilizers or fresh manure, which will burn the roots. Tamp the compost down firmly so that the root ball won't later sink and put the trunk below ground level. If the tree is large and the trunk is weak, now is the time to add a stake for future support.
3. Take the excavated soil and mix it, if necessary, with some crushed leaves or leaf litter.
4. Place the ball in the hole so that ground level will be at the same point on the trunk as it was at the nursery. Do not remove the burlap; it will soon rot. Just re-

move any wrapping that would stick out in the open air and, like a wick, draw moisture from the soil. If the wrap is plastic, wait until the ball is in place, then cut away as much as possible. All this care is needed so the tiny rootlets that absorb water and nutrients are not disturbed.

5. Fill the remaining hole with water and allow it to settle. Then using your fingers, firmly pack the soil around the roots and push it down hard. This step is very important; if air pockets remain around the ball, many fragile rootlets will die. Leave a slight lip around the edge of the hole to act as a catch basin for water.

If the ground isn't soaked on the day you plant, water thoroughly. Continue to water during the rest of the growing season. Too often, gardeners plant a tree with care but neglect to keep up the watering chores, so the plant dies.

A SELECTION OF SMALL TREES

The following trees do best in full sun. Some, as noted, will adapt to shade. I left out flowering cherries and crabapples because they are so common at garden centers but picked some that are more unusual, and I included the American dogwood. Even though this beautiful tree is threatened by a terrible disease, I've included descriptions and advice in helping them survive. All of the trees are hardy to Zone 5, unless noted in the text.

Albizia julibrissin 'Rosea', the silk or mimosa tree, is a deciduous tree that grows to about thirty feet. It has a spreading form and lacy leaves composed of many small leaflets. Fluffy clusters of pink flowers with long stamens appear in midsummer and look like pink powder puffs. It's a good specimen tree for a lawn. Moist soil is ideal, but I've seen it do well on dry, rocky soil where few other plants thrive. Silk trees are so easily grown from seed, they can become weedy. (Pull up unwanted plants when very young as the roots are tough.) Young plants in the North must have winter protection; established plants do well in Zone 6. Unfortunately this tree is subject to a soilborne disease called fusarium wilt; if this fungus affects your other plants, do not plant or transplant silk trees.

Amelanchier canadensis is commonly called the serviceberry, juneberry, or shadblow. Jens Jensen, one of America's pioneer landscape architects, described the tree in his book *Siftings* (Ralph Fletcher Seymour, Chicago, IL, 1939): "To see the real beauty of the juneberry is to see its frail blossoms intermixed with snowflakes on a stormy day in early spring—youth daring the tempest." A deciduous tree with a rounded form, it can reach a height of thirty feet. The young leaves are silvery, but it is the clusters of white flowers appearing in early spring that make it such a desirable tree. In the Northeast it blooms when shad come up the rivers to spawn—hence the name shadblow.

The edible purple fruit is attractive to birds (rarely are enough berries left to make jelly). This tree does best in well-drained loam, but will tolerate a wide range of soils. It is hardy to Zone 4.

Amelanchier laevis has larger flowers and is usually found in nurseries as the cultivar 'Rosea', having flowers flushed with pink. *Amelanchier* × *grandiflora (A. arborea* × *A. laevis)* is often called *A. lamarckii* and is offered as the cultivar 'Autumn Brilliance', having better-than-type autumn foliage of orange and red; it reaches a twenty-five-foot height at maturity.

Betula pendula 'Youngii', Young's weeping birch, has a weeping habit with an irregular top. A cultivar of the European white birch, it ultimately reaches a height of fifteen feet and is exceptionally attractive for a small garden. We enjoyed this tree for many years in our northern garden. It is hardy to Zone 4.

Betula populifolia, the gray birch, is an underestimated tree. Instead of being papery white like the canoe birch, this tree has a chalky white bark with distinct triangular black marks below the branches. It is graceful in habit until well into old age—about thirty years. The normal height is about thirty-five feet with a trunk diameter of one foot. Multiple trunks will arise but the unwanted can be cut off. The natural range is from Nova Scotia to Delaware, so it is a very hardy tree.

Large numbers of gray birch trees grew in the abandoned fields between our northern garden and the woods proper.

We noticed their ability to bend under the weight of heavy snow without breaking. Once the snow was removed they quickly straightened up again.

In a New Jersey garden belonging to Florence and Robert Zuck, several old gray birch volunteers were left to form an allée of great charm. In one place in the Zuck garden, a gray birch is surrounded by rings of creeping blue phlox (*Phlox divaricata*) and primroses (*Primula vulgaris*), and English ivy grows up the multiple trunks.

Catkins appear on the branches in autumn and bloom the following spring. The seeds provide excellent food for wildlife, including ruffed grouse and songbirds. Deer leave these trees alone unless there is nothing else to eat.

Caragana arborescens, the Siberian pea tree, is often mentioned in old garden books as a perfect windbreak for the windswept plains of Alberta, Manitoba, and Saskatchewan. But I've seen it used to great effect in small gardens and rock gardens around the Northeast. My garden friend Budd Myers used *C. arborescens* forma *lorbergii* as a spring focal point at the edge of his Pennsylvania rock garden.

The Siberian pea tree is fast-growing when young. Its soft oval leaves grow in pairs and are in groups of four to six, giving a cloud effect from a distance. The main branches have thorns, with smaller spines at the leaf axils. In May, clusters of bright yellow pealike flowers appear, followed by pods, which remain on the plant after opening. The leaves turn yellow in autumn, and during winter months the greenish stems add interest to the landscape, especially if the red-stemmed dogwood (*Cornus alba* 'Sibirica') is planted nearby for contrast. This is an especially valuable plant for small gardens that survives where the winters are bleak and frigid.

'Pendula' is an exceptionally beautiful cultivar of the pea tree, introduced into the Imperial Botanical Gardens of St. Petersburg in 1730. It is usually grafted to a three-foot trunk of *C. arborescens* and is perfect for the small garden or as a border centerpiece.

Cercis canadensis, the Eastern redbud, is a small deciduous tree that stays under thirty feet. In spring, red-budded pealike flowers appear directly on branches and quickly turn to rose-mauve or pink. They are followed by heart-shaped leaves that turn yellow in the autumn. There is a white-flowered cultivar called 'Alba'. Provide a well-drained, slightly acid or neutral pH. This is a good tree for small spaces but be sure to move it while it's still young, since it's difficult to transplant larger trees.

Chionanthus virginicus, the fringe tree or old-man's-beard, is an American native that grows to thirty feet in the wild. It has an irregular form and eight-inch-long oval leaves that turn bright yellow in autumn. But it's in spring when the fringe tree excels, because the six-inch clusters of fragrant white flowers with one-inch petals look like waving pieces of translucent white jade. This is a spectacular tree in flower and worth having just to see it in bloom. The garden designer who lived next door to us here in North Carolina planted a fringe tree at the entrance to his Japanese moss garden. He weighted the trunk down with a concrete block tied to a rope, and today it gracefully bends to the ground. These trees need a moist, fertile soil with good drainage.

Cornus florida, the American flowering dogwood, is a great small tree for the garden. The horizontal branches give the tree a distinctive flat top. Mature specimens sometimes reach forty feet tall. The four-inch oval leaves have sharp points and turn varying shades of scarlet in the fall. In many parts of the nation the small flower clusters surrounded by four large, showy white or pink bracts are a sure sign that spring is here.

Unfortunately, many of these beautiful trees are dying as a result of dogwood anthracnose, a plant disease caused by several types of fungi. It attacks trees both in the woods and in home gardens, although the disease hits woodland plants hardest because the environment there is usually cooler and wetter. The first symptoms are spots on the leaves, followed by leaf scorching. When the leaves die, they remain on the tree, carrying infection. Sometimes an infected tree grows water sprouts, which carry the disease back into the bark. The bark then gets cankers or eventual dead spots.

To help keep your dogwoods from getting the disease, try the following:

1. Practice good sanitation by pruning dead twigs that carry spores; water trees well during extended dry spells and fertilize every year in spring or late fall.

2. If the fungus is reported in your area, spray trees with a fungicide when the young leaves appear in spring and twice again, at two-week intervals.

3. Replace lost trees with the Chinese dogwood (*C. kousa*), which is resistant, though not immune. This tree is smaller (to twenty-five feet), with an upright, spreading form. Flower clusters are surrounded by large showy white pointed bracts. The berrylike fruits are attractive to birds. Give these trees full sun in cooler climates (they'll grow in open shade, too). They prefer a light, well-drained acid soil that is rich in organic matter.

Cotinus coggygria, the smoke tree, has always had a place in our garden. Our first specimen was the cultivar 'Pink Champagne', raised from seed collected by Kew Garden in London. In our present garden is a very old 'Royal Purple' that has been in place over twenty years.

Smoke trees are considered either small trees or bushy shrubs according to their habit of growth. The individual flowers are insignificant but the pedicels, or stems, of the nonfertile flowers are long and covered with silky hairs, looking just like wisps of smoke.

In our northern garden, we grew a common smoke tree at the edge of a slope with mugho pines in front and the rising fields behind. To the right of the conifers was a wide bed of cordgrass (*Spartina* spp.), and the effect of the green needles, the waving grasses, and the gray smoke of the smoke tree blossoms was truly beautiful.

A number of cultivars are available, including 'Flame', which bears purplish pink flower heads and green leaves that turn a brilliant orange-red in autumn. 'Pink Champagne' has fluffy pink flower heads, and the leaves are purple-red in the fall. 'Purple Supreme' has deep purple foliage in the spring, turning bright red in autumn. 'Royal Purple' has deep pink plumes and deep purple leaves that usually keep their color all summer.

Franklinia alatamaha, the Franklin tree, was introduced into cultivation in 1770, then disappeared from the wild around 1790. Today, it is found only in gardens and arboretums. Usually some twenty feet tall, this deciduous tree has an upright form and oblong, glossy green leaves that turn a beautiful orange-red in autumn. Three-inch white flowers with prominent yellow stamens appear in late summer or early fall. Franklinias need moist, well-drained soil and do beautifully along the bank of a stream. They do best with an eastern exposure and morning sun; they also like open shade. Usually these trees are not hardy north of Zone 6, but garden specimens will send up new shoots every spring if the crown is mulched against severe cold.

Halesia carolina, the Carolina silver-bell, reaches about twenty feet and has a round-headed, spreading form. The four-inch-long oval leaves turn yellow in autumn. Small, dangling, bell-shaped white flowers appear in spring. Plant this tree in fertile, moist but well-drained loam in partial shade. Avoid windy sites and, in the North, low, cold spots where late frost can damage the flowers. Use as a specimen plant or in a woodland garden.

Hibiscus syriacus, the rose of Sharon, was introduced into English gardens back in 1596, so it's been around for a long time. This deciduous small tree or shrub grows about twelve feet high with upright branches that bear three-lobed leaves and, in summer, funnel-shaped, five-petaled flowers of purple, red, or white. Most gardeners plunk the tree in the middle of a lawn, alone in the hot sun, and it survives. But it will do better—and look better—in company with other plants, especially if provided with somewhat moist soil and a bit of lime in areas where acidity is high.

There are many cultivars but the best two are 'Blue Bird', bearing large azure-blue flowers about four inches wide, and 'Diana', an introduction of the U.S. National Arboretum. It bears pure white flowers that open to six inches across and remain open at night when most of the other roses of Sharon are closed. These shrubs are hardy to Zone 5.

Kolreuteria paniculata, the golden-rain tree, grows about thirty feet tall. This deciduous tree has an upright form and bears feathery compound leaves that sometimes turn yellow in autumn. In late spring and early summer, long clusters of small yellow fragrant flowers appear, followed by attractive seedpods, which the Chinese use to make necklaces. The trees grow in practically any garden soil and tolerate both drought and wind.

Magnolia tomentosa (M. stellata), the star magnolia, is the only magnolia that is reliably hardy in Zone 5, and even there it needs protection from the worst of winter winds. Even on one dismal wet day in early March when most of the United States was suffering from wind-chill temperatures below zero, the buds of our star magnolia were doing fine. Garden dirt was soft underfoot and the fallen leaves were soaked through; the garden was, in fact, a dismal place to be. But those buds were perfectly comfortable under their coat of furry fuzz.

This small tree or shrub has an attractive compact growth habit and is a great tree for the small garden. The large and lovely double white blossoms have floppy petals tinged with pink and fill the garden with fragrance in spring. The five-inch-long leaves add interest in summer.

Buy a star magnolia that is container grown and plant it in your garden before growth really starts for the year. You will find an occasional seedling tree in the vicinity of the parent; it will flower at a very young age.

Recently, a new hybrid between the star magnolia and *M. kobus,* a tree from Japan, has produced *M.* × *Loebneri.* Of particular interest is the cultivar 'Merrill', a rapid grower that reaches twenty-five feet, with blossoms larger than the star magnolia. This tree is reportedly hardy in Zone 4.

Oxydendrum arboreum, the sorrel or sourwood tree, reaches a height of twenty-five feet. It has a pyramidal form and small glossy green leaves that resemble those of a a mountain laurel, turning bright red in fall. Drooping clusters of fragrant, bell-shaped white flowers bloom in summer, followed by attractive seedpods in autumn. Sorrels must have full morning sun, but do best in some shade as the day heats up. The soil should be well drained and somewhat acid. Grow this fine tree as a specimen, or use it as the background for a formal border. It is hardy to Zone 6.

All the following members of the willow family have had a part in our garden at one time or another. My only cautionary remark is this: Never plant a willow close to a sewer system or drainage pipe, especially when the pipes are old and ceramic. In their search for water, the roots have an uncanny ability to ferret out the tiniest crack in any system—and will enlarge it to the breaking point.

Salix matsudana 'Tortuosa', the dragon-claw or corkscrew willow, is a flower arranger's delight. In summer it's just another pretty tree, but in the winter, the twisted, corkscrew-shaped branches are beautiful against a stormy sky. The ultimate height is thirty feet, and a healthy specimen will grow about fifteen feet in eight years. This tree grows beautifully in a large pot. The dragon-claw is hardy to Zone 4.

Salix melanostachys, the black pussy willow, is far more interesting than the wild pussy willow (*S. caprea*). The catkins are so dark that they appear black, in stark contrast to the reddish stems that bear them. Then as they mature, the pollen-yellow stamens are supported by red filaments, again in sharp contrast to the catkin "fur." These shrubs eventually reach a height of ten feet, with a twelve-foot spread. They are hardy to Zone 4.

Wisteria spp. are deciduous vines, but when properly trained by pruning, wisteria can become a small tree with a weeping habit. The delicate compound leaves surround large, drooping clusters of fragrant pealike lilac, white, or pink flowers in spring. Plants need only full sun, and a moist but well-drained soil with an acid pH. To start a tree, choose a vine that stands at least three feet in its pot. Pick one stem, stake it, and remove all side shoots; it will eventually reach the height you wish. Cut back shoots in early autumn to two to three buds. If there are any flower buds at the base of the shoot, the pruning will encourage them to develop next spring. The process can be time consuming, but it's worth the effort when the blooms finally appear. If you don't have the time to start your own tree, check with specialty nurseries, which often have standards in stock. Although vines are hardy to Zone 5, the flower buds need protection from bitter winter winds.

PLAN FOR A GROVE OF SMALL NATIVE TREES

Not only are shrub and small tree borders perfect as backgrounds for perennial borders (and much cheaper than building an old stone or brick wall), they are especially useful for screening an unwanted view or filtering both noise and dust from a nearby roadway.

The following design can be adapted to almost any situation and features shrubs and trees for spring color, summer shade, and autumn glory.

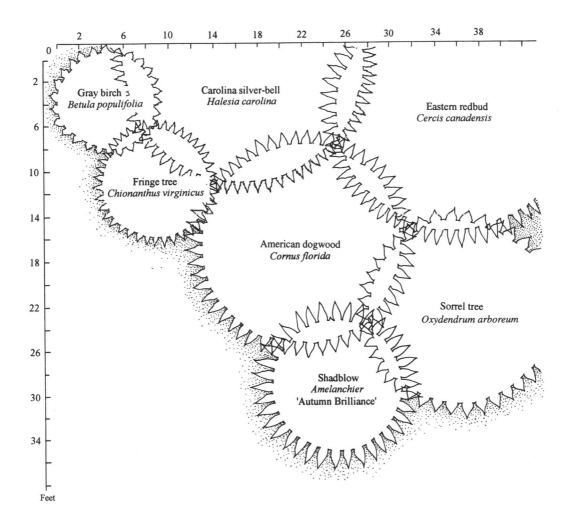

Thirteen

Shrub Gardens and Hedges

~

THE BEAUTY OF INCLUDING SHRUBS IN THE HOME LANDSCAPE STEMS FROM THEIR VERSATILITY. Most of these plants have either lovely flowers or interesting foliage or both. Then their ultimate size fits into the new small landscape, and with their speed of maturation, shrubs give a mature look to the landscape decades before some trees make the mark.

Just a few shrubs can endow a garden with an established look; even young lilacs, rhododendrons, azaleas, or heaths and heathers will soon bloom and bring continuity to the scene. Hedges can halt most dogs from running rampant. They can conceal effective—but aesthetically ugly—wire fencing.

A wall of, say, hybrid rhododendrons, or forsythia or honeysuckle (*Lonicera* spp.), or clipped Canadian hemlocks (*Tsuga canadensis*) can turn a mass of perennials from dull clots of color to an invigorating diorama by providing that dark background color that so many flowers need to be effective. And shrubs set in a rough row then underplanted with ferns, hostas, or other perennials, or shrubs simply planted in a line make great delineators that bring privacy to a garden room and mark boundaries around a property. A single hybrid rhododendron can become that focal point that unites all the other plants in the garden. Shrubs and high hedges become walls without plasterboard; with judicious pruning, they can even have windows in them that allow glimpses into the garden room next door.

At the Elspeth and Jamie Clarke garden in Fairview, North Carolina (he was for many years the congressman from the Asheville area), a very old boxwood hedge was planted behind an old stone wall. Over the years the shrubs grew up, over, and across the wall. The Clarkes cut a three-foot-wide, three-foot-high, and two-foot-deep enclosure from the living hedge, and a present-day wall-sitter has a cozy shelter, protected from all but the worst rains.

The procedures for planting shrubs are much the same as for planting small trees (chapter 12).

LILACS

Syringa vulgaris, the common lilac, is one of the toughest members of the clan of small trees and large shrubs. Almost every front yard of an abandoned farmhouse has an old Persian lilac, with lavender blossoms or sometimes white.

Among the more attractive *Syringa vulgaris* cultivars are 'Ellen Willmott', which bears double white flowers; 'Mont Blanc', with single white flowers; 'President Lincoln', which has single blue flowers; and 'Belle de Nancy', with double pink flowers. 'Firmament' is a particularly beautiful cultivar with single blue blossoms; 'Sensation' bears lovely single purple picotee flowers with white edges.

Syringa patula 'Miss Kim' is a dwarf Korean lilac, five by five feet when mature and in perfect scale for a very small garden. It's one of the few lilacs that will bloom in the cooler parts of the South. ('Lavender Lady' is another such shrub.) *Syringa lacinata,* the cut-leaf lilac, is also adaptable to warm areas, but still, southern lilacs never bloom with the beauty of those in the North.

There are two important things to know about lilacs. First, they need full sun; lilacs will bloom in partial shade, but not at their best. And they must have a period of winter cold; south of the northern reaches of Zone 7, lilacs do not bloom with any regularity.

Lilacs need a reasonably fertile, well-drained soil, preferably with a high organic content. A layer of organic mulch helps conserve soil moisture, reduce weeds, and protect the plants from mechanical injuries caused by aberrant lawn mowers.

Left to their own devices, many lilacs, like those in abandoned gardens, bloom year after year. But after flowering is over, it's a good idea to cut out any diseased canes and the suckers growing around the base. Dead-head spent flowers to save on the shrub's energy—and for cosmetic reasons. Just be careful not to remove next year's flower buds, which are located on the branches below the dead flowerheads.

To control pests that affect lilacs, keep plants healthy, prune when necesssary, and choose the proper plant for your climate. If necessary, applications of horticultural oils and soaps will keep pests in check.

(Powdery mildew usually occurs in areas with high summer humidity, but though unsightly, usually doesn't harm the shrub itself. To control it, use Bordeaux mixture, a fungicide discovered many years ago in

France. Made from copper sulfate and lime, it was a garden standard until 1940, when it was superseded by chemicals produced by the oil companies. It's still a cheap and effective fungicide that leaves a conspicuous but relatively harmless residue.)

RHODODENDRONS AND AZALEAS

Rhododendrons and azaleas belong to the genus *Rhododendron*. Azaleas are either evergreen or deciduous and have flowers shaped like funnels, and rhododendrons are usually evergreen and have bell-shaped flowers.

There are so many species and cultivars that choosing one can be bewildering. Thousands of pages are needed to describe all the species and cultivars of the rhododendrons and azaleas available on the market today. Interested gardeners usually join the American Rhododendron Society (see the Appendix) to meet local experts who can help them decide what plants to choose.

Among the better rhododendrons I've grown or seen in other gardens are 'Vulcan' and 'Mars', both of which have rich red flowers; 'Blue Peter', an old cultivar whose pretty near-blue flowers have a contrasting dark eye; and 'Wheatley', with fragrant flowers of a lovely soft pink. 'Blue Diamond', hardy to -5°F, is only three feet tall by two feet wide and needs more sun (at least a half day of direct sun) than larger-leaved plants to flower well. It is covered with small blue blossoms that seem to glow. 'Baden-Baden' grows just over eighteen inches high and has a three-foot spread. Its flowers are luminous red bells. Finally, *R. yakusimanum* and hybrids of *R. yakusimanum* and *R. smirnowii* are noteworthy for their silvery new growth and the indumentum (downy covering) on their leaves.

Azaleas boast a bewildering number of cultivars that belong to groups developed in Europe, Japan, and America. Hundreds of these hybrids and cultivars have proven to be outstanding and include the Kehr azaleas from North Carolina, the Linwood azaleas from Linwood, New Jersey, the Girard azaleas from Ohio, the Schroeder azaleas from Evansville, Indiana, and the Greenwood azaleas from Oregon.

Some of the best include 'Pyrored', a new introduction from the National Arboretum. It may not yet be widely available, but watch for it. Its glowing red flowers and small evergreen leaves are particularly attractive when paired with white flowering dogwood. The Robin Hill hybrids were developed by Robert Gartrell of Wyckoff, New Jersey. 'Sir Robert' and 'Nancy of Robin Hill' both offer large, frilly, pastel pink flowers on low, spreading, semideciduous plants. *Rhododendron kaempferi* 'Othello' has good autumn color and flowers profusely with blossoms of a soft, warm pink with a lot of orange. The above are reliably winter hardy to Zone 6.

Many of the Exbury hybrids were introduced after World War II. They bloom in spectacular two-tone blends, such as 'Salmon Orange' or 'Gibraltar', with glowing orange flowers. These hybrids look wonderful when planted near other flowers of complementary colors. They are hardy to Zones 5 and 6 but resent extremes of heat and are better in northern gardens.

There is even an azalea for the extreme northern parts of the United States. 'White Lights' is one of a series of azaleas developed at the University of Minnesota. The fragrant blossoms are white with a dash of gold at the center, and the plants are hardy to -50°F.

Cultural requirements for rhododendrons and azaleas are the same. Both need a well-drained, acid soil composed of leaf mold combined with sphagnum peat moss; heavy clay and alkaline soils are slow death to the clan. Their root systems are shallow and thinly branched, so the soil must be continually moist.

Rhododendrons prefer a location that protects them from both the continuous heat of a summer sun and the harsh winds of winter.

Although some species are quite hardy (to -25°F), most prefer winter temperatures above 0°F.

Generally, rhododendrons and azaleas should be planted out in early spring when the plants are waking from their winter slumber and ready to grow and flower. This schedule is especially important in the North, since it gives plants adequate time to settle in before winter.

Planting preparations are much the same as for other balled-and-burlapped or container-grown shrubs: the hole must be large enough for the roots to spread out. Set the root ball so that the crown is at the same depth it was in the container. Fill the hole with a mixture of three parts soil to one part shredded leaves or compost. Firm the soil mix lovingly around the roots to remove large air pockets, but don't pack it so hard that you compact the soil; remember that these plants have roots close to the surface and need the oxygen that a porous soil provides.

Water thoroughly after planting. Keep the soil moist and follow a careful watering schedule for the remainder of the growing season. Make a donut of mulch around the shrub so that water will run into the root ball.

If you garden in an area of poorly drained or decidedly alkaline soil, set the root ball of a small rhododendron or azalea directly on the surface of the soil. Then mound additional soil around the ball, and mulch the entire hummock. Instad of growing down into the packed earth, the roots will grow horizontally into the new soil. This process is not recommended for large shrubs and trees.

If you plant rhododendrons or azaleas next to a masonry wall of brick or stone, over the years the rain will leach the lime out of the wall. Eventually, the soil will become alkaline and the plants will suffer. Adding ferrous sulfate should rectify the situation for a time, but it's a good idea to consult your local extension agent for a correct reading of the soil pH and the right amount of chemical to add. Don't be tempted to use aluminum sulfate; it can have an adverse effect on rhododendrons and azaleas.

Unlike most evergreens, rhododendrons and azaleas can be moved with relative ease, since their root systems are shallow and so close to the stems. Just be sure the hole is large enough and that you use enough water to settle the plant into its new home.

After the plants flower, remove the spent blossoms to prevent seed formation and to channel the plant's energy into next year's crop of blooms.

Except to remove diseased or damaged wood, rhododendrons need little pruning. If there is a dead branch on a plant, cut it back to the next largest branch. In general, cutting branches back to one foot on old, overgrown plants will encourage compact growth. I've seen rhododendrons cut to the ground by knife and saw, and still bounce back. But if you have a valued rhododendron and wish for rejuvenation, remove only one-third of the plant each year, just to make sure you don't kill it. If pruning is necessary, start in early spring so that new growth has a chance to harden before winter sets in.

Azaleas can be pruned for shape by cutting back a long stem to the point where branching should begin. Because dormant vegetative buds are located all along the branches of azaleas, pruning cuts can be made just about anywhere. This is why azaleas can be sheared in Japanese gardens and always put out new growth. But get the job done by the end of July so that the azalea has time to develop flower buds for the following year.

TREE PEONIES

I've grown peonies for years, but I've never been particularly pleased with the results. Peonies are wonderful when in bloom, but once their silky petals have fallen to the ground, for the rest of the season you've got a rather dull mound of leaves. But there *are* peonies that I think are extra special and belong in every small garden; they are called tree peonies.

Tree peonies—chiefly *Paeonia suffruticosa, P. lutea,* and *P. delavayi*—can cause even the most hardened garden visitor to gasp. In old Chinese tapestries, those magnificent blossoms that look like idealized peonies are instead realistically rendered tree peonies.

The tree peony is not really a tree but a shrub, reaching a height of about five feet and a spread up to six feet. Individual flowers are between six and eight inches wide, but those of the more exotic Japanese cultivars can be a foot across. The soft green foliage is also attractive. Unlike other peonies, the branches develop a bark and should never be cut off unless you are pruning an old plant.

Because this plant is so spectacular, you should make it the focal point of your garden. Site it so that you can easily walk up to it or at least see it from inside the house. The smallest city garden would not be complete without a tree peony, complemented with small roses and hostas.

Many cultivars are available. 'Age of Gold', winner of the Gold Medal of the American Peony Society, bears fully double golden blossoms with a light red tracing on some of the petals. Also look for 'Angelet', with semidouble yellow flowers edged with rose; 'Black Pirate', with single deep maroon flowers; 'Godaishu', a large semidouble that bears globe-shaped white flowers of pure white with a yellow center; 'Hesperus', bearing single rose-pink flowers with yellow overtones; 'Ori-hime', with double blossoms of Chinese red (the color of the lacquer); 'Shin-shium-ryo', whose semidouble flowers are deep purple and have fringed edges; and 'Yuki Doro', sporting double white flowers with red markings in the center.

Tree peonies are expensive, especially when you buy grafts that are at least three years old. These older plants are worth it, however, since they are more established and have a higher success rate than younger grafts.

New tree peony plants need a deep, sandy, rich soil that is neutral or slightly acid. Add plenty of humus and compost, plus one cup of bonemeal per plant. If your soil is too heavy, add sand to lighten it.

Dig a hole about two feet deep and three feet wide and fill it with the soil mix well before planting time, giving the mix a chance to settle. Tree peonies have been known to live for over eighty years, so it's worth the effort to plant them properly.

The best time to plant is late September or early October, depending on your climate. Set the plants the same depth as they were at the nursery. Use plenty of water and muddy-in the roots with a slurry of water and soil. Most tree peonies are grafted onto regular peony roots; the graft junction should be about six inches below the ground level so that the graft will develop its own root system. For a season or two your peony might send up two kinds of leaves: the deeply cut leaves are those of the tree peony, but any other shoots growing from the rootstock should be removed. If you are planting more than one tree peony, space them at least four feet apart.

Keep the plant well watered until frost. For the first winter, protect it from bitter winds with an inverted bushel basket topped with a stone.

Tree peonies are chancy in climates colder than Zone 5 and need extra protection and care; if winter temperatures in your area drop below -20°F for any length of time, it's a good idea to cover the tree every year with a wooden box filled with dried leaves or straw.

A tree peony develops a strong system of feeder roots that lie close to the soil surface, so take care when cultivating. Every spring, scratch in a cup or so of bonemeal. The plant will increase in size each year, sending up new branches from the crown. Prune out dead wood when it is in full foliage.

Every so often a branch of a tree peony will wilt without any obvious cause. The problem is a fungus blight called botrytis. Quickly sever the wilted branch and burn it. Pick up any leaf litter around the plant and remove all the old plant debris in the fall. Botrytis usually does not bother plants that have good drainage and plenty of air circulation. Ants are attracted to the sweet sap of peony buds but are not known to cause any damage.

OTHER SHRUBS FOR THE SMALL GARDEN

Abeliophyllum distichum, the so-called white forsythia, is a very valuable shrub. Even where winter temperatures can plunge to -25°F, this beauty blooms every April, long before the yellow forsythias ever think of opening up. A native of central Korea, *A. distichum* has been growing in American gardens since 1924, but it still doesn't have the popularity it deserves.

The flower buds appear in late summer, so always prune in the spring, after blossoming is over for the year. The shrub needs protection from winter winds because the flower buds remain on the stems all winter and can be damaged by severe weather.

A good-sized container-grown plant should become six feet tall and four feet wide in about three years. Prune if it becomes too large. Root the cuttings for your garden friends and force the branches to provide flowers for the winter table.

A new cultivar called 'Rosea' is now on the market. It bears light pink flowers and is especially beautiful in early spring gardens.

Baptisia australis, blue false indigo, is an American wildflower that bears attractive blue-green leaves on strong four-foot stems. This bushy perennial acts like a deciduous shrub; in the fall, the foliage turns coal-black, then falls off. Spikes of dark blue pea-like flowers appear in late spring, followed by attractive seedpods. Blue false indigo is especially striking when planted with goldenrods and little bluestem ornamental grasses (*Andropogon* spp.).

I still remember many of the plants that grew in our first formal garden. Three false indigos stood in a row on top of the bank and did a great job holding the soil. They overlooked slopes of myrtle, hay-scented ferns and, farther down, our red Japanese maple.

Because they are legumes, baptisias grow moderately well even in poor soil and are excellent plants for preventing erosion on banks. But plan ahead because the root system becomes so extensive that old plants are not easily moved. Seedlings should be set out by the second spring. In time, they will cover an area of several feet with their graceful foliage. Baptisia adapts to filtered shade but does best in full sun.

Elaeagnus angustifolia, the Russian olive, gets its generic name from the Greek word for sacred olive tree (the leaves resemble those of olive trees); the species name means narrow-leaved. The plants in our garden began to bloom by mid-June of the second year. Their small flowers gave off a delightful though heavy odor over the whole garden; visitors would stand for minutes, enjoying the perfume. Then in late summer flocks of birds turned up to devour the berries.

In the winter, when the leaves have fallen, the gray bark of the Russian olive provides more interest in the garden. (Some say it's a dirty tree because of shedding bark, but we never had this problem.) These shrubs age quickly, and before ten years have passed, their trunks are gnarled and wrinkled. It's a look that many gardeners fight for decades to have.

Russian olive is an especially good tree for the small lawn, or as backdrop for other shrubs. It's also a popular shrub for seaside gardens, where it serves as a windbreak when planted in long rows. Plants are hardy to Zone 2.

Hydrangea includes the popular species *H. macrophylla,* a shrub that bears pink or blue flowers according to the acidity of the soil. But my favorite is *H. quercifolia,* the oak-leaved hydrangea. This beautiful American native reaches a height of eight feet with very attractive leaves that resemble those of an oak. As an added bonus they turn scarlet to burgundy in autumn. Upright panicles of very beautiful, fragrant white flowers appear from July to September. (They make great dried flowers for winter bouquets.) 'Snow Queen' is a remarkable new cultivar that blooms profusely and offers magnificent autumn color. It grows to seven feet high and seven feet wide in about six years.

Oak-leaved hydrangeas make wonderful backdrops for a bed of flowers or are attractive just simply as hedge borders. They are hardy to the warmer regions of Zone 5, provided they are protected from bitter winter winds. If you have room in your garden for only one shrub, consider this in your top ten choices.

Ilex crenata 'Helleri', Heller's Japanese holly, is a small evergreen shrub that grows

between three and four feet tall with glossy half-inch oval leaves and very compact but dense twiggy growth. The flowers and fruit are inconspicuous so these plants are used for their neat and tidy growth habit. Provide sun to shade with average garden soil but add plenty of compost for good fertility. These hollies also need plenty of moisture, especially when rains are sparse. The growth rate is very slow and pruning is not necessary unless plants get leggy. Spider mites can be a problem when summers are dry; wash them off with the hose. This shrub makes a great substitute for dwarf boxwood. Heller's holly is hardy only to Zone 6.

Ilex verticillata, the winterberry, is best seen in late autumn, when its carmine berries dot the landscape like bunches of red BBs. Many gardeners wonder why berries so plentiful in fall are usually gone by midwinter. The answer is the birds. As other food supplies dwindle, resident chickadees, blue jays, and such zero in on these tasty fruits.

These deciduous shrubs are members of the holly family. They can grow to a height of twenty feet but are easily kept in check by pruning. The flowers are small and white, blooming in late June and early July, and escape the notice of all but the most careful observer. Not until late autumn, when most leaves have fallen, do the beautiful, brilliant red berries begin to attract notice.

Winterberries, like all hollies, are dioecious, meaning they have male and female flowers on separate plants, so when buying plants, make sure you have both kinds. The staminate, or male, flowers have many anthers and cluster where the leaf stems meet. There are fewer female flowers, and each has a prominent stigma.

This is the only species of holly that is fully winter-hardy. Plants do well in poor soil and even partial shade. They also thrive in a wettish or swampy site yet will surprise knowledgeable collectors by appearing on the steepest of dry hillsides. Winterberries are hardy from Zone 3 southward. Plant them out in spring or fall and protect them from deer until they are established.

Potentilla fruticosa, the potentilla or cinquefoil, is a member of the rose family. Although it is considered by many to be a weed, it makes an excellent edging plant, ground cover, or plant for the perennial border. We first used it as a low hedge along the top of the bank behind our perennial border. Three specimens of the cultivar 'Goldfinger' curved around the front of a golden-thread Sawara cypress (*Chamae-cyparis pisifera* 'Filifera Aurea') and were bounded on the other side by a carpet juniper (*Juniperus* 'Gray Owl'), a combination that ensured color interest through-out the season.

There are dozens of cultivars that have been developed over the years. They usually grow to a height of two to three feet, blooming from May until September. Look for 'Abbottswood', with large white flowers that hover above dark blue-green foliage; 'Day Dawn', which bears peach-pink flowers suffused with cream; 'Dakota Sur-prise', with light yellow flowers sparkling

on dense growth; and 'Goldfinger', which has two-inch-wide bright yellow flowers and deep green foliage.

No matter how hot the sun or how dry the summer, once established, the potentil-las thrive, often blooming until the blossoms are cut down by the frosts of late September. They prefer full sun and will tolerate partial shade—but produce fewer flowers. Remove any seed cases in the fall. If pruning is nec-essary, cut out older wood in early spring. These shrubs also do well in containers, as long as they get enough water, especially during hot weather. Like all members of the rose family, potentillas are often ravaged by Japanese beetles. Well-placed beetle traps keep most of the pests away; and it's also easy to pick off these shiny-backed pests with your fingers and toss them into a can of soapy water.

Rubus odoratus, the flowering raspberry, Virginia raspberry, or thimbleberry, is a deciduous American shrub with eight-foot-high upright canes. The five-lobed leaves alone are a lovely green but there are also beautiful purple flowers. Even the shed-ding bark is attractive, providing winter color in many shades of reddish brown.

The flowers are fragrant, measure up to two inches across, and bloom most of the summer and often into fall. There are many yellow stamens, and when fertilized the flowers become dry and tasteless drupes, completely unlike the delicious fruit pro-duced by many other members of the genus.

Years ago I asked a garden friend for one of the suckers that these shrubs freely produce. I planted it along the slope behind the perennial border—just to the right of a Japanese maple—so that the leaves and flowers would overhang an old concrete birdbath. The shrub soon grew large enough that the leaves touched the water's surface and the birds that visited splashed among those leaves as though they were strutting on a watered stage.

Don't look for this plant at fancy nurs-eries, since flowering raspberry is often considered too coarse for the garden. But William Robinson, a great English gardener, wrote, "There is no finer shrub for planting under the shade of large trees and in rough places."

If left to their own devices, flowering raspberries will form large colonies, spreading with suckers that are easily removed if not wanted.

PLAN FOR AN INFORMAL SHRUB GARDEN

The following plan uses a selection of shrubs to form a private little grove within a small backyard, providing a place of peace and quiet.

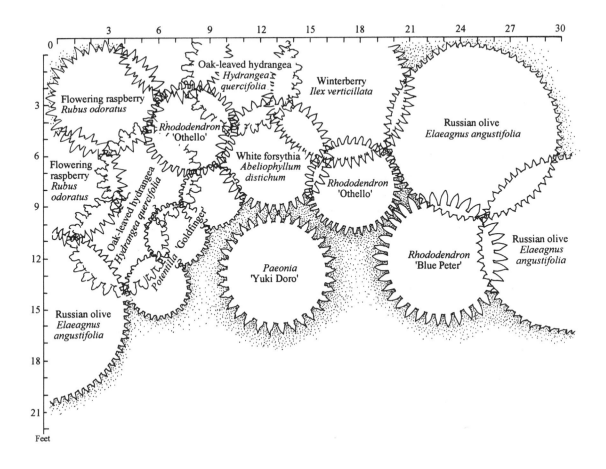

Fourteen

Roses

~

GROUCHO MARX ONCE SANG, "SHOW ME A ROSE OR SHOW ME A STAG AT BAY," AND FOR years I laughingly chose the stag, leaving roses for those other gardeners. But recently I've included roses in my garden plans, a move that came about when I learned that rose culture includes more choices than just hybrid teas.

My wife's grandfather grew hybrid teas—in Buffalo no less. He spent hours in his rose garden, taking infinite pains in efforts that included heavy mulching for winter. Frankly, I never had any luck with hybrid teas; for a time during the first year of planting they would do well, but soon the Japanese beetles would chew the leaves. Then with the fall I would forget to mulch properly for our Catskill winters, and invariably the roses would perish from the cold.

A SELECTION OF ROSES

All of the roses I describe are reasonably disease resistant, but you should always be on the lookout for spider mites, especially on miniatures. These arachnids, about the size of a small typographical period, spin visible webs, reproduce, and soon destroy most leaves in their path. Use an insecticidal soap for control. Japanese beetles love roses but can be kept in check if you pick them off by hand in the cool of the morning, a time when their flight muscles are slow to move. Or use one of the scented baits now available at most garden centers.

If you yearn for a yard full of roses, see the Bibliography for a good book on roses in general. But if, like me, you wish for only a few roses at a time, let me suggest the following rose cultivars.

'Archduke Charles', a China rose (originally from China), belongs to the group called old garden roses and has been cultivated for more than 160 years. The three-inch-wide flowers open to a pink blended with white. Unlike most flowers, in sunlight the color intensifies, to a light rose. The bush reaches a height of about three feet and has smooth glossy leaves that are brushed with red when young. Unfortunately, this rose is not hardy for areas north of Zone 6.

'Baron Prévost' is a wonderful old-fashioned rose that bears lightly fragrant, flat pink blossoms with dozens of petals, beginning in early summer with repeat blooming until fall. A mature bush is between four and five feet high. If planted in a protected place and mulched, this rose will live through the average winter in Zone 5.

'Cécile Brunner' has been popular since 1881. Back at the last *fin de siècle,* fashion dictated that men wore flowers in their buttonholes. High on the popularity list was this very small rose bred for that very purpose. Now that another one hundred years are soon to be marked, 'Cécile Brunner' is still one of the most beloved roses in the garden. The blossoms are lightly fragrant and look like perfect tea roses, only they measure an inch and a half across.

The long-lived, three-foot-high bushes bloom heavily in late spring, then on and off throughout the summer until they are nipped by frost. The small dark green leaves are semiglossy and disease resistant. And if the ordinary height of three to four feet is too much for your garden, the bushes can be trimmed back. In areas with hard winters and little or no snow cover, this rose must be mulched.

For gardeners with a bit more space, there is 'Climbing Cécile Brunner', introduced in 1894 and considered by many rosarians to be the finest climbing rose ever created. Without support it will eventually form an umbrella-shaped bush eight to ten feet across, but it can also be led to climb a trellis and kept within reasonable grounds.

'Rosa Mundi' is the oldest striped rose on record. This cultivar of *Rosa gallica officinalis* has enjoyed a place in rose history since 1581. A cultivar of the apothecary rose (so called because the petals remain fragrant when stored in airtight glass jars), no two blossoms are ever alike; each variation of color is subtly different. Gardeners who dislike variegated petals, or variegated plants in general, make exceptions for this lovely blossom.

The somewhat fragrant, semidouble flowers average about three inches across with medium to deep pink petals, striped with blush or white. The lovely golden stamens look more like Victorian curtain pulls than flower parts. Plants grow about three and a half feet tall in a rounded, compact habit. The medium green leaves are borne on stems with few thorns but many bristles. Round red hips appear in the fall. This rose was hardy in our Catskill garden with protection from winter winds.

'Rose de Rescht' bears double, very fragrant deep pink flowers that are brushed with mauve. They first appear in summer with a good repeat bloom until fall. The leaves are medium green and semiglossy, and it's hardy in areas with cold winters, especially with snow cover or mulching. The bush reaches a three-foot height. After its fifth birthday it may lose its ability to re-bloom, but this can be remedied by severe pruning.

'Souvenir de la Malmaison' is a small bush rose reaching a height of about three feet. It dates from 1843 and was named in honor of Malmaison, the country estate of Empress Josephine, located outside Paris. The double flowers are up to five inches across, with as many as seventy-five light pink petals each, and are wonderfully fragrant. They begin to appear in summer and continue on and off into the fall. The medium green leaves are semiglossy. With some protection, this rose is reasonably winter hardy.

Rosa 'Petite Pink' is perfect for a very small garden. This cultivar was discovered by Jackson M. Batchelor in 1949 at an old plantation site near Wilmington, North Carolina. A little too large to be a true miniature, this rose forms thirty-inch mounds of foliage that is evergreen except in extremely cold areas. Small pink roses appear in early summer. Like many roses, this is a tough plant; it is highly resistant to disease, extremely hardy, and ravaged only by Japanese beetles. Give it good, fertile soil and full sun.

Rosa rugosa, the Japanese or rugosa rose, is a sturdy shrub with upright, prickly stems covered with leaves that closely resemble the much-maligned multiflora rose (R. multi-flora). It grows to a height of four to six feet and has a five-foot spread. The lovely flowers appear in spring, but if deadheaded, it will continue to bloom on and off until fall. Depending on the cultivar, the blossoms are usually about three and a half inches wide of purplish rose to white petals and are followed in fall by large orange-red hips. The foliage turns orange with the coming of frost. Pruning is limited to removing old and dead branches and suckers.

Try rugosa as a specimen in the flower border or as a dependable hedge. These roses are one of the best bets for a seaside garden. 'Alba' has flowers of white, and 'Rubra' has blooms of magenta-red. 'Sir Thomas Lipton' bears fragrant snow-white, double flowers.

The new landscape rose. The Meidi-land (pronounced may-d-land) landscape roses came from France and are perfect as ground covers or for hedges in a small garden. Unlike many specialized roses, they are reproduced by cuttings and grow on their own roots. Because of this root hardiness, they will survive even in Zone 4.

I can't say enough about the Meidilands. For gardeners who want roses without the fuss, these are the answer; anywhere grass will grow, so will these roses. They require little—if any—pruning, some have attractive fruits, and most bloom from spring until fall.

Unless otherwise noted, plant on three-foot centers if you want a blooming hedge.

'Alba Meidiland' is a white everblooming rose that bears clusters of small white blossoms on plants that reach two feet in height with about a four-foot spread. This is a great rose for carpeting a difficult bank or slope. For a hedge, plant these roses on four-foot centers.

'White Meidiland' bears three-inch-wide, pure white double flowers that begin to open in June and continue blooming throughout the summer. The plants grow about two feet high and spread to five feet. Leaves are a glossy dark green. Deadheading will prolong bloom.

'Pink Meidiland' is everblooming, with single two-inch flowers that are bright pink with white centers. Plants are three to four feet high and two to three feet wide.

'Bonica' has three-inch double pink flowers on a plant eventually reaching five feet in height. The spread is five feet but it can be trimmed to a desired height. This particular Meidiland produces bright red fruit.

'Scarlet Meidiland' flowers with vivid scarlet blooms that measure up to one and a half inches across, lasting up to two weeks on the bush and one week as cut flowers. The shrubs grow to a height of three feet with a five-foot spread and will adapt to some shade. Plant on four-foot centers.

Miniature roses. Miniature roses are thought to have descended from a chance seedling (of *Rosa roulettii* or *R. chinensis* 'Minima', depending on which reference you read), discovered in a window box in a Swiss village back in 1815.

Miniature roses have the same cultural requirements as their larger relatives, with one exception: it's not easy to dig up a hybrid tea rose or a rose that clambers up a wall and bring it indoors for the winter but with the miniatures, there's no problem at all.

Outdoors, these roses need good garden soil, good drainage, and for reliable blooming at least eight hours of sun every day. Grow them in containers, as edgings in the garden, or in small beds of their own. In areas with very cold winters, especially where snow cover is lacking, mulch them with hilled-up soil or straw. Trim the dead tips back in the spring. Inside they must have plenty of sunlight or supplemental artificial light to grow properly.

'Beauty Secret' grows about eighteen inches high and bears highly fragrant, medium red blossoms; 'Cupcake' has medium light pink flowers and is slightly shorter; 'Green Ice' is an eight-inch bush with slightly fragrant white flowers that turn greenish as they age; and 'Starina' grows to sixteen inches high and bears orange-red blossoms.

PLAN FOR A SMALL ROSE GARDEN

The following plan uses a selection of recommended roses surrounding an old-fashioned gazing globe with a white picket fence at one side.

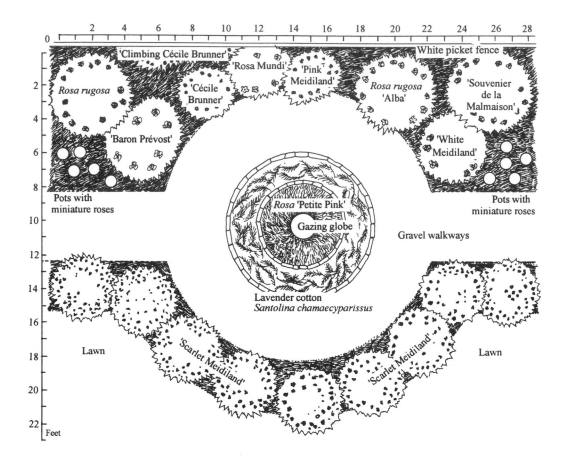

0 2 4 6 8 10 12 14 16 18 20 22 24 26 28

White picket fence

'Climbing Cécile Brunner'

'Rosa Mundi'

'Pink Meidiland'

Rosa rugosa

'Cécile Brunner'

Rosa rugosa 'Alba'

'Souvenier de la Malmaison'

'Baron Prévost'

'White Meidiland'

Pots with miniature roses

Rosa 'Petite Pink'

Gazing globe

Gravel walkways

Pots with miniature roses

Lavender cotton
Santolina chamaecyparissus

Lawn

'Scarlet Meidiland'

'Scarlet Meidiland'

Lawn

Feet

Fifteen

Espaliered Trees

~

A LEXANDER POPE SAID OF THE EARL OF BURLINGTON IN HIS *MORAL ESSAYS,*

Behold Villerio's ten years toil complete,

His quincunx darkens, his espaliers meet.

It's a poetic way to mark the passage of time in the garden.

The quincunx in this case was not the title of a contemporary novel but an old arrangement of five trees, four at each corner of a square and one in the center.

Espalier is from the French word *epaule,* or shoulder, and the Italian word, *spella,* a special wainscot construction to lean the shoulders against. Through the evolution of language, it eventually came to mean the process of growing shrubs and trees against flat supports or trellises either in front of or upon a wall.

The technique of espaliering began in Roman times and was perfected in Europe, where gardens were enclosed because of both enemies and climate. Weather conditions are often cool and cloudy, and such fruit trees as apples and pears greatly benefited from being trained against a sunny and heat-retaining wall. Here in America the process has been used more for decoration than for fruit growing, and such plantings have become living screens, or have added interest to large blank walls and fences.

I'll admit that espaliering trees is not exactly up my alley. For some reason, I've had the patience to wait five years for a seedling plant to flower, but the idea of training a tree to grow up a wall does not appeal to me.

A few years ago, I asked Honorio H. Ignacio, superintendent of horticulture at the

Brooklyn Botanic Garden, about this method of growing trees in small spaces. He is in charge of all the espaliers in the garden, including six weeping flowering crabapples, and he offered the following step-by-step procedure.

1. The plant chosen for espalier against a wall should have small leaves: because light comes from only one direction, a leaf more than three inches wide will cast too much of a shadow for healthy growth. The tree should also have a long life span, since the technique involves a great deal of work. In addition, it must be reasonably resistant to pests and disease.

2. Choose a design. A more formal approach is usually better in the long run than an informal design. Espaliered trees can be trained in the shape of fans, gridirons, or pyramids, or in oblique, upright, or horizontal cordons. In fact, the only limit is one's imagination and the time available for pruning and care. Fruit trees are especially good with the cordon design and U shapes; yews are best as fans. "Sometimes you will find a single stem but no side branches," said Mr. Ignacio. "It might be cheaper but it's no good for espaliering. Often the plant that is available will dictate the design you want."

3. Because these plants will be in place for a long, long time, the initial planting must be done with care. Choose the site carefully. Western or southern exposure is best; north of New York City an eastern exposure is also acceptable. According to Mr. Ignacio, if you don't want to damage a stone wall, you can use a trellis in front of the wall. That way it's easier to trim the tree. And in many walls, anchors in the mortar between the stones are not a strong enough support, so once again a trellis is better. And if the tree is too close to the wall, insects can escape oil sprays or soap sprays by hiding behind the branches and in the crevices of the stone.

4. Use good soil and a decent sized hole prepared at least eighteen to twenty-four inches deep and up to thirty inches wide. If you aren't using a trellis, position the base of the plant at least six inches away from the wall. Use plant stakes when the tree is young, until the branches are strong enough to support themselves. Use special soft ties, garden twine, or rubber bands—not wire—for holding branches. Twigs bend best when they are young; hold them in place for a year or so until the branch growth has matured.

5. Prune as little as possible the first three years. According to Mr. Ignacio, you should remove "any branches that sweep up instead of falling directly down." In addition, remove any suckers. There should be just one branch or trunk coming from the base. It's a good idea to have a sketch of the desired result in front of you as you prune or you could inadvertently remove the wrong branches and shoots.

6. Prune lightly three or four weeks after blooming, then again in early summer, and finally in late September. Prune if the new growth is over three inches long, to

prevent heavy branches from breaking. Called "winterizing" the tree, the last pruning for the year should be minimal. It is a precautionary measure because a severe winter could bring heavy snow and ice that could break branches.

A FEW SUGGESTED TREES FOR ESPALIERING

Acer palmatum cultivars, Japanese maple

Camellia japonica, common camellia

Cercis canadensis, Eastern redbud

Chaenomeles spp. and cultivars, Japanese quince

Cornus florida, flowering dogwood

C. kousa, Japanese dogwood

C. mas, cornelian cherry

Cotoneaster horizontalis, rockspray cotoneaster

Euonymus alata, winged euonymus

Forsythia spp.

Fruit trees: apples (including *Malus* 'Red Jade'), pears, plums, cherries, peaches, nectarines, and apricots

Hamamelis spp., witch hazel

Jasminium nudiflorum, winter jasmine

Magnolia grandiflora, Southern magnolia

M. tomentosa, star magnolia

Philadelphus coronarius, mock orange

Pyracantha spp. and cultivars, fire thorns

Taxus spp. and cultivars, yew

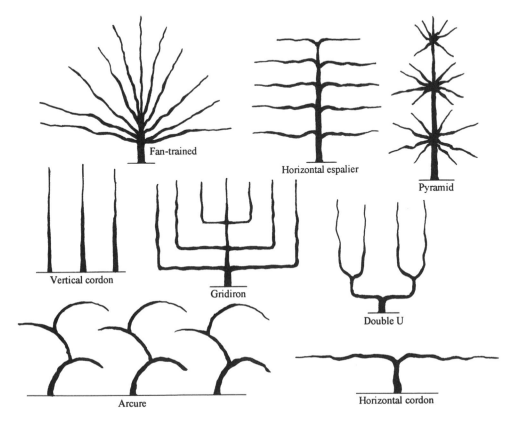

Fan-trained

Horizontal espalier

Pyramid

Vertical cordon

Gridiron

Double U

Arcure

Horizontal cordon

Dwarf Conifers

～

LATE IN THE SUMMER OF 1980, OUR OLD FARMHOUSE IN COCHECTON WAS REROOFED. IT was a heck of a job, and it provoked the following comments in my garden notes: "During the roof installation various pieces of shingle sailed through the air like square Frisbees, impaling themselves in the earth in a number of places; old nails pierced the leaves of shrubs and trees like straight pins in a dress pattern; and globs of tar piled up until they melted again to the ground under the late spring sun. The result of the week's roofing activity was that some sedums and sempervivums on the front rock garden survived and some did not; most of the saxifrages lost their long spikes of bloom; a number of dwarf iris in one of the target areas were obliterated until next year; and other specimens of rather unique plant life literally bit the dust.

"But all was not lost. All my dwarf and small evergreens survived the bombardment. My collection of hemlocks—bent under the weight of old shingles—sprang back like unhooked springs when the debris was removed. Two small Japanese pines planted on the upper slope of the backyard returned to their previous positions when the accumulations of tarry boards and bits of paper were picked up. In fact, not one of the dozens of varieties of evergreens was bothered by the workout."

And as if that weren't enough, earlier in the year, we had had the driest late spring and summer that anyone could remember, and I noted the following: "Walking in the garden I pass my collections of evergreens. They still glow with color: The needles on the creeping hemlocks shine in the waning light; the arborvitae is still a fresh and vibrant green; and even the waxy leaves of the wild ginger have fought the drought and retain a bit of luster. And all around them the lilies die back and the ornamental grasses turn brown and shrivel, and the back lawn looks exactly like a rather large woven doormat. Yet the evergreens remain true to their calling."

Not only are these great plants for the small garden, they are made of tough stuff.

The term *evergreen* refers to plants whose foliage remains green through more than one growing season. Small evergreens are dwarfs (three feet high or less at maturity) or small plants (usually under twelve feet high when mature, although a few specimens might reach sixteen feet). There are at least six reasons a particular plant qualifies for the title:

1. It is genetically predisposed to be dwarf or small. The Japanese stone pine (*Pinus pumila*) rarely exceeds nine feet in height when mature, and paxistima (*Paxistima canbyi*), an evergreen angiosperm, never gets beyond sixteen inches even under the best conditions.

2. It grows slowly. A particular species might take two or more human lifetimes to reach its ultimate height—and even with present advances in medicine, such a tree will not be a problem until at least 2080. A western red ceder (*Thuja plicata*) might be thirteen feet high in ten years, but because of its slow growth, it will be fine in a small backyard for fifty or sixty years; by the age of two hundred, however, it could be two hundred feet high.

3. Its growth habit causes it to appear small. The branches might droop, spread out and sweep the ground, or creep along the earth. The tree never increases in height; instead, it grows outward.

4. The plant is pruned by man, browsed by animals, or clipped as a hedge. Bonsai trees, for example, remain small and are at home in a container the size of a soup bowl.

5. It is the result of a chance mutation that caused a young seedling to become shorter than its parents. These seedling mutations can often result in other changes, too, such as the color, shape, and size of the leaves.

6. It is the result of a sport, or bud mutation, in which only one branch of a particular species gives any evidence of a change from the parent. Were the embryo in a seed to undergo a genetic shift, the entire plant would change its appearance, but in a sport, only a comparatively few cells in one branch or twig change their DNA programming. The result is a tree that might have one touch of yellow amid a mass of green, or a few contorted needles standing out in a collection of others that are long and straight. Propagation of these sports is by asexual methods.

Witches'-broom is a bud mutation. This condition usually occurs on species of larch, spruce, or pine. In this case a tightly fisted branch of dwarf or congested needles appears on the tip of a normal branch. These growth variations are easily mistaken for birds' nests or, as folklore would see it, a witch's traveling aid. Plants that are propagated by cuttings from the brooms grow into dwarf or small specimens, and many conifers now common in gardens were first reproduced in this manner.

Normal-size branches may also develop and, unless removed, ultimately kill the smaller ones by choking off all light and air. Whatever the initial cause of a broom—mutation, insect attacks, fungi, or viruses—the results have led to a most valuable addition to the stable of plants for the small garden.

Even though dwarf conifers are tough plants that can survive many adverse conditions, it's important to give them proper attention and care if they are to thrive.

Unlike herbaceous plants and trees, evergreens can suffer from desiccation during the first winters after planting out. If the needlelike leaves lose moisture to cold winter winds, the plants cannot replace it, since the roots are sealed fast in the frozen earth. Water them well in late fall.

To lessen the possibility of drought or to help a warm-weather tree survive the cold, you can improvise screens for protection against winter winds. Some gardeners surround their trees with burlap stapled to wooden stakes or snow fencing held up with metal fence posts. Others construct small slatted, wooden pyramids to set over plants. Even an old Christmas tree can be propped up next to small evergreens to deflect icy blasts.

When building a windscreen, it's important to put the foundation stakes around the plant *before* the ground freezes up or you'll never be able to pound them in. But wait until winter really begins before adding the burlap. And in a dry autumn, water each conifer liberally before the ground freezes.

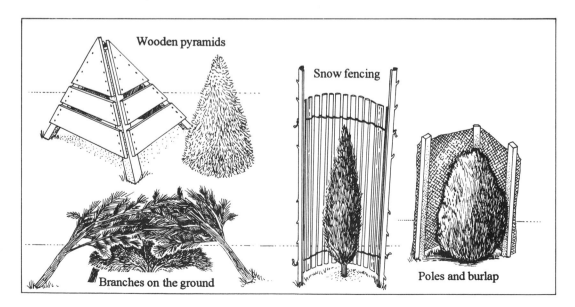

Wooden pyramids

Snow fencing

Branches on the ground

Poles and burlap

The alternate freezing and thawing of ground during winter cold combined with winter sun will cause poorly rooted plants to push out of the soil, thus exposing their roots to wind, cold, and sun. Those roots must be promptly pushed down into the soil once again. Winter mulching is the best prevention; snow cover is ideal. Although snow must be knocked off weeping trees to keep the weight from breaking the branches, melting snow keeps the temperature of the soil constant.

Promptly remove all weeds growing close to your evergreens. Also, keep all grass at least one foot away from the outside edge of any tree or shrub planted in your lawn. Grass and weeds take nourishment, water, and sunlight away from small trees. When using a lawn mower or weed trimmer, be careful not to scrape the bark.

Cover all exposed earth around the trees with a mulch—wood chips, pine needles, crushed leaves, pine branches, and the like—to inhibit weeds and conserve moisture. Do not use sawdust, grass clippings, or sphagnum peat moss; they will pack down too tightly and peat moss will actually repel water.

Keep an eagle eye out for insects and disease. Dwarf conifers are very tough, but even they can succumb to an army of insects ganging up on them, especially when they have been recently planted. When the needles turn a dull green or are streaked with gray, look for spider mites; if necessary, use insecticidal soap or frequent blasts of water to dislodge them. Try some of the newer insecticidal soaps or the biological controls to help kill aphids and caterpillars. Use chemical insecticides only as a last resort.

Finally, anticipate the ravages of deer, dogs, rabbits, and mice. Deer in many parts of the country are enjoying a revival, and when winters are bad (or even when they're not), these marauding Bambis move right in and rape, pillage, and destroy. And remember, wildlife fans, that deer, mice, rabbits, woodchucks, and so forth continue to chew everything in sight even if they have plenty of food.

Nothing discourages wildlife more than the gardener's early-morning or late-evening walks; such unscheduled meanderings generally upset the precise schedule of most animals. In our northern garden, I often went out just before sunrise to enjoy the sound of deer snorting in rage because there was a human in the vicinity.

Pruning conifers. Most conifers need no pruning to improve their shape; their natural form is usually attractive from the start. Occasionally, though, a plant grows too large for its location and cannot be moved without great difficulty. In this case, you can prune the branches vigorously (early spring is the best time) and maintain the tree's shape.

Pruning is also needed when the trunk and main branches are obscured by heavy growth of secondary branches on the outer parts of the tree. In this case, you can often improve the tree's appearance by thinning the outer branches. To facilitate weeding and mowing around older trees, remove any branches that are resting on the ground.

When there is winter damage, remove any branches that were affected. If the needles on the branch ends are depriving the undergrowth of sufficient light, you'll need to cut these off, too.

Always use a sharp and clean knife, saw, or pruning shears. Never just break off a branch; nine times out of ten, small wounds rarely become infected, but it isn't worth taking a chance. By the way, tree wound dressings are no longer considered beneficial. The open air will keep the cut clean until it begins to heal over.

If you must move a dwarf or small conifer and you cannot find—or afford—a tree-moving machine, you will need to prune the roots first. A year before you plan to move the tree, encircle it with deep spade cuts to encourage a new and healthy root system closer to the tree's center. That way, when you do move the tree, it will have a greater chance of survival.

Growing dwarf conifers in containers. One of the charms of the smaller evergreen conifers is the comparative ease with which they can be grown in containers. And that's a plus, especially for those gardeners who have a city terrace or a small lot in the suburbs.

Evergreens in small containers do best if they are sunk in the ground for the winter and allowed to enjoy the cold. If a potted plant is left outside without being buried or protected in some way, the bitter winds or repeated freezing and thawing will soon kill it. If evergreens are brought under shelter, they must be exposed to average temperatures of no more than 40° to 45°F for at least three months. If these conditions are not met, the plants will eventually die.

If you live in Zone 6 or south and have no backyard in which to store plants, you can put them behind a parapet or wall or anyplace where they are out of the direct wind and out of the winter sun. Or you could put the pots in small boxes surrounded with Styrofoam pellets or dry foam insulation.

In the colder parts of the country, clay pots may break when the water in their pores freezes and expands, so the best thing to do is use plastic pots and put them inside more decorative containers.

Conifers are defined as woody plants, many of them shrubs, sometimes deciduous, but usually evergreen, and use cones for reproduction rather than flowers. When listing small evergreen conifers, most catalogs specify a particular shape: pyramidal, dwarf conical, prostrate, round, ovoid, columnar, rounded bush, weeping, or spreading. (Often a plant has two or more of these labels.) A kind of standard horticultural shorthand has evolved to describe these plants:

UH, ultimate height. Refers to the height a particular plant will ultimately reach (to the best of the grower's knowledge).

US, ultimate spread. Refers to the limits of outward growth.

AGR, annual growth rate. Refers to the increase in the length of one branch per year. Thus a round bush with an AGR of five inches will increase its girth by approximately ten inches each year.

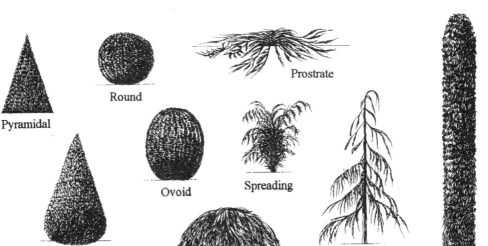

Pyramidal

Round

Prostrate

Dwarf conical

Ovoid

Spreading

Rounded bush

Weeping

Columnar

A SELECTION OF DWARF CONIFERS

Abies balsamea 'Nana', the dwarf balsam fir, has a rounded form and is a short version of a seventy-five-foot-tall tree. The deep blue-green leaves are flat on the upper side. The cones stand upright on the branch and mature during the summer, changing from violet, blue, green, or yellow to brown. These firs prefer good moist soil and resent shallow or alkaline ground. Smaller trees benefit from mulching, especially during hot, dry summers. Unlike many conifers these trees do not tolerate pollution and are not recommended for city gardens. Eventually this nana form makes a round bush with a diameter of three feet and has an AGR of two to three inches. It is hardy to Zone 3.

Abies concolor 'Candicans' is a short form of the white fir, a tree that can top two hundred feet in the wild. The upper leaves are a silver-blue and one of the most beautiful blues in the conifer clan; the tree is cone-shaped, and the cones themselves are purplish before maturity. 'Candicans' can tolerate some heat and dryness. It has an AGR of six inches and grows to twenty in forty years.

Cedrus atlantica 'Glauca Pendula', the weeping blue cedar, can be a hundred feet tall in the wild. Trees have stiff, bluish, needle-shaped leaves and upright brown cones that ripen in two to three years. They require a fairly well-drained soil with a slightly acid pH. This beautiful cedar is not a dwarf and must be raised as a standard or be grafted onto a standard to prevent the foliage from growing flat on the ground; most nurseries list it as a four- to five-foot tree. After fifty years, the diameter at the base is twenty-five to thirty feet. It is hardy to Zone 6, with some protection from bitter winter winds.

Chamaecyparis lawsoniana, the Lawson cypress, can reach a hundred feet in the wild, but after ten years the cultivar 'Fili-formis Compacta' forms a three-foot-high bun with about the same width. The AGR is three inches. Threadlike sprays of aromatic foliage have a blue-green hue. Cones are small, round, and brown. These dwarf trees do best in a moist, well-drained, slightly acid soil. Perched on a bank, they are a great accent in a small rock garden or evergreen planting. They are hardy to Zone 6 but need protection from winter winds.

Chamaecyparis obtusa 'Nana' is the dwarf form of the Hinoki cypress. It bears dark green threadlike foliage, with white lines on the leaf undersides that resemble stick figures. This is one of the oldest evergreens in continual cultivation; the Japanese have been using it in rock and stone gardens for centuries. Culture is the same as for the false cypress. After thirty years, a tree is thirty inches high and thirty inches wide and has a rough oval shape. Since it can be easily damaged by snow, it's a good idea to grow it in a pot. It's hardy to Zone 5 but needs protection from heavy snows, which can break the branches.

Chamaecyparis pisifera, the sawara cypress, is another giant in the wild, reaching a height of a hundred feet. These trees often exhibit one of several types of foliage and are grouped accordingly: juvenile, which is soft and feathery to the touch and called squarrosa; intermediate, which is a compromise between soft and prickly,

called plumosa; and the adult form, which is sharp and called pisifera. There is also a fourth, threadlike leaf called filifera.

A fine example of the squarrosa type is the blue-gray 'Boulevard'. (It was called *Retinispora pisifera squarrosa cyano-viridis* when it was introduced in 1934, but happily the name was changed.) The tree has a pyramidal form, reaching a height of six feet in ten years and twenty feet in thirty years. The AGR is six inches.

'Plumosa Albopicta' is a plumosa type that bears fan-shaped branches of small-leaved dark-green foliage that is splotched here and there with small dots of creamy white. In ten years this tree grows to about six feet high and three feet wide. It's an excellent tub plant.

'Compacta' is a very small plant that exhibits adult foliage with distinct white markings on the underleaf. I have one in the conifer bed that still looks like a green mop head after five years. After ten years, this little plant is about eight inches high and a foot across. The rich blue-green foliage turns brownish green in winter.

Among the many excellent filiferas, look for 'Filifera Aurea', with bright yellow foliage that turns golden brown in winter and is so dense it's hard to push through to the plant's center: a beautiful plant at home in most gardens. It ultimately reaches twelve to sixteen feet in height with a spread of five to eight feet; its AGR is eight inches. 'Filifera Nana' has green, trailing, threadlike foliage that weeps and will spread to three feet wide and one foot high in ten years. All are hardy in Zone 5.

Juniperus chinensis, the time-honored juniper, reaches a height of sixty feet in its native habitat of eastern Asia. Juvenile leaves are awllike or needle shaped; adult leaves are scalelike, overlapping and clasping the stem. The berrylike fruit (really a modified cone coated with resin and dusted with a whitish bloom) is used to flavor gin and adds a special zip to stuffing for roasted wild game.

'Iowa' is blue-green and has an upright habit. In ten years a tree grows to six feet high with a base of three feet. 'Kaizuka', the Hollywood juniper, has normally upright growth, but the branches are easily pruned, which allows the tree to spread. It grows to ten feet in ten years, with a spread of four feet; the ultimate height is twenty-five feet. This tree withstands pollution's rigors and adapts to climates from southern California to Iowa. 'Kaizuka Variegated' grows in a column and has foliage with patches of creamy yellow, but my wife thinks it looks more like a "sick and twisted thing" than a conifer, so I've learned to overlook this cultivar.

'Mountbatten' originated as a mutant seedling in a Canadian nursery and is hardy to the frigid grip of Zone 3. If not pruned back, it will ultimately reach a height of sixteen feet; in ten years, it will be ten feet tall and have a pyramidal form. 'Pyramidalis' grows in the shape that its cultivar name implies. It eventually reaches sixteen feet with a five- to six-foot-wide base. Its blue-green color makes it a very attractive specimen tree. Soil should have a slightly acid to neutral pH; most of these trees do well in calcareous soils. Provide water during extended dry spells and prune in spring to remove winter-damaged branches.

Juniperus communis, the common juniper, stops growing at twenty-five feet in the wild. This low shrub or tree is found growing on rocky hillsides and pastures in the cooler northern states and is very picturesque in windswept locations. The bark is thin and sheds easily. The needles are sharp, blue-green on top, and a gray-white underneath. Berries turn from green to dark blue as they ripen. Culture is the same as for *J. chinensis.* The cultivar 'Echiniformis' is named because of its supposed resemblance to a sea urchin but looks more like a profile of a European hedgehog. This light green, bun-shaped plant grows slowly to a one-foot diameter and a height of six inches. *J.c.* var. *depressa* 'Aurea' is a yellow-bronze carpet that turns green with the approach of winter. It spreads to four feet in ten years and rarely exceeds a height of one foot. Prune to keep it within bounds.

Juniperus horizontalis, the creeping juniper, will stay about eighteen inches high and has a low spreading or creeping habit. The foliage may be needlelike or scalelike and medium green, blue-green, or gray-green, often turning purple in winter. This shrub tolerates a wide range of soils as well as hot, dry, or city conditions—hence its popularity as a landscape plant around service stations where unimaginative landscapers have taken the contracts. It makes an excellent ground cover and can be pruned back to promote bushy growth. 'Douglasii' originated in the 1850s, in

Waukegan, Illinois, and is also known as the Waukegan juniper. The main branches hug the ground, and side shoots swerve upward. Plants are blue-green in summer and purple-blue in winter. The AGR is fifteen inches. This small juniper is especially good for seaside gardens.

Juniperus procumbens, the Japanese garden juniper, grows to about one foot high. Discovered in the mountains of Japan many hundreds of years ago, this prostrate evergreen conifer has a low creeping habit and blue-green needles all year long. The AGR is six inches, and a plant will, in thirty years, fill a twenty-foot circle.

Juniperus procumbens 'Nana', the dwarf Japanese juniper, is smaller than the species. The color in spring is light green, eventually turning to blue-green. This is a great bonsai subject and makes a lovely specimen tree. It is also attractive cascading over rocks.

Juniperus virginiana, the native red cedar, is a hardy tree that can reach a height of fifty feet in the wild. There are dozens of cultivars, including 'Skyrocket', found in 1949 growing in the wild, and often used as a vertical accent in the small garden. In ten years it reaches twelve to fifteen feet tall. At maturity it is twenty-five feet tall but only one foot wide at the base. The color is a silvery blue-green. This cedar is hardy to Zone 3. *Note:* If your garden is close to a working apple orchard, this tree is not for you, as it is an alternate host for the apple-rust fungus.

Picea abies, the Norway spruce, can top 150 feet in its native habitat. The sharp needles are attached to branches with a tiny stem (sterigma), so when needles fall, the branch feels rough to the touch. The cones are blue or green when young, ripening to brown, and hang from the branch. The popular phrase "spruced up" is derived from the neat appearance of these trees.

'Nidiformis' is known as the bird's-nest spruce because of the slight depression at the top of young plants. The spring buds are light green; older needles are dark green. This dense, flat-topped tree has an AGR of three to four inches. It reaches a height of four to five feet, with a six-foot spread. 'Pygmaea', the pygmy spruce, has a round form with an AGR of two inches, and after ten years it makes a globe about one foot in diameter. Then it slows its growth by one-third. These trees are tolerant of most urban pollutants and do well in a variety of soils but prefer a mildly acid condition. They are hardy to Zone 3.

Picea glauca, the white spruce, often reaches a hundred feet in the wild, but in a garden it grows to only six feet high in ten years. Needles are dark green with a definite bloom and a beautiful light green in spring. The AGR is six inches a year. 'Conica', the dwarf Alberta spruce, bears grass-green needles that are so tightly packed, the tree looks like a solid inverted cone. It grows to fifteen feet but can be pruned to keep it smaller; the AGR is four to six inches. This is a great accent plant and looks especially attractive in a terracotta pot.

'Echiniformis' is a true dwarf among dwarfs. A small pincushion of glaucous gray-green needles, it originally appeared in France during the mid-1800s, and it's been popular ever since. It grows to only thirty inches, with a spread of some three feet; the AGR is one to two inches a year. Both 'Conica' and 'Echiniformis' need a good, well-drained moist soil.

Pinus densiflora, the Japanese red pine, grows more than a hundred feet high in the wild. It bears large woody cones and long green needles in bundles of two, three, and five. Although these pines prefer full sun, they will tolerate some shade. They will grow in poor soil as long as it is deep enough for good root systems to develop, but they resent wet feet. Japanese reds usually grow about ten feet in ten years and can be kept small by pruning. The bending stems, graceful needles, and red bark make this a beautiful small tree. It is hardy to Zone 4 with protection from bitter winter winds. 'Umbraculifera' is the Japanese umbrella pine, a slow-growing cultivar with branches that grow up and around from the trunk. After thirty-five years, it is fifteen feet tall.

Pinus parviflora, the Japanese white pine, is a fifty-foot evergreen conifer with widespread, horizontal branches and twisted blue-green needles that grow in groups of five, making dense tufts; the ovoid cones are pale brown. There are many unusual compact cultivars, including 'Glauca', with decidedly blue foliage, and 'Gimborns Ideal', which eventually forms a tall but still compact shrub. The Japanese white pine is a valuable plant for bonsai cultivation. Provide full sun and a well-drained soil of a reasonable fertility.

Pinus strobus, the Eastern white pine, is an evergreen conifer reaching a height of 120 feet in the wild. The trunks were once used to make the masts on sailing ships of the Atlantic. Needles are blue-green and very soft; the cones are long and brown. The cultivar 'Contorta' develops twisted branches that in turn bear densely packed, twisted needles. It is not a threat to the small garden because in forty years, it grows just eighteen feet high. 'Nana' has needles so tightly bunched, the trunk is usually hidden. It grows about eight feet high and has an AGR of two to four inches. 'Pendula', the weeping white pine, reaches a height of twelve to fifteen feet with a slightly smaller spread; the AGR is one foot. The trunk bends over and bears weeping branches. Full sun is best, but these plants tolerate some shade. Any well-drained or evenly moist soil will do for white pines, since they are very adaptable. Trees are hardy to Zone 3.

Pinus sylvestris, the Scotch pine, is another conifer that reaches a height of a hundred feet or more in its native habitat. Three-inch stiff and twisted blue-green needles grow in bunches of two. Cones are two and a half inches long; the trunk is reddish. 'Fastigiata' is an excellent choice for a small garden: this columnar tree reaches an eight-foot height in ten years but has very little growth at the base; a thirty-foot tree may have only a three-foot spread. It bears blue-green needles and is hardy to Zone 3. 'Viridis Compacta' bears twisted and contorted needles that are a lighter green than those of the species. This slow-growing tree will reach a height of six feet in fifteen years and is hardy to Zone 4. Any well-drained, average garden soil will do.

Sequoia sempervirens 'Adpressa' is the dwarf redwood. In the wild this evergreen conifer can reach a height of three hundred feet—or more. The medium green, scalelike leaves are one-half inch long, and have a bluish bloom underneath; the bunches of new growth are tipped with white. Our dwarf redwood spent ten years up North in a large terracotta pot; each year we brought it into the house for Christmas and decorated it with tinsel. Once the holidays were over, it passed the rest of the winter in our unheated garage.

To keep this tree in harness, remove any leaders that might develop. Then it might reach a height of sixteen feet in the gardener's lifetime, certainly a manageable dimension. The tree does well in a pot, needing plenty of winter light, occasional watering, and temperatures between 35° and 40°F. It's a beautiful tree but hardy only to Zone 7 and even there best in a protected spot. Any good and well-drained garden soil is acceptable.

Thuja occidentalis 'Hetz Midget', the dwarf white cedar, belongs to a genus of conifers that can reach a height of sixty feet in the wild. In the garden this plant grows to just one foot high in ten years; after thirty years it will only be two feet high. Dark green scalelike leaves appear on flattened branches. The cones are small, brown, and about a quarter inch across. Provide well-drained, slightly acid soil of

average fertility. 'Lutea' grows to sixteen feet with a three-foot spread when mature; it has an AGR of six inches. During active growth the tips of the branches are a cream yellow but turn a golden bronze as winter approaches.

Tsuga canadensis, the American hemlock, is an evergreen tree with graceful arching branches and shiny dark green needles that have two white bands underneath. The cones are small and brown. In the woods these trees reach a height of a hundred feet or more. Luckily for gardeners, there are approximately seventy recognized cultivars that are classified as dwarf or slow-growing. Most dwarf hemlocks like full sun but adapt to partial shade, especially in the South. Soil should be average, well drained or moist, and slightly acidic. Needles might fall in times of drought, so water as needed. Hardy to Zone 5.

My favorite dwarf hemlock is 'Cole', a prostrate tree that actually hugs the ground as it runs in, over, and around rocks like water in a rill. It prefers some shade and does not do well in hot sun or under very dry conditions. Plants cover a four-foot circle in ten years; AGR is three inches.

Other favorites include 'Jervis', which forms an irregular pyramid of very compact growth. In my garden it has yet to grow larger than fifteen inches in any direction after twenty-some years. 'Gentsch White' has branches with a lacy look and tips of silvery white; it grows two feet high with a two-foot spread. 'Pendula', or Sargent's weeping hemlock, is the Rolls-

Royce of the hemlock world. It was discovered by General Joseph Howland in 1870 on the summit of the Fishkill Mountains near Fishkill, New York. A mature tree looks like a green and glossy mammoth without tusks and is best as a specimen tree set off by a sweep of lawn. It reaches twelve to fifteen feet in height and spreads twelve to twenty-five feet; AGR is two to three inches.

PLAN FOR A TAPESTRY HEDGE

The following plan is based on the tapestry hedge that I've been planting in the area above the wall in our garden room. I decided on these conifer combinations after seeing Jordan Jack's experimental tapestry hedge at his nursery in Asheville, North Carolina. The idea was to create a wall of texture and color that is effective both in winter and in summer. Interspersed among the conifers are various bulb species that begin blooming in spring and continue until late fall.

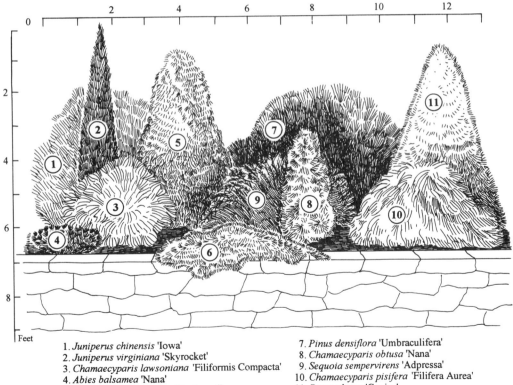

1. *Juniperus chinensis* 'Iowa'
2. *Juniperus virginiana* 'Skyrocket'
3. *Chamaecyparis lawsoniana* 'Filiformis Compacta'
4. *Abies balsamea* 'Nana'
5. *Chamaecyparis pisifera* 'Boulevard'
6. *Juniperus procumbens* 'Nana'
7. *Pinus densiflora* 'Umbraculifera'
8. *Chamaecyparis obtusa* 'Nana'
9. *Sequoia sempervirens* 'Adpressa'
10. *Chamaecyparis pisifera* 'Filifera Aurea'
11. *Picea glauca* 'Conica'

PLAN FOR A CONIFER BED

The conifer bed is adapted from the garden I've planted just below our terrace. Here, a number of dwarfs pop up amid the rocks and share the space with various alpine plants and unusual bulbs. A few exotic annuals and tender perennials round out the collection.

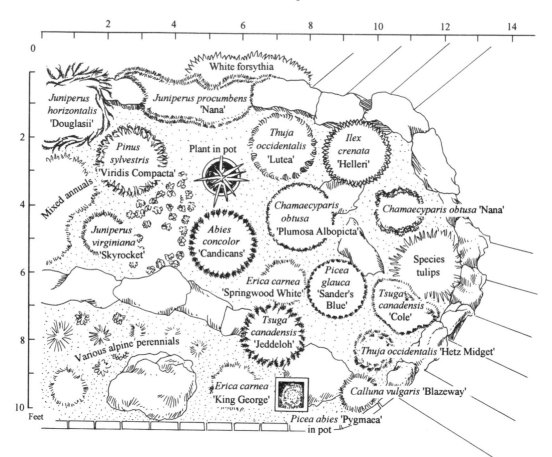

Annuals

～

WHEN WINTER WINDS BLOW ABOUT THE CABIN DOOR OR ACROSS CITY STREETS, THERE IS one entertainment I know of (shy of a fully paid vacation to the tropics) that will gladden the sad heart of a snow-weary gardener: looking at seed catalogs from around the world.

This year I've already set my garden charts for 'Imperial Frosty Rose' pansies, Swan River daisies called 'White Splendor', rich dark purple nemophilas billed as 'Pennie Black', and 'Peach Melba' nasturtiums that look good enough to eat.

Americans did not always look to seed catalogs for their annual flowers. According to Alice Morse Earle in *Old Time Gardens,* many women of the American colonies found selling flower seeds a "congenial occupation." Miss Earle adds,

> I think it must have been very pleasant to buy packages of flower seed at the same time and place where you bought your best bonnet and have them all sent home in a bandbox together.

The charming seller of seeds seems to be missing from today's garden scene—and I haven't bought a hat since college—but for over twenty-five years I have been a sucker for the bright and slick pages of seed catalogs. My perennials usually come from mail-order nurseries or gardening friends and a few begin with seeds gathered by the various seed exchanges or plant societies like the American Rock Garden Society. But all of my annuals come from those florific catalogs with their endless pages featuring the most blatant new zinnea, the most brilliant cosmos, the brightest coleus, and the loudest proclamations: "If you thought last year's petunias were something, wait until you see this year's *giant* pastel hybrids!''

Annuals are great plants for filling up empty spaces in a perennial border while you are waiting for other flowers to bloom, or for providing instant color when other plants are past their prime. But annuals are also valuable used on their own, and a small garden of nothing but annuals can add excitement and color to the backyard.

Getting a jump on the seasons is always important. To plant annuals, prepare the soil in autumn or in early spring, as soon as the ground is workable. If you need to add compost and organic matter, be sure to give it time to mellow before planting. In all climates, avoid planting in very hot weather.

Planting in the North. Start seeds of hardy and half-hardy annuals (and perennials that masquerade as annuals) indoors in late winter, and start to harden off seedlings in April and May. Direct-sow hardy annuals as soon as the soil can be worked in spring.

Plant tender annuals in late spring or early summer, when the danger of frost is past and the soil is warm. Harden off seedlings started indoors before moving them to the garden.

Planting in the South. For annuals that bloom in late spring and summer, start seeds indoors in winter and start planting out in early spring. Direct-sow cold-tolerant flowers. In the warmest climates, set out bedding annuals in early spring.

Sow hardy and half-hardy annuals (such as ageratum, sweet alyssum, bachelor's-buttons, calendula, larkspur, candytuft, poppies, snapdragons, and sweet peas) in autumn, to bloom in winter and spring. Or sow in January for early-spring flowers.

Plant out tender annuals in midspring. Direct-sow annuals in summer for fall flowers. In early summer, replace early annuals and spring bulbs with heat-tolerant flowers, such as cosmos, marigolds, and portulaca.

Caring for annuals. Water new plantings regularly until they become established, then water as needed during hot, dry weather. Check the soil by sticking your finger one or two inches below the surface; if dry, it's time to water. Be sure to water deeply. Annuals in containers should be watered every day—sometimes twice a day—in summer.

Fertilize garden annuals at least once a month during the growing season with seaweed extract, fish emulsion, or an all-purpose plant food (5-10-5 is a good ratio). Container-grown plants should be fertilized every two weeks because watering eventually leaches out the nutrients in potted soil.

Remove fading or dead flowers to prolong bloom. Pinching back bushy plants, such as impatiens, will encourage more flowers. For a bushier shape and more flowers, shear back small-leaved plants, like sweet alyssum. Shear once or twice during the growing season, then feed and water.

Keep the garden clean of plant debris because that material becomes a breeding ground for pests and diseases. Weed and mulch beds and borders and cultivate often if no mulch is used, so that the soil stays open to air and water circulation. If disease occurs, immediately remove the infected plants. At the first sign of pests, spray with insecticidal soap or take other appropriate measures. If you use pesticides, be extremely cautious and follow package directions carefully; any product that lists an 800 number for medical help should be treated with respect, if not completely shunned.

After the first frost, pull and discard all tender annuals; many others adapt to colder temperatures. In warm climates, pull them when they stop blooming in late fall.

You can dig and pot up marigolds, nasturtiums, petunias, and other annuals in fall for continued bloom indoors. Take cuttings of begonias, geraniums, and impatiens for winter flowers indoors.

SOME FAVORITE ANNUALS

I've left out some of the more common annuals found at garden centers and included only those usually grown from seed. A few perennials are included that are grown as annuals. Unless otherwise noted, these plants need plenty of sunlight.

Amaranthus caudatus grows to five feet high, then brings forth long twisted ropes of tiny blood-red flowers that hang to the ground (or other plants and garden structures)—hence the common names kiss-me-over-the-garden-gate and the downright macabre love-lies-bleeding. 'Viridis' bears vibrant green flowers. Both plants make an unusual statement at the back of the border.

Ammi majus, bishop's weed, belongs to the same family as Queen Anne's lace but is a more attractive plant and very popular with the cut flower trade. Stems are two and a half feet high and topped with five- to six-inch flower heads, each consisting of hundreds of tiny white flowers. For a striking display, mass these flowers in the center of the border with love-lies-bleeding (*Amaranthus caudatus*) so that the red flowers drape over the white clusters.

Ammobium alatum is an Australian perennial that is treated as an annual. The common name, winged everlasting, refers to the flattened winglike part of each three-foot stem. The silvery white flowers with yellow centers are up to two inches wide. These plants are best planted in masses. To keep as dried flowers, cut the stems just before the blossoms open and hang them upside down in a dry place.

Brachycome iberidifolia, the Swan River daisy, is another Australian native. This long-blooming plant bears sweet-smelling daisy-like blossoms on foot-high stems. The delicate flowers—in white, rose, pink, or lilac—bloom for a long time, their pinwheels hovering over ferny foliage that will in turn gracefully drape over other plants or the edge of a pot. Try growing these beauties in a large urn, either alone or with a seedling cabbage palm (*Cordyline australis*) at the center.

Canna × *generalis,* or as it's sometimes called, Indian shot (calling attention to the cannonball seeds), is a large tropical perennial grown as an annual in areas with freezing winters. Most plants are large and flashy but a new cultivar called 'Seven Dwarfs' is useful where space is limited. Plants are eighteen inches high; flowers come in red, rose, orange, yellow, and salmon. Also look for 'Ambrosia', which is twenty-four inches high and bears pink flowers.

Celosia spp., the woolflowers, are probably the most artificial-looking flowers in the garden. Both color and form are often bright and bizarre. For example, *C. cristata* should be overlooked because it resembles an alien in the 1950s science fiction film *The Brain from Planet Arous.* But one particular variety called pink spiked celosia (*C. cristata* var. *spicata*) should be in every garden because of the rare beauty of the drooping flowers. It's been in cultivation since 1790. I first saw it at Jefferson's garden at Monticello. The three-foot bushlike plants with their drooping flowers look great along a walkway.

Cleome hasslerana, the spider flower, gets its common name from the flowers that feature long waving stamens—followed by seedpods—that wave about like the legs of harvestmen or daddy long legs. Plants reach six feet in a typical growing season and can almost fill an entire garden bed with their long-lasting floral display. There are a number of cultivars, with colors ranging from white to pink and rose to purple. For a beautiful display, mass spider flowers tightly together inside a hedge of boxwood bushes or hollies.

Cobaea scandens, the cup-and-saucer vine, is a tropical perennial vine that flowers the first year from seed. Two-inch-long rosy purple flowers sit on a saucer-shaped green calyx and look like elegant Victorian china. The flowers are green as they open and have an unpleasant odor that attracts flies, but soon the smell turns to honey and the bees appear—this plant would have it both ways! The oblong leaves are four inches long; the tendrils cling to any available support. Move plants into the greenhouse or onto the sunporch at the end of the garden season for winter bloom. These vines need a good, moist, well-drained soil coupled with full sun in the North and partial shade in the South.

Convolvulus tricolor, the bush morning glory, does not climb like others of its kin but merely grows about one foot high and then spreads in all directions, making it perfect for a hanging basket or falling over the edge of a wall. Plants are constantly in bloom; the one-and-a-half-inch flowers are blue, pink, or purple, with a white area that descends to a yellow center. The handsome leaves are splashed with white and green. Start plants in three-inch peat pots; nick the seed with a file to hasten germination. In warmer areas, bush morning glories will reseed.

Datura spp., angel's trumpet, flowers in just under four months from seed. Five-foot plants bear four-inch trumpetlike blooms that scent the night air with the sweet smells of the tropics. 'La Fleur Lilac' has pale lilac flowers. Grow plants in fancy pots and provide partial shade in the afternoon. Watch for the moths that visit during the long summer evenings.

Digitalis purpurea 'Foxy' is the only foxglove cultivar that blooms the first year from seed. The first flowers appear about five months after the seeds are sown. The two-inch blossoms have freckled throats and come in white, yellow, pink, or cerise. They cover stems up to three feet tall, blooming from the bottom up. Plants are most effective when massed in the border or planted at the edge of a woodland lot. They are also striking against a background of evergreen shrubbery.

Dolichos lablab, the hyacinth bean, is a tropical perennial vine that blooms the first year from seed. The leaves look like those of lilacs. Fragrant, pealike purple flowers produce elegant purple-brown seedpods that resemble the sound box of a rare cello. These fast-growing vines will clamber up and soon cover a four-by-eight-foot trellis or a tall tripod. The flowers of 'Daylight' are white. Start plants indoors in early spring; sow three seeds in each pot, then remove the two weakest seedlings.

Eschscholzia californica, the California poppy, is a perennial or biennial where winters are warm; everywhere else it is a charming annual. Each flower has four satiny petals that bloom on twelve- to fifteen-inch stems and exhibit a number of colors, including white, orange, golden yellow, purple-violet, and lemon yellow. There are also double flowers. The small disc at the base of each flower is called a *torus.* Even the foliage is attractive, so use California poppies to provide drifts of color, or plant along edges or in a wild garden.

Helianthus annuus 'Stella' and 'Italian White' are elegant cultivars of the common sunflower but instead of looking like gigantic Van Gogh still lifes, they resemble slightly oversized daisies with four-inch flowers. The first cultivar is primrose yellow and the second soft ivory. Depending on the size of your border's width, place them at the back or in the middle, massed for the best effect. Plants grow to four feet high.

Ipomoea alba, the moonflower, is another tropical perennial that is grown as an annual. This white morning glory opens its sweetly scented blossoms in late afternoon or evening, the petals unfolding as in a slow-motion nature film. Grow it on a wooded or stringed trellis, and be sure to have a party when the flowers begin to open. Nick the seeds to hasten germination.

Kochia scoparia forma *trichophylla,* the summer cypress or burning bush, originally came from southern Europe and Japan. It resembles a dwarf conifer and is perfect for a temporary summer hedge, along borders, as a single garden accent, or in selected pots set around the terrace. With the arrival of fall, the foliage turns scarlet red, hence the name burning bush. Plants range between two and three feet tall, depending on the variety. 'Acapulco Silver' has light green leaves dusted on the tips with silver.

Lavatera trimestis, the tree mallow, is an annual plant that looks like a perennial. One of the most sumptuous books on container gardening that I ever saw (*The Art of Gardening in Pots,* Wappinger's Falls, New York: Antique Collectors' Club, 1990), features a photograph of eight clay pots—four small and four large—holding white ('Mont Blanc') and pink ('Silver Cup') mallows, reaffirming my belief that tree mallows with their bushlike growth habit and their hollyhock trumpets are among the finest of annuals for the home garden. Flowers are three to four inches across on two-foot plants.

Linaria maroccana, the toadflax, is an elfin snapdragon from Morocco. (It requires a stretch of the imagination to see the mini-amphibians of the common name in the flowers.) It is available in a number of colors, including red, yellow, blue, lavender, violet, pink, and white. Because of the discreet charm of these flowers, the cultivar 'Fairy Bouquet' is aptly named. Plants require well-drained soil and full sun or partial shade. Toadflax looks great at the edge of a wall or growing in cracks between paving stones.

Mirabilis jalapa, the four-o'clock, blooms in late afternoon, producing a sweet lemonlike fragrance. The tubular flowers are one inch wide and two inches long; they come in red, yellow, magenta, crimson, and white, and some are even striped. Flowers bloom on bushy growth that can reach a height of three feet. They are perennials in their native home of tropical America. Where the soil freezes in winter, dig up the long thin black tubers in the fall and plant them again the following spring. I use four-o'clocks in the border and in pots.

Moluccella laevis, or bells-of-Ireland, hail from the Molucca Islands west of New Guinea. The shamrock-green bell-like flowers are really enlarged calyxes, the small leaves that in most plants wrap around an unopened blossom. The tiny white flowers sit within. Three-foot stems are ringed with these green bells, making them among the most beautiful of everlasting flowers for the garden and especially attractive in winter bouquets. Bunch the plants at the back of the border. The seeds need good light for germination.

Nicotiana alata, jasmine tobacco, is a true perennial from the tropics that is grown as an annual; it's very popular as a bedding plant, in the border, and as a cut flower. As an annual it is especially valuable because it does well in light or open shade. Breeders have been busy and produced a number of cultivars, which range in height from one to three feet and bear two-inch flowers that bloom throughout the day (older cultivars held off opening until late afternoon). 'Sensation Mixed' is a three-foot plant that produces fragrant flowers in shades of maroon-red, pink, yellow, and white. 'Domino' bears pink, rose, lime, or white flowers on foot-high stems. *Nicotiana sylvestris* is another perennial grown as an annual, with long-tubed white flowers that are over three inches long and resemble shooting stars in the garden. Finally *N. tabacum,* the true tobacco of commerce, can reach seven feet in one season and bears pinkish blossoms one and a half inches long. The plants are very attractive in large pots on the patio.

Nigella damascena, commonly called love-in-a-mist or fennel flower, has been cultivated for more than four centuries. The first common name refers to the pastel blossoms that hover over a tangle of light green fernlike foliage. The aromatic seeds are used in the Orient in cooking and medicine, and in India, seeds and leaves are used to repel moths in the closet. The best cultivars are 'Miss Jekyll', with bright blue semidouble flowers, and 'Miss Jekyll Alba', with white semidouble blooms. Fertilized flowers form balloonlike seedpods with tiny projections and closely resemble a jester's cap. They are perfect in dry-flower arrangements. Use these plants as an edging at the front of the garden.

Oxypetalum caeruleum, or Southern stars, bears five-lobed, one-inch pale blue flowers that turn purple with age, eventually fading to lilac as they wither. The downy leaves are heart shaped. These warm-weather perennial shrubs bloom the first year and can be wintered over in the greenhouse or on the sunporch. Since they belong to the milkweed family, the brown seedpods eventually open to release silky parachutes that fly off in autumn breezes like windblown umbrellas. We plant ours in the herb

garden along with a number of silver leaved plants like lamb's-ears (*Stachys byzantina*) and dusty miller (*Centaurea cineraria*).

Papaver somniferum, the opium poppy, has for some years been responsible for giving the whole poppy family bad press. In the United States growing opium poppies is illegal, so seed producers now call it the peony-flowered poppy. Opium poppies are spectacular in the garden; even if you have a very limited space, I suggest you include a few. But leave room for *Papaver burseri* (*P. alpinum*), which hugs the ground with rosettes of long, wavy gray-green leaves and satiny-petaled flowers on eight- to ten-inch stems. The blossoms, all of which have a sweet delicate fragrance, come in orange, yellow, pink, apricot, and white. Then, in honor of John McCrae's poem, "In Flanders' fields the poppies blow between the crosses, row on row," be sure to include the field poppy, *P. rhoeas,* whose flowers, up to three inches across, are scarlet, crimson, salmon pink, pink, or white with petals that look like crushed silk. Plant all poppies directly in the garden or start in individual pots; their taproots make the seedlings difficult to transplant.

Phaseolus coccineus, the scarlet runner bean, is a perennial twining vine that is grown as an annual and blooms the first year from seed. Dark green compound leaves spring from vines that can reach eight feet by midsummer. When days are warm, clusters of scarlet pealike flowers appear. Years ago, my mother grew these vines in front-porch windowboxes by stretching strings, ten inches apart, from the porch rail to the edge of the roof above. These vines make excellent screens in small gardens.

Phlox drummondii is a native phlox discovered in Texas in the 1830s. The newer dwarf cultivars stay between six and eight inches high and are covered with blossoms measuring over an inch across. Colors range from pure white to purple, crimson, yellow, and lavender; some plants are bicolored. 'Twinkle' has fancy star-shaped blossoms, usually in two colors. Use these flowers in borders, rock gardens, or little pots. They also make excellent cut flowers.

Portulaca grandiflora, the moss rose, is so tough it will bloom under almost any conditions; parched, dry, and generally poor soil—plus the hot sun—will not even slow the onward march of this creeping plant. Single or double flowers come in red, yellow, orange, scarlet, magenta, and white. The silky blooms appear on succulent reddish stems, dotted with small cylindrical leaves. Use moss roses as edgings, or plant them between rocks or along the edge of a wall.

Rhodochiton atrosanguineum, the purple bell vine, was found growing in Mexico in 1755. Masses of flowers the color of venous blood quickly cover this fast-growing vine, which can grow ten feet in a season. The five-lobed, inch-wide calyx of each flower is bell shaped and a lighter shade of purple than the two-inch-long tubular corolla, which flares at the bottom into five lobes of unequal size. Purple bell vines are well suited for covering a trellis or fence.

Salvia farinacea is another perennial from

Mexico. It is commonly called mealy-cup salvia because the blossoms are said to be *puberulent,* both unfortunate words to describe the minute, soft hairs that cover the flowers. 'Victoria' has deep blue flowers, and the blossoms of 'Silver' are silvery white. Plants are up to two feet tall and bloom throughout the summer. They tolerate high heat and humidity, and are splendid in dried bouquets.

Salvia splendens, or scarlet sage, is a Brazilian perennial that blooms the first year from seed. This subshrub has deep green, glossy leaves and fire engine red flowers that look like elongated snapdragons. It is found in almost every park in America. Plants are one foot to thirty inches high, depending on the cultivar. 'Blaze of Fire' does not disappoint, and 'Flare' is almost as flashy. Find a place in your border for a clump of these stunning flowers, but don't use them for cutting, since the flowers fade in water.

Sanvitalia procumbens, the creeping zinnia, is an annual from Mexico and perfect for a rock garden, a hanging basket, or a pot for the sunporch or greenhouse. It also makes a good edging plant and is especially effective falling over the edge of a wall. Flowers are one inch wide and look like zinnias. The species flower is yellow; the cultivar 'Mandarin Orange' bears double flowers of bright orange, which appear in July. A well-grown plant will cover a two-foot radius. Creeping zinnias do not transplant well, so start plants in individual pots.

Thunbergia alata, or the black-eyed Susan vine, is a perennial from tropical Africa that blooms the first year from seed. Flowers are one and a half inches across and are available in white, orange, and yellow; most have a purple to black throat or eye. These plants are not rampant growers; they will clamber along the ground, winding in and out of other plants, or trail from baskets, or climb wires to a height of six feet or more. We have black-eyed Susan vines growing on three wires on the side of our house, and in Zone 7 and warmer, they reseed and come up every year in the same place.

Tithonia rotundifolia, or Mexican sunflower, creates large dots of color for bed or border. Today, the species is difficult to find, but luckily two cultivars are available. 'Goldfinger' bears three-inch-wide, bright orange-scarlet flowers on thirty-inch stems. The chrome-yellow flowers of 'Yellow Torch' are slightly smaller and appear on three- to four-foot stems. These plants are great for covering up fences or other structures better left hidden. They are fine cut flowers but to prevent wilting, seal the hollow stem ends with a match or gas flame as you would with poppies.

Venidium fastuosum is the monarch-of-the-Veldt, a South African annual whose blossoms, like many African flowers, close at night. The four- to five-inch flowers are somewhat like sunflowers but the colors are far more unique: bright orange petals are feathered with black toward the base and all surround a dark brown-purple disc that is almost black. Flowers of 'Zulu Prince' are creamy white and have the same striking black centers. The deeply cut leaves, up to six inches long, are covered with fine silvery hairs that sparkle in the sun. These two-foot-tall plants from the grasslands dislike damp conditions.

PLAN FOR A SMALL ANNUAL GARDEN

Annual gardens are full of color beginning about eight weeks after their inception, and the plants will continue to produce flowers until the days shorten and autumn frosts arrive. The following design tries to use annuals to their best advantage and guarantees both color in the garden and bouquets for the table.

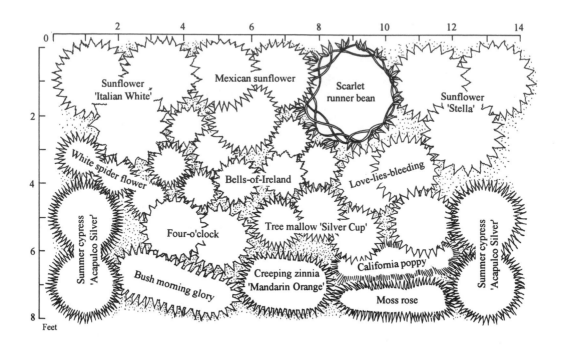

Eighteen

Great Plans for Small Gardens

TWO PITHY SAYINGS SHOULD COME TO MIND WHEN GARDEN PLANS ARE MENTIONED. ONE dates to the first century B.C., when Publius Syrus penned his Maxim 469, "It is a bad plan that admits of no modification." The other was voiced by John Henry Cardinal Newman in 1868, when he said: "Living Nature, not dull Art shall plan my ways and rule my heart."

Both are important to keep in mind when planning a garden. The first because something always comes up at the last minute that forces a change of plans. One of the trees that you've built your garden around can be struck by lightning, or the special clematis that you ordered a year in advance has succumbed to a viral infection, or the nursery loses your order, or you find out that your live-in mother-in-law is allergic to all the hostas.

The second because a garden is a living entity. Except for pathways, sculpture, and other manmade objects, it is subject to the laws of entropy. This means that your garden, like the universe, is on a continuing slide to complete disorganization, and only you, the gardener, stand in the way.

If you don't believe this, abandon your garden for one month—preferably in late spring—and see what happens. Depending on the area of the country you live in, once past the slugs, voles, deer, and insects (not to mention general disease), you will confront rampant growth, unbridled grass, and a sea of weeds.

The following ten plans are simply meant to stimulate ideas or to serve as jumping-off points, and not to be slavishly followed.

A TREE ISLAND

Judy Ferris, one of my garden friends in Ohio, has a very large walnut tree in her backyard. After years of frustration with many ornamentals, she learned that the black walnut (*Juglans nigra*) exudes a self-protective poison called *juglone* into the surrounding soil, discouraging many ornamentals with its chemical attacks. Instead of searching for resistant perennials, Judy surrounded the tree with flagstones and the flagstones with a wide ring of common—and very tough—garden violets (*Viola nephrophylla*). Next, she added an old concrete garden bench and two concrete putti she had found at a roadside antiques barn. Now the Ferrises and the putti have a cool place to sit on summer afternoons and watch the Ohio heat haze.

At our first house in the country, we had an ancient apple tree that was gnarled and covered with lichens, yet it still produced a small crop of Russian Astrachans every odd year or so. I surrounded the furrowed trunk with a large square of fieldstones. Then I edged the stones with various daylily cultivars so that blooms would appear from late May to early September. Finally, I set out various pots of annuals and wrought iron garden furniture.

Unless you are underplanting a black walnut, there are ground covers you can use to create a tree "island." Try cultivars of English ivy (*Hedera helix*), Alleghany spurge (*Pachysandra procumbens*), lily turf (*Liriope* spp.), winter creeper (*Euonymus fortunei*), or one of the best, the Lenten rose (*Helleborus orientalis*).

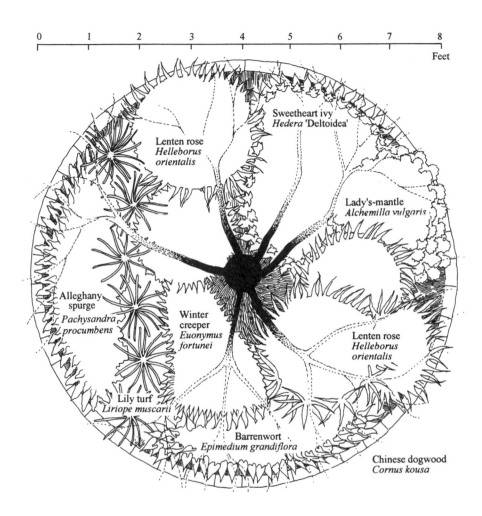

Sweetheart ivy
Hedera 'Deltoidea'

Lenten rose
*Helleborus
orientalis*

Lady's-mantle
Alchemilla vulgaris

Alleghany
spurge
*Pachysandra
procumbens*

Winter
creeper
*Euonymus
fortunei*

Lenten rose
*Helleborus
orientalis*

Lily turf
Liriope muscarii

Barrenwort
Epimedium grandiflora

Chinese dogwood
Cornus kousa

0   1   2   3   4   5   6   7   8
Feet

A GARDEN ROOM

Like a house, a garden can be divided into a number of areas, each with a different theme. If these areas are walled in with hedges or borders, they can feel like individual rooms. It is this design principle that makes the great garden at Sissinghurst so appealing.

The grass floor of our partially walled garden room measures twenty-five by thirteen feet and is surrounded by planted borders that are about five feet wide. In the center of the lawn is a flagstone square; in summer, it sports a twenty-year-old potted cabbage palm (*Cordylene australis*), and in the winter, a concrete pot that holds a dwarf conifer.

The small trees and shrubs in this small garden room include a very mature specimen of *Viburnum* × *carlcephalum,* which bears large balls of fragrant flowers in the spring and brilliant autumn foliage that turns orange-red long after other leaves have fallen. There are also two rhododendrons ('Blue Peter' and 'Red Peter'), and a star magnolia (*Magnolia tomentosa* [*M. stellata*]), which shades many of my houseplants in the summer.

The dwarf conifers include a ten-year-old specimen of a dwarf redwood (*Sequoia sempervirens* 'Adpressa'); remove the fast-growing upright leaders to keep it under ten to sixteen feet. Others are a dwarf spruce (*Picea glauca* 'Echiniformis'), which resembles an English hedgehog, and a beautiful hemlock (*Tsuga canadensis* 'Cappy's Choice'), which bears finely textured light green needles tinged with gold and reaches a height of eighteen inches in ten years.

In addition to daylilies, hostas, and a number of spring bulbs, there are Lenten roses (*Helleborus orientalis*), a large clump of gold-banded Chinese lilies (*Lilium auratum*), and for fall, colchicums (*Colchicum autumnale* 'Waterlily') and other autumn crocuses.

This garden requires little effort. We have a small hand-propelled lawn mower to cut the lawn, and aside from removing dead flowers and some weeding, the most work is removing leaves that fall from two towering white oaks at the rear of the garden.

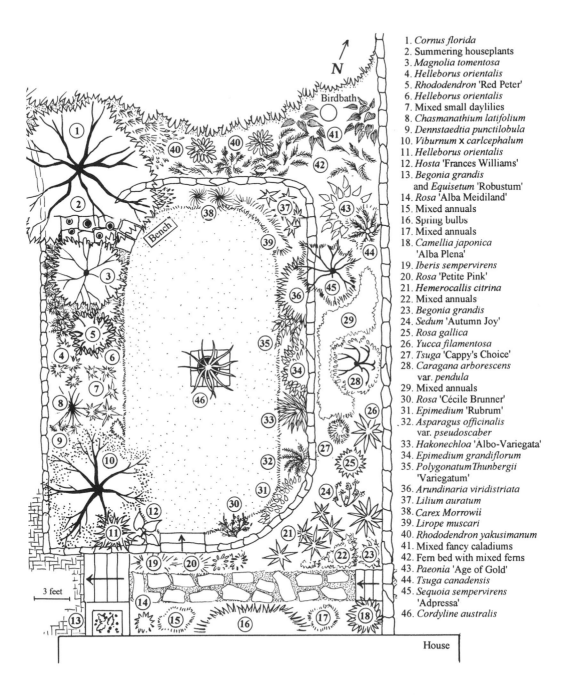

1. *Cornus florida*
2. Summering houseplants
3. *Magnolia tomentosa*
4. *Helleborus orientalis*
5. *Rhododendron* 'Red Peter'
6. *Helleborus orientalis*
7. Mixed small daylilies
8. *Chasmanathium latifolium*
9. *Dennstaedtia punctilobula*
10. *Viburnum* x *carlcephalum*
11. *Helleborus orientalis*
12. *Hosta* 'Frances Williams'
13. *Begonia grandis*
    and *Equisetum* 'Robustum'
14. *Rosa* 'Alba Meidiland'
15. Mixed annuals
16. Spring bulbs
17. Mixed annuals
18. *Camellia japonica*
    'Alba Plena'
19. *Iberis sempervirens*
20. *Rosa* 'Petite Pink'
21. *Hemerocallis citrina*
22. Mixed annuals
23. *Begonia grandis*
24. *Sedum* 'Autumn Joy'
25. *Rosa gallica*
26. *Yucca filamentosa*
27. *Tsuga* 'Cappy's Choice'
28. *Caragana arborescens*
    var. *pendula*
29. Mixed annuals
30. *Rosa* 'Cécile Brunner'
31. *Epimedium* 'Rubrum'
32. *Asparagus officinalis*
    var. *pseudoscaber*
33. *Hakonechloa* 'Albo-Variegata'
34. *Epimedium grandiflorum*
35. *Polygonatum Thunbergii*
    'Variegatum'
36. *Arundinaria viridistriata*
37. *Lilium auratum*
38. *Carex Morrowii*
39. *Lirope muscari*
40. *Rhododendron yakusimanum*
41. Mixed fancy caladiums
42. Fern bed with mixed ferns
43. *Paeonia* 'Age of Gold'
44. *Tsuga canadensis*
45. *Sequoia sempervirens*
    'Adpressa'
46. *Cordyline australis*

A GARDEN IN THE CITY

Because of its built-in feeling of formality, the following garden seems best within a city lot. There its straight borders echo those of the surrounding buildings, and its various plants offer relief from the institutional gray of concrete and the dull red of city brick.

It's assumed that buildings will provide partial shade at least part of the day, so many of the chosen plants do well with limited sunlight. The pool can hold small waterlilies but only if they receive at least six hours of sunlight every day. Even without flowers, the pool is worth including for the gentle sound of splashing water.

The plants include horsetails (*Equisetum* spp.) for the pool, various impatiens, some ivies, and a number of different ferns, and vacationing houseplants, such as philodendrons.

The scheme also includes two ornamental grasses that do well in moist soil and water-side plantings. The first is variegated reed manna grass (*Glyceria aquatica* 'Variegata'), a cultivar that bears long straplike leaves with creamy yellow stripes. It responds to partial shade and can actually be planted directly in shallow water. The second is fountain grass (*Pennisetum alopecuroides*). When in bloom, the drooping panicles of these grasses are unbeatable; in the morning light, their bristles are often dotted with dew. 'Hameln' is a dwarf variety that forms two-foot mounds.

If city soot is a problem, lay down paving stones or used bricks and a terrace rather than gravel or crushed marble, since the stones and brick are much easier to keep clean.

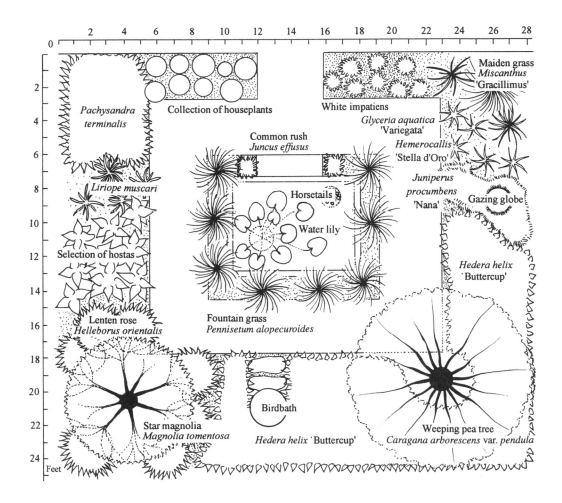

Maiden grass
Miscanthus 'Gracillimus'

White impatiens

Glyceria aquatica 'Variegata'

Hemerocallis 'Stella d'Oro'

Juniperus procumbens 'Nana'

Gazing globe

Pachysandra terminalis

Collection of houseplants

Common rush
Juncus effusus

Liriope muscari

Horsetails

Water lily

Hedera helix `Buttercup'

Selection of hostas

Fountain grass
Pennisetum alopecuroides

Lenten rose
Helleborus orientalis

Birdbath

Star magnolia
Magnolia tomentosa

Hedera helix `Buttercup'

Weeping pea tree
Caragana arborescens var. *pendula*

Feet

A PETITE POTAGER FOR COLORFUL VEGETABLES

I've never been much of a vegetable gardener, having left all such work to my wife while I went out to do battle with the blossoms. So I owe Jean for most of what I know about garden vegetables. And from reading the works of Beverley Nichols I also learned a lot about vegetable history (including the fact that a beanfield killed Pythagoras: this vegetarian Greek philosopher had such reverence for plants and flowers that when angry nonbelievers chased him toward a beanfield, he refused to cross lest he trample the plants, so he kept to the road and was killed).

The French, who never waste anything—including beauty—are famous for a type of garden called a potager, in which vegetables and flowers are grown together. Combining aesthetics with nutrition, I offer the following plan.

The center features a small square of fieldstones, bricks, or concrete paving bricks for a fashionable terracotta pot or a sundial. Four brick paths follow the four main compass points. The overall shape can be either circular or elliptical, depending on the amount of space available.

Among the plants featured are edible annuals, such as variegated nasturtiums (*Tropaeolum* 'Alaska'); borage (*Borago officinalis*), whose leaves lend a great flavor to iced drinks; calendulas (*Calendula officinalis*), especially 'Bon Bon'; and pansies, which my mother used to decorate cakes.

The best poppies for such a garden are the opium poppies (*Papaver somniferum*), certainly the double-flowered cultivars (now called peony-flowered poppies or *P. somniferum* var. *paeoniaeflorum*). An older cultivar of great beauty is 'Pink Chiffon'. Today's catalogs usually feature 'White Cloud', 'Golden Paeony', or 'Oase', whose scarlet petals have white splotches. The flowers are followed by decorative seedpods that become sculptural additions (the seeds can be used to dress up dinner rolls).

This garden also includes clouds of the bronze-leaved fennel called 'Bronze Form'; Florence fennel (*Foeniculum vulgare* var. *azoricum*) for its the beautiful foliage; many thymes (*Thymus* spp.); and ornamental cabbages and kales.

Among the perennials featured are garlic chives (*Allium tuberosum*) and common chives (*A. schoenoprasum*). The asparagus bed is valuable not only for the spears but also for the ferny plumes.

Finally, there are the greens: red-stemmed Swiss chard, called 'Vulcan'; white-stemmed 'Swiss Chard of Geneva'; 'Red Giant' mustard greens; and bronze-red 'Red Sails', pink 'Selma Lollo', and green 'Green Ice' lettuce.

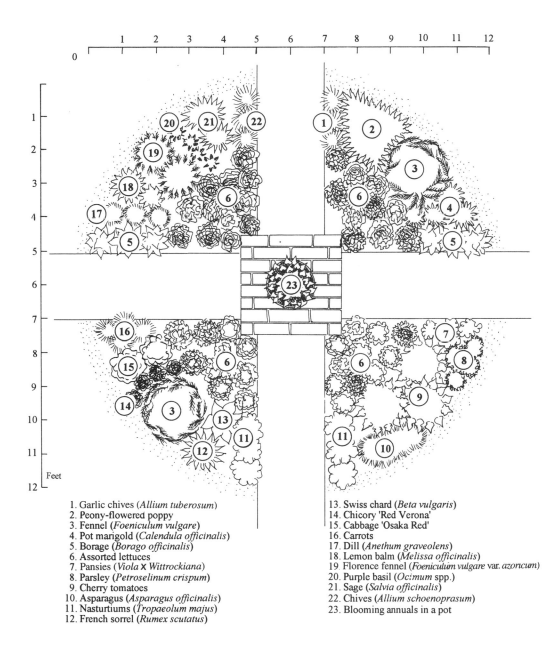

1. Garlic chives (*Allium tuberosum*)
2. Peony-flowered poppy
3. Fennel (*Foeniculum vulgare*)
4. Pot marigold (*Calendula officinalis*)
5. Borage (*Borago officinalis*)
6. Assorted lettuces
7. Pansies (*Viola* X *Wittrockiana*)
8. Parsley (*Petroselinum crispum*)
9. Cherry tomatoes
10. Asparagus (*Asparagus officinalis*)
11. Nasturtiums (*Tropaeolum majus*)
12. French sorrel (*Rumex scutatus*)
13. Swiss chard (*Beta vulgaris*)
14. Chicory 'Red Verona'
15. Cabbage 'Osaka Red'
16. Carrots
17. Dill (*Anethum graveolens*)
18. Lemon balm (*Melissa officinalis*)
19. Florence fennel (*Foeniculum vulgare* var. *azoricum*)
20. Purple basil (*Ocimum* spp.)
21. Sage (*Salvia officinalis*)
22. Chives (*Allium schoenoprasum*)
23. Blooming annuals in a pot

A WILDFLOWER WALK

Our wildflower garden began as an area full of weeds, predominantly American bitter-sweet (*Celastrus scandens*). This stranglehold vine is lovely when fruiting, but a terror if left unchecked. And poison ivy requires constant vigilance to keep from spreading, since birds eat the berries, then drop the seeds everywhere.

An old concrete bench, scarred with a number of lichens, sits in the middle of this garden. From its center, three pathways of old bricks set in sand radiate in three directions.

Among the plants are maidenhair fern (*Adiantum pedatum*), hay-scented fern (*Dennstaedtia punctilobula*), Virginia bluebells (*Mertensia virginica*), and many different trilliums, including the large whites (*Trillium grandiflorum*), whippoorwill flowers (*T. cuneatum*), and painted trilliums (*T. undulatum*). There are also dogtooth violets (*Erythronium* spp.), columbines (*Aquilegia vulgaris* and *A. canadensis*), and Alleghany spurge (*Pachysandra procumbens*), an excellent native American ground cover that bears gently toothed, deep green leaves etched with faint silver lines. At the back of this garden is a wall of rhododendrons (*Rhododendron maximum*), cork-barked or winged euonymus (*Euonymus alata*), and Carolina hemlocks (*Tsuga caroliniana*), plus a whole line of jack-in-the-pulpits (*Arisaema triphyllum*).

I have also allowed a few interlopers to establish themselves. These include autumn-flowering colchicums (*Colchicum* 'Waterlily') and red spider lilies (*Lycoris radiata*), whose strap-like leaves appear in spring and red spiderlike flowers appear in mid- to late September.

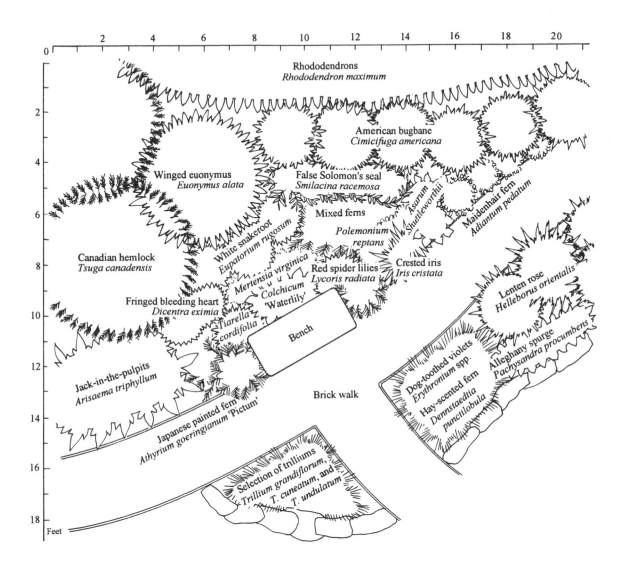

Rhododendrons
Rhododendron maximum

American bugbane
Cimicifuga americana

Winged euonymus
Euonymus alata

False Solomon's seal
Smilacina racemosa

Asarum Shuttleworthii

Maidenhair fern
Adiantum pedatum

Mixed ferns

White snakeroot
Eupatorium rugosum

Polemonium reptans

Canadian hemlock
Tsuga canadensis

Mertensia virginica

Red spider lilies
Lycoris radiata

Crested iris
Iris cristata

Lenten rose
Helleborus orientalis

Fringed bleeding heart
Dicentra eximia

Colchicum 'Waterlily'

Tiarella cordifolia

Bench

Dog-toothed violets
Erythronium spp.

Alleghany spurge
Pachysandra procumbens

Hay-scented fern
Dennstaedtia punctilobula

Jack-in-the-pulpits
Arisaema triphyllum

Brick walk

Japanese painted fern
Athyrium goeringianum 'Pictum'

Selection of trilliums
Trillium grandiflorum,
T. cuneatum, and
T. undulatum

A FORMAL GARDEN

This formal garden is based on three city gardens I have seen in Asheville, plus part of our own. The Plesses' garden has boxwood hedges that are trimmed low and surround mowed grass. The corners are filled with perennials like peonies and poppies. The Coles' garden consists of a wide perennial border separated by a strip of mowed grass originating from their rear terrace. The border contains Russian sage (*Perovskia atriplicifolia*) and a number of ornamental grasses, chiefly fountain grass (*Pennisetum alopecuroides*). Boxwood hedges are also featured at Peggy Pennell's garden. At one corner is a low brick panel about three feet wide and four feet tall. Set into a bank of ivy, it surrounds an architectural fragment of great beauty and is fronted by a small birdbath and an Italian putto of black iron.

If you live in a cold part of the country, the ground cover at the garden's center could be Japanese pachysandra (*Pachysandra terminalis*). A better choice, however, would be one of the more unusual ivy cultivars, such as *Hedera helix* 'Baltica'. This plant bears small leaves with whitish veins and makes an excellent ground cover even in Zone 4. In Zones 7 or 8, look for 'Brokamp', a German ivy with dark green, glossy leaves that turn a beautiful shade of bronze in winter (a color that is heightened by growing the plant in poor soil). 'Ivalace' is also a good choice. Its gray-green leaves have white margins and turn copper in the winter.

The large evergreen shrub could be a rhododendron. Or for an especially elegant look, plant one of the more unusual Japanese maples instead of an evergreen (see chapter 16).

This garden is made for sculpture, including many of the reproductions sold by museums. Our favorite is a fiberglass reproduction called "Fat Persian Cat" by American sculptor Richard H. Recchia and sold by the Boston Museum. Be sure to leave a spot for a large concrete or terracotta trough filled with beautiful annuals.

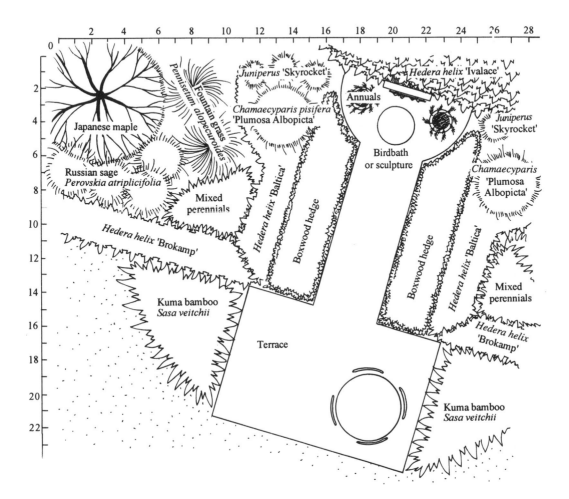

Japanese maple

Russian sage
Perovskia atriplicifolia

Hedera helix 'Brokamp'

Kuma bamboo
Sasa veitchii

Terrace

Pennisetum alopecuroides
Fountain grass

Mixed
perennials

Juniperus 'Skyrocket'

Chamaecyparis pisifera
'Plumosa Albopicta'

Hedera helix 'Baltica'

Boxwood hedge

Annuals

Hedera helix 'Ivalace'

Birdbath
or sculpture

Juniperus
'Skyrocket'

Chamaecyparis
'Plumosa
Albopicta'

Boxwood hedge

Hedera helix 'Baltica'

Mixed
perennials

Hedera helix
'Brokamp'

Kuma bamboo
Sasa veitchii

A SHADY BORDER

Everybody knows what is meant by the term *sunny*. A sunny day, as Gertrude Stein might say, is a sunny day is a sunny day. But shade has many different colors.

Light shade is the same as *open shade*. It's the shade found beneath a tall and stately tree, where sun is available in the early morning and late afternoon but the area is protected from the intense light of midday.

Medium shade (or partial shade) is found under a group of trees, where sunlight is dappled as in the woods; you will see reflected sunlight but not the direct sun.

Full shade is getting darker. Closely grouped trees and thickets intertwine and effectively cut out direct sun and even bright indirect light.

Deep shade is truly dark. Buildings, trees, natural or artificial barriers, or a combination of all four cut off most of the sun's light. Few plants can exist here except potted jungle-types like philodendrons and then only for a short time.

Seasonal shade occurs when deciduous trees and shrubs leaf out. It disappears from late fall through winter and into early spring, when the sun shines through the naked branches.

When gardening in the shade, add plenty of leaf litter and garden compost to the soil. The combination of poor drainage and deep shade can be deadly to plants.

This shade garden plan is based on our own backyard. Three large oaks provide a canopy of high or open shade, leaving enough light that grass grows and daylilies bloom. A quartet of young dogwoods (*Cornus florida*) creates an area of medium shade that supports hostas, ivies, and a seasonal display of impatiens. This garden is a source of enjoyment every time we walk through it. Yet it requires very little work: just cutting the slow-growing lawn three or four times a summer, removing spent flowers, and raking up leaves in the fall.

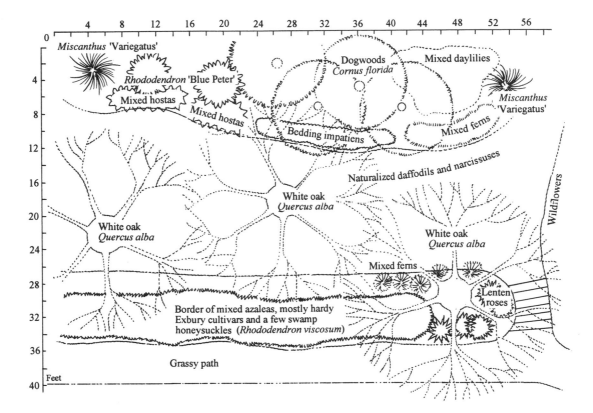

Miscanthus 'Variegatus'

Rhododendron 'Blue Peter'

Mixed hostas

Mixed hostas

Dogwoods
Cornus florida

Mixed daylilies

Miscanthus
'Variegatus'

Bedding impatiens

Mixed ferns

Naturalized daffodils and narcissuses

White oak
Quercus alba

White oak
Quercus alba

White oak
Quercus alba

Wildflowers

Mixed ferns

Lenten
roses

Border of mixed azaleas, mostly hardy
Exbury cultivars and a few swamp
honeysuckles (Rhododendron viscosum)

Grassy path

Feet

A GARDEN OF SEDUMS AND SEMPERVIVUMS

Over the years, I've thought of a lot of garden schemes, but the idea of a plan devoted to sedums and sempervivums did not, as Minerva sprang from the forehead of Jupiter, spring directly from the author's mind. Rather, it came to me after reading three books: Anne Ashberry's *Alpine Lawns* (London: Hodder and Stoughton, 1966), Rhoda Tarantino's *Small Gardens Are More Fun* (New York: Simon and Schuster, 1972), and Helen Payne's *Plant Jewels of the High Country* (Medford, Oregon: Pine Cone Publishers, 1972).

The idea was also inspired by a picture of Harlan Hand's marvelous frost-free garden, which overlooks the San Francisco Bay in El Cerrito, California. Hand has created a living stream of Mexican snowballs (*Echeveria elegans*) that churn over and around a rocky bottom; the river's edge is shaded by a grove of coral aloe hybrids (*Aloe striata*). His garden is geared for warmer climates, but for those of us who suffer from the icy finger of frost, these mostly tropical Mexican snowballs can be replaced by the hardier species of the sempervivums.

Sempervivums (*Sempervivum* spp.) are commonly known as houseleeks or hen-and-chickens. The first name is a salute to the well-known *S. tectorum* and its habit of growing on slate roofs in Europe; the second refers to parent plants that are usually surrounded by tiny offspring. These succulents are impervious to drought and the hot sun. Their many leaf colors, lovely starlike flowers, and small stature make them valuable for rock gardens, spaces between pathway stones, trough and pot gardens, and small ornamental lawns. All they need is poor soil and perfect drainage.

There are hundreds of hen-and-chickens. *Sempervivum arachnoideum* alone is responsible for dozens of varieties and cultivars. From the Alps comes *S. montanum,* with purple-edged leaves and violet-purple flowers. From the Pyrenees and central France comes *S. tectorum,* a large-leaved plant that usually colors up when the weather gets cool, and *S. soboliferum,* which forms two-inch rosettes of green leaves edged with russet red.

Other plants to consider for this type of garden are the common yellow stonecrop (*Sedum acre*) and its diminutive kin, gold moss (*S. acre* 'Minus'). From the Swiss Alps comes *S. dasyphyllum,* with pale blue leaves and pale pink flowers. Also from Switzerland is *S. hispanicum,* which bears tiny pointed and tufted leaves and white flowers. There are two forms of *S. kamtschaticum:* the first, the species from Siberia, has green leaves and orange flowers, and the cultivar 'Variegatum' has green leaves edged with a narrow band of white. From the Caucasus Mountains comes *S. spurium* 'Album', with white flowers; 'Roseum', bearing brilliant rosy red flowers; and of course, the ever-popular 'Dragon's Blood'. There is that great species from Japan, *S. spectabile,* an eighteen-inch sedum with blue foliage, and all its variations. Then, from the Cascade Mountains of our own Northwest, there is *S. spathulifolium,* a beautiful species with gray-green leaves that grow in rosettes and make creeping mats—and all its subpecies and cultivars.

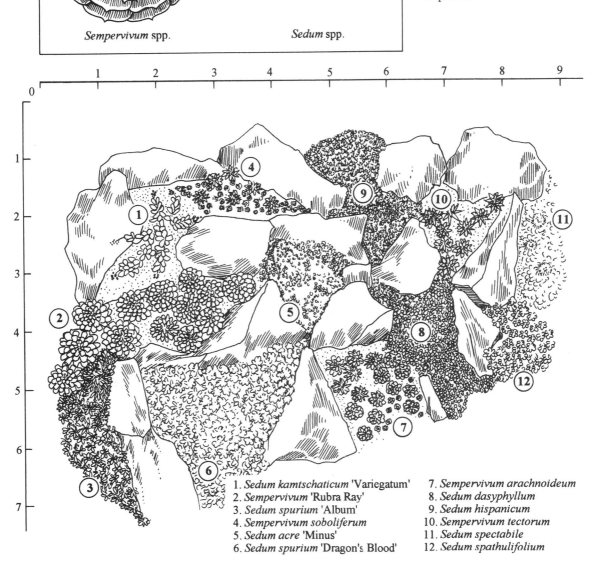

Sempervivum spp. *Sedum* spp.

By placing stepping-stones through your bed of sedums and sempervivums, you can make any number of crazy-quilt designs with patches of plants.

1. *Sedum kamtschaticum* 'Variegatum'
2. *Sempervivum* 'Rubra Ray'
3. *Sedum spurium* 'Album'
4. *Sempervivum soboliferum*
5. *Sedum acre* 'Minus'
6. *Sedum spurium* 'Dragon's Blood'
7. *Sempervivum arachnoideum*
8. *Sedum dasyphyllum*
9. *Sedum hispanicum*
10. *Sempervivum tectorum*
11. *Sedum spectabile*
12. *Sedum spathulifolium*

A CARPET BED GARDEN

Carpet bedding began in the Victorian era and hit its peak when London's Crystal Palace was built. Such gardens were so popular that their colors blazed from every corner of England, and the style spread throughout Europe and America. And to this day, municipal park departments still mass great numbers of florific annuals in designs whose original inspiration came from the nineteenth century's interpretations of Turkish Oriental rugs.

William Robinson described this garden style in *The English Flower Garden and Home Grounds* (London: John Murray, 1883): "The flower garden planting was made up of a few kinds of flowers which people were proud to put out in thousands and tens of thousands, and with these, patterns, more or less elaborate, were carried out in every garden save the very poorest cottage garden. It was not easy to get away from all this false and hideous 'art.'"

Nonetheless, carpet bedding gardens can be showstoppers—when executed tastefully, that is. Garden design is a personal thing, and luckily, there are beautiful gardens created by individuals who, drawing on both instinct and common sense, have created striking examples. Whenever I think I've seen it all, I remember the Shamrock Garden at Mount Stewart in Northern Ireland, where a giant hand over ten feet long is silhouetted in dwarf red begonias. It commemorates the Bloody Hand of Ulster—a tribute to the apparent loser of two Scottish clans, both racing by boat to Ireland, who cut off his hand and threw it ashore to claim the prize—demonstrating that there is always room for the unique.

At the center of the garden plan is a potted cabbage palm (*Cordyline australis*), which could easily be replaced by a potted yucca or a large container full of petunias. There are also pink and red geraniums, dusty millers (*Centaurea cineraria*), pink woolflowers (*Celosia cristata*), blue flossflowers (*Ageratum houstonianum*), and white sweet alyssums (*Lobularia maritima*).

Feet

1. Dusty millers
2. White sweet alyssum
3. Blue flossflowers
4. Pink woolflowers

5. Pink geraniums
6. White geraniums
7. Cabbage palm

A SUNDIAL GARDEN

On a sunny day after Thanksgiving I walked next door to make a map of the sundial garden created by Doan Ogden some twenty-five years ago. The heart of the garden is a capsule-shaped bed about twenty-five feet long and six feet wide. In the very center is a modern sculpture of a six-foot bird. Originally, the centerpiece was an old sundial with a gnomon (the triangular plate that casts the shadow) engraved, "Hours fly, flowers die, new days, new ways pass by—love stays!"

On either side of the centerpiece are ornamental grasses, including two specimens of Ravenna grass (*Erianthus ravennae*). Each of these plants is flanked by zebra grass (*Miscanthus sinensis* 'Zebrinus'). The rest of the bed—outlined by common bricks laid edgewise on the horizontal—is composed of black-eyed Susans (*Rudbeckia hirta*). The central garden is surrounded by a four-foot strip of grass that, at one end, leads through a tunnel of age-old rhododendrons (*Rhododendron catawbiense*); at the other end are steps made of railroad ties.

Among the other plants in this garden are both wild and domesticated goldenrods (*Solidago* spp.), New England asters (*Aster novae-angliae*), Tartarian asters (*A. tataricus*), smaller rhododendrons, and epimediums for spring bloom and all-season leaves. There are also a number of Japanese anenomes, including *Anemone* × *hybrida* 'Queen Charlotte' and *A. hupehensis* 'September Charm', which seeds all over the garden.

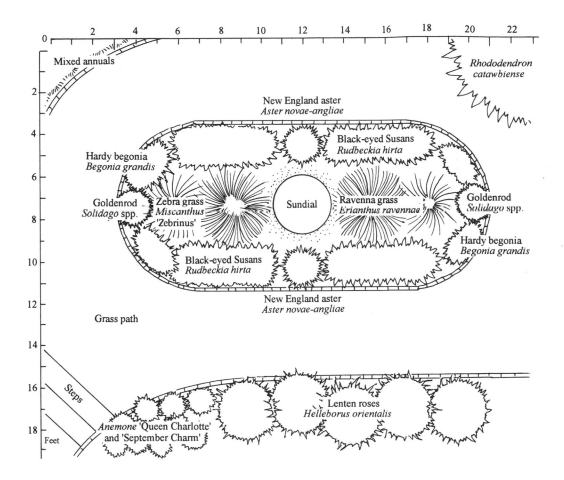

Mixed annuals

Rhododendron catawbiense

New England aster
Aster novae-angliae

Hardy begonia
Begonia grandis

Black-eyed Susans
Rudbeckia hirta

Goldenrod
Solidago spp.

Zebra grass
Miscanthus 'Zebrinus'

Sundial

Ravenna grass
Erianthus ravennae

Goldenrod
Solidago spp.

Hardy begonia
Begonia grandis

Black-eyed Susans
Rudbeckia hirta

New England aster
Aster novae-angliae

Grass path

Steps

Feet

Anemone 'Queen Charlotte' and 'September Charm'

Lenten roses
Helleborus orientalis

Around the Garden

~

THE PLANTS DESCRIBED IN THIS BOOK RANGE FROM THOSE HAPPY IN DAMP OR WET SOIL to those that prefer a thin layer of the the driest dirt. Most will get by in average soil, some like a bit of added humus or compost, and a few will persist in solid clay.

The first thing a gardener should do is to check the soil. Is it solid clay, rich loam, sandy, or a combination? Is it well drained, or does water stand in puddles even after a light rain?

Clay soils are sticky. If you roll a lump of wet soil between your fingers, as if rolling a cigarette, and it forms a heavy lump that sticks together, that's clay. Clay can become rock hard when it is completely dry. Instead of sinking into that soil, water simply rolls to the lowest level and sits there. Soil with lots of organic matter drains, and sandy soil drains immediately. If you need help determining your soil types, contact your local extension agent.

Many plants with coarse roots, such as roses, will do very well in clay soil. Plants with fine roots, or those that demand perfect drainage, such as alpine and mountain plants, usually perish in heavy clay soils.

For plants with no special requirements, try to prepare a garden soil that strikes a balance between clay, sand, and loam. Add organic matter, which provides food for healthy growth. If you have clay soil, add as much as you can; the more organic material, the better the soil becomes.

Take advantage of the weather. Whenever possible, dig your garden in the fall and let it sit over the winter; the action of the frost helps to break up the soil.

Double-digging. If your soil is especially poor and you can devote an afternoon to a seemingly thankless job, try your hand at double-digging.

First mark out the area you wish to dig. Cut all weeds or grass with a mower or a scythe. Put down a tarpaulin or some plastic sheeting and rake the vegetation into piles for later use as filler for the trenches you will dig.

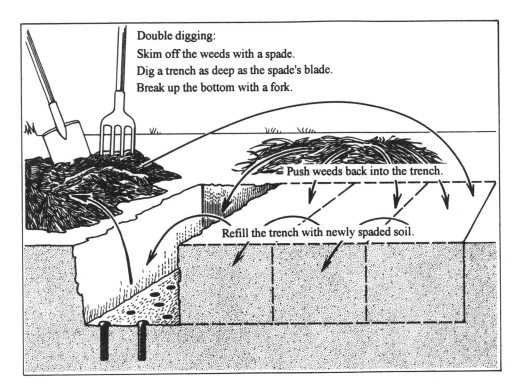

Double digging:

Skim off the weeds with a spade.

Dig a trench as deep as the spade's blade.

Break up the bottom with a fork.

Push weeds back into the trench.

Refill the trench with newly spaded soil.

Do not use a Rototiller; the idea of double-digging is to break up the garden's subsoil and to add organic matter to the rest. Surface tilling is only for soil that has already been sufficiently worked.

Peat moss. For many years I tried to work around having a compost heap because I thought it was messy. So I bought bales of peat moss instead, fooling myself into believing that it would at least help loosen the packed earth.

But in order to get the peat moss to the garden, I had to go to the nursery center, drag that tightly packed bale to the garden, open the tough plastic wrap, then dig into that dry and unpleasant stuff, trying to get it into a workable state while the dust made its way up my nose.

Then, after all that, I found out the same thing every year: peat moss really doesn't mix well with soil, and if allowed to dry out, it actually repels water, thus becoming useless as a mulch.

The best way to build good soil is to add organic matter, not peat moss. I have done a lot for my garden soil simply by mixing crushed leaves directly into the dirt when I plant bulbs in the fall and putting the rest into small heaps scattered throughout the property so that compost is always within reach.

I save money by using composted leaves and vegetable matter; all that cash used to buy fertilizers and garden conditioners can go for buying plants. And the plants I grow using compost are healthier than those grown with artificial fertilizers and peat moss. Compost adds valuable trace elements to the soil, too. Finally, there's the added benefit of knowing you're helping to alleviate the solid waste problem.

I do add some fertilizers to our gardens, especially because they lay fallow for so many years. They consist of blood meal, cotton meal, and greensand. This last substance is an iron potassium silicate that began as an undersea deposit and is a great source of potash. Then I always crumble a bit of bonemeal at the bottom of every hole that I dig for a daffodil or species tulip bulbs.

Compost. This soil amendment is easy to make. Choose an out-of-the-way spot that is accessible to the garden. The spot should be level and well drained and receive at least half a day of sunlight. You can either buy a ready-made compost bin or build your own. Just make sure that your creation has adequate venting in the sides and bottom to allow for air circulation. If the air does not circulate, the aerobic, or oxygen-loving, bacteria and fungi will be replaced by anaerobic organisms, which will slow down the decaying process and produce an odor.

Once the bin is set up, you can begin to add all sorts of organic matter. In addition to shredded leaves, you can add leaf litter to your compost heaps, plus sawdust, shredded paper, wood ashes, shredded bark, grass clippings, weeds, kitchen scraps, and even black-and-white newsprint (but not color because of the chemical dyes).

Materials that are *not* suitable for a compost heap include animal feces, bones, meat products, and plant material that has been treated with herbicides or pesticides.

Smaller is better. A chunk of tree limb can take months to break down, but if broken into small pieces, it will decompose in just weeks.

Alternate vegetable matter with layers of soil. Once every week or so, turn the pile to keep the ingredients mixed and the decomposition process working efficiently. Occasionally add water. A dry compost heap will not "work" because moisture is needed for the chemical actions. Eventually the bacteria will break down the collection of organic matter into a rich, beautiful, dark brown humus that is odor-free and will do wonders for your garden.

Soil pH. The pH is a measurement of the relative acidity (or sourness) and alkalinity (or sweetness) of the soil. A pH of 7 is neutral. Lower numbers indicate acidity; higher numbers indicate alkalinity. Each number represents a multiple of 10, so that a soil with a pH of 6 is 10 times more acidic than one with a pH of 7, and one with a pH of 5 is 100 times more acid than neutral soil.

Most plants grow in soil with a pH between 5.0 and 7.0. Swamps and bogs that have a high percentage of peat are extremely acidic. In humid regions—and in most woods and forests—the soil is moderately acid to slightly alkaline. Arid regions have soil with a moderate to a strong alkaline content, and many desert areas in the Southwest have vast alkali flats.

To test the pH of your soil, you can buy an inexpensive paper tape, available at most garden centers. When you hold it against a sample of moist soil, it will turn colors to indicate the degree of acidity. Or, if you prefer, you can call your county extension agent about the acidity of the soil in your area.

Farmers often add lime to their fields, since many crops do best in soil that is close to neutral. Most of the plants in this book, however, are not lime lovers.

You can lessen acidity by adding lime and you can lessen alkalinity by adding sphagnum peat, but these changes are usually only temporary. I recommend getting advice on changing soil pH from your local extension service.

Mulches. When the hot days of summer arrive in your garden and that sun beats down on dirt and plant alike, the soil and the roots begin to bake and what water there is quickly evaporates. That's the time to apply a garden mulch.

Mulches help to slow the evaporation of moisture from the soil, cut work for the weeding brigade, and depending on the material used, improve the appearance of the garden by giving beds, borders, and edgings a neat and orderly look.

Organic mulches are plant-based materials that gradually decompose, thereby adding organic matter to the soil. (I don't advise using peat moss for a mulch, since it packs down and repels water with a vengeance.) Stone mulches are excellent for rock gardens and for drought-resistant plants. A mulch of pea gravel, for example, keeps mud from splashing onto dainty rock garden plants during heavy rains. And stones hold warmth from the sun, radiating it back at night and producing condensation that benefits many plants. (Just promise not to use black plastic: about the only thing it's good for is the vegetable garden, where it keeps the ground warm for crops like melons.)

In the winter mulches do an entirely different job. Once the ground freezes in your garden, mulches keep the ground frozen until the following spring. Plants hardy in your climate are not damaged or killed by the cold but by the alternate freezing and thawing of the ground, as days warm up, then nights get cold again. This heaving eventually pushes plant roots right out of the ground.

Mulching mowers. The small lawn acts as an elegant frame for a small garden. Grass pathways are very desirable additions to the garden scene, if they are not subject to too much traffic.

The new mulching mowers are designed to cut up grass clippings and return them directly to the lawn, where they quickly decompose. Many older mowers cut up the grass, too; remove the grass-collection bag and close the opening on the mower to prevent dangerous objects from flying out. To keep clippings from piling up, never mow the grass when it is wet because the grass blades pack together. Also, keep the cut high—never remove more than one-third of the grass blades in a single mowing. Too many clippings will also foul up the blades.

If you don't have a mulching mower or your older mower won't work for this purpose, bag the clippings and add them to the compost heap. They will eventually decompose, along with the other compost ingredients. (A new grass-clippings compost maker will turn them into compost in less than thirty days.)

Watering and watering systems. Water is a limited resource, so when you water the garden, do it well. Use enough to soak into the soil, down where it will do the most good. As water penetrates the soil, roots grow down to reach it, and plants with longer roots will survive dry spells. Surface watering forces roots to grow upward, where they are easily destroyed when there is no water.

According to tradition, gardens need about one inch of water per week. The actual amount, of course, depends on temperature and wind, since high heat and strong winds speed evaporation. Soil type is another factor, since fast-draining soils dry quicker than clay. A plant's requirements are also important. For example, shallow-rooted plants need water more often than deep-rooted ones, and new plantings need constant moisture to establish new roots. If you get one good soaking rain per week, you will probably not have to water. The best way to tell when the garden needs water is to stick your finger down into the soil; if it feels dry a couple of inches below the surface, it's time to water.

Overhead sprinklers are the least efficient way to water, especially in areas with high temperatures, strong winds, and porous soils. Soaker hoses are far better, and drip irrigation systems that deliver water directly to the roots are the best.

Soaker hoses have tiny holes that let water out slowly, soaking the ground. They can be installed underground or under mulch, or laid directly on top of the soil. Drip systems use slender plastic tubing with tiny pores that allow water to percolate slowly. Kits are available that supply all the parts you need.

There are several kinds of water timers to add to your system. A simple wind-up timer meters any amount of water up to 1,400 gallons from five minutes to three and a half hours, then shuts the water off automatically. A computerized control, operating on two AA batteries, turns sprinklers or irrigation systems on and off and can be programmed for seven days.

Microclimate adventures. One of the marvelous adventures in gardening is growing unusual plants. It's especially rewarding when you have success with a rare specimen that everyone said could not possibly grow in your area.

Take advantage of your garden's microclimates: the spot that's sheltered from the worst of the winter winds by a small hill, the area where summer heat is moderated by a nearby lake or pond, the place that gets warmth from a stone or brick wall or a tree trunk. Often the earth around the foundation of a house receives a great deal of heat from relatively warm basements. Air temperatures are relative; when the outside temperature is 15°F, 35°F can feel like a heat wave.

Although we garden in Zone 7, there are a few nights every year when the temperatures fall below 0°F. But I still have a gunnera (*Gunnera chilensis*) that has survived such indignities because the roots are protected by a three-sided Styrofoam box with the fourth, or open, side facing our house foundation. The roots are heavily mulched, but that alone would not keep the plant alive; it's the heat leaking from the house that does it. That's one example of a microclimate. So if you find protected areas on your property, try growing plants that other gardeners in your area list as failures.

Six-legged pests. Walk into that section of any garden center that sells pesticides and you will be bowled over by the smell of chemicals. Those rows and rows of brightly colored boxes and brown plastic bottles are poison, and the user is warned in very small type of chances not worth taking. Magazine ads encourage the purchase of these brews by showing beautiful pictures of perfect gardens: only with chemicals, they insist, can you have great flowers and a perfect lawn. But there are other ways to garden without resorting to sprays that give you an 800 number to call if the stuff gets in your lungs.

Pest control starts with well-conditioned soil, good fertility, and adequate watering; a healthy plant can fight off attacks that kill a weaker cousin. Never allow diseased or decaying plant material to lie about.

Our worst garden problem has always been slugs. These are snails without shells that glide about on a glittering trail of slime and chew holes in just about everything. We've tried trapping slugs with pans full of beer (we refuse to use poisoned bait because of possible danger to Miss Jekyll, our garden cat) but have never found them to be entirely reliable (especially when it rains). So I resort to the easiest method: taking a flashlight out into the garden at night, spotlighting slugs, and sprinkling a few grains of salt on their bodies. This starts the process of reverse osmosis, which kills them quickly.

You can pick Japanese beetles off the plants and drop them in a can of soapy water. The resulting mixture can be buried when the can is full. Or you can use one of the new chemical bait traps that lure the males with sex attractants and the females with the smell of roses.

You can control insects like flea beetles, aphids, and spider mites by spraying with insecticidal soaps or using insecticides derived from the dried flower heads of the pyrethrum daisy (*Chrysanthemum cinerariifolium*), a plant that resembles the common field daisy. Pyrethrum has one drawback, however: its chemicals are quickly broken down by the action of light, so it should be applied in late afternoon.

Rotenone is another plant-based insecticide, manufactured from the roots of the tuba root (*Derris elliptica*) and the lancepods (*Lonchocarpus* spp.). It is sold as a dust and is an extremely potent control for many insects. Unfortunately, if inhaled, it can cause severe irritation to human lungs, but like pyrethrum, it safely breaks down in the environment.

BIBLIOGRAPHY

IN ADDITION TO THE BOOKS CITED IN THE TEXT, THE FOLLOWING ARE ALSO INTERESTING from a small-gardening point of view.

Allen, Oliver E. *Gardening with the New Small Plants.* Boston: Houghton Mifflin Company, 1987.

Baumann, Ernst. *New Gardens.* New York: Wittenborn and Company, 1955.

Brookes, John. *Room Outside.* New York: The Viking Press, 1969.

David Hicks Garden Design. Editor, Andrew Wheatcroft. London: Routledge & Kegan Paul, Ltd., 1982.

Evans, Hazel. *The Patio Garden.* New York: Viking Penguin, Inc., 1985.

Grasby, Nancy. *Imaginative Small Gardens.* New York: Hearthside Press, Inc., 1963.

Halpin, Anne. *Great Gardens from Everyday Plants.* New York: Simon & Schuster, 1993.

Loewer, H. Peter. *Growing and Decorating with Grasses.* New York: Walker and Company, 1977.

———. *A Year of Flowers.* Emmaus, Pennsylvania: Rodale Press, 1989.

Miles, Bebe. *Wildflower Perennials for Your Garden.* New York: Hawthorne, 1976.

Storm, Katharine and Arthur. *The Small Garden.* New York: Frederick A. Stokes Company, 1939.

Tarantino, Rhoda Specht. *Small Gardens Are More Fun.* New York: Simon & Schuster, 1972.

Taylor's Guide to Roses. Boston: Houghton Mifflin Company, 1986.

Yang, Linda. *The City Gardener's Handbook.* New York: Random House, 1990.

APPENDIX

SOURCES FOR PLANTS

Bulbs
Bio-Quest International
P.O. Box 5752
Santa Barbara, CA 93150
(805) 969-4072

McClure & Zimmerman
P.O. Box 368
108 West Winnebago
Friesland, WI 53935
(414) 326-4220

Daylilies
Daylily Discounters
Route 2, Box 24
Alachua, FL 32615
(904) 462-1539

Dwarf conifers
Washington Evergreen Nursery
P.O. Box 388
Leicester, NC 28748
(704) 683-4518

Espaliered gardening
Henry Leuthardt Nurseries, Inc.
Montauk Highway, Box 666
East Moriches, Long Island, NY 11940
(516) 878-1387

Fragrant plants and herbs
Companion Plants
7247 North Coolville Ridge Road
Athens, OH 47501
(614) 592-4643

Sandy Mush Herb Nursery
Route 2, Surrett Cove Road
Leicester, NC 28748
(704) 683-2014

Ferns, ivy, mosses
Logee's Greenhouses
141 North Street
Danielson, CT 06239
(203) 774-8038

Merry Gardens
Camden, ME 04843
(207) 236-9064

Lilies
B & D Lilies
330 P Street
Port Townsend, WA 98368
(206) 385-1738

Rhododendrons, small trees, magnolias, native plants

Camellia Forest Nursery
125 Carolina Forest
Chapel Hill, NC 27516

Forestfarm
990 Tetherah Road
Williams, OR 97544
(503) 846-6963

Girard Nurseries
P.O. Box 428
Geneva, OH 44041

Greer Gardens
1280 Goodpasture Island Road
Eugene, OR 97401
(503) 686-8266

Klupenger's Nursery
24075 Klupenger Rd., N.E.
Aurora, OR 97002
(800) 237-0768

Louisiana Nursery
Route 7, Box 43
Opelousas, LA 70570
(318) 948-3696

Mountain Maples
5901 Spy Rock Road
Laytonville, CA 95454

Woodlanders
1128 Colleton Avenue
Aiken, SC 29801
(803) 648-7522

Ornamental grasses

Kurt Bluemel
2740 Greene Lane
Baldwin, MD 21013
(410) 557-7229

Mostly perennials, but ferns and roses, too

Appalachian Gardens
Box 82
Waynesboro, PA 17268
(717) 762-4312

Coastal Gardens & Nursery
4611 Socastee Boulevard
Myrtle Beach, SC 29575
(803) 293-2000

Holbrook Farm and Nursery
Route 2, Box 223 B
Fletcher, NC 28732
(704) 891-7790

Lamb Nurseries
East 101 Sharp Avenue
Spokane, WA 99202
(509) 328-7956

Primrose Path
RD 2, Box 110
Scottdale, PA 15683
(412) 887-6756

Andre Viette
Route 1, Box 16
Fishersville, VA 22939
(703) 943-2315

Wayside Gardens
Hodges, SC 29695
(800) 845-1124

White Flower Farm
Litchfield, CT 06759
(203) 496-9600

Seeds
The Fragrant Path
P.O. Box 328
Fort Calhoun, NE 68023

Chiltern Seeds
Bortree Stile, Ulverston
Cumbria LA12 7PB
England
(0229) 581137

Park Seed Company
Cokesbury Road
Greenwood, SC 29647
(802) 223-7333

Plants of the Southwest
930 Baca Street
Sante Fe, NM 87501
(505) 983-1548

Thompson & Morgan
P.O. Box 1308
Jackson, NJ 08527
(908) 363-2225

Water lilies
Lilypons Water Gardens
6800 Lilypons Road
P.O. Box 10
Buckeystown, MD 21717
(301) 428-0686

Wildflowers
Niche Gardens
1111 Dawson Road
Chapel Hill, NC 27516
(919) 967-0078

We-Du Nurseries
Route 5, Box 724
Marion, NC 28752
(704) 738-8300

SOURCES FOR TOOLS AND SUPPLIES

General garden tools, pots, etc.
The Walt Nicke Company
P.O. Box 433
36 McLeod Avenue
Topsfield, MA 01983
(508) 887-3388

Mellingers, Inc.
2310 West South Range Road
North Lima, OH 44452
(216) 549-9861

Hypertuffa troughs
Karen Harris
200 East Genesee Street
Fayetteville, NY 13066
(315) 637-8209

Sculpture
Museum of Fine Arts, Boston
Catalog Sales Department
P.O. Box 1044
Boston, MA 02120
(800) 225-5592

Design Toscano
7 East Campbell Street
Arlington Heights, IL 60005
(800) 525-0733

Gazing globes
Milaeger's Gardens
4838 Douglas Avenue
Racine, WI 53402
(414) 639-2371

Societies with seed exchanges
Alpine Garden Society
AGS Centre, Avon Bank
Pershore, Worcestershire WR10 3JP
England
0386-552657

American Conifer Society
P.O. Box 314
Perry Hall, MD 21128
(410) 882-5595

American Horticultural Society
7931 East Boulevard Drive
Alexandria, VA 22308
(800) 777-7931

American Rock Garden Society
221 West 9th Street
Hastings, MN 55033
(612) 437-4390

Arizona Native Plant Society
P.O. Box 41206
Tuscon, AZ 85717

The Hardy Plant Society
710 Hemlock Road
Media, PA 19063
(215) 566-0861

The Royal Horticultural Society
80 Vincent Square
London SW1P 2PE
England

Scottish Rock Garden Society
21 Merchiston Park
Edinburgh EH10 4PW
Scotland
031-229-8138

Index of Plant Names